Bloom's Modern Critical Views

Bloom's Modern Critical Views

EUGENE O'NEILL
Updated Edition

Edited and with an introduction by
Harold Bloom
Sterling Professor of the Humanities
Yale University

BLOOM'S
LITERARY CRITICISM
An imprint of Infobase Publishing

Bloom's Modern Critical Views: Eugene O'Neill—Updated Edition

Copyright ©2007 Infobase Publishing

Introduction © 2007 by Harold Bloom

Bloom's Literary Criticism
An imprint of Infobase Publishing
132 West 31st Street
New York NY 10001

ISBN-10: 0-7910-9366-2
ISBN-13: 978-0-7910-9366-5

Library of Congress Cataloging-in-Publication Data
Eugene O'Neill / Harold Bloom, editor. ——Updated ed.
    p. cm. -—(Bloom's modern critical views)
  Includes bibliographical references and index.
  ISBN 0-7910-9366-2 (hardcover)
  1. O'Neill, Eugene, 1888-1953—Criticism and interpretation. I.
Bloom, Harold. II. Title. III. Series
  PS3529.N5Z634 2007
  812'.52—dc22   2006036859

Contributing Editor: Gabriel Welsch
Cover designed by Takeshi Takahashi
Cover photo © Hulton Archive/Getty Images

Printed in the United States of America
Bang EJB 10 9 8 7 6 5 4 3 2 1

This book is printed on acid-free paper.

Contents

Editor's Note

My Introduction praises O'Neill's theatricality in his masterworks, *Long Day's Journey into Night* and *The Iceman Cometh*, while questioning the adequacy of the prose in both plays.

Laurin Porter consider's time's revenges in *Iceman* and *Hughie*, while Doris Alexander investigates the biographical context of *Mourning Becomes Electra*.

For Kurt Eisen, the aesthetic failure of *The Great God Brown* was a necessary prelude to the success of *Long Day's Journey* and *Iceman*.

Long Day's Journey is interpreted by Edward L. Shaugnessy as a product of O'Neill's Catholic sensibility, which survived his disbelief.

Margaret Loftus Robinson surveys the early plays, a labor performed for the middle dramas by James A. Robinson.

Anna Christie is uncovered as a work of uncertainty by Barbara Voglino, after which Zander Brietzke meditates upon O'Neill's mixed achievement in the use of theatrical masks.

In an overview, Romulus Linney regards O'Neill's career as a self-finding, while Andrew Graham-Yooll takes us to Buenos Aires to look at the importance for the dramatist's development of his down-and-out days in Argentine metropolis.

That sojourn was part of O'Neill's experience of mixing with working class people, the subject of the essay by Patrick J. Chura.

Bound East for Cardiff, a play informed by such experience, is mulled over by Egil Törnqvist, after which Doris Alexander concludes this volume with a study of O'Neill's last play, the intensely autobiographical *A Moon for the Misbegotten*.

HAROLD BLOOM

Introduction

I

It is an inevitable oddity that the principal American dramatist to date
should have no American precursors. Eugene O'Neill's art as a playwright
owes most to Strindberg's, and something crucial, though rather less, to
Ibsen's. Intellectually, O'Neill's ancestry also has little to do with American
tradition, with Emerson or William James or any other of our cultural
speculators. Schopenhauer, Nietzsche, and Freud formed O'Neill's sense of
what little was possible for any of us. Even where American literary tradition
was strongest, in the novel and poetry, it did not much affect O'Neill. His
novelists were Zola and Conrad; his poets were Dante Gabriel Rossetti
and Swinburne. Overwhelmingly an Irish-American, with his Jansenist
Catholicism transformed into anger at God, he had little active interest in
the greatest American writer, Whitman, though his spiritual darkness has
a curious, antithetical relation to Whitman's overt analysis of our national
character.

Yet O'Neill, despite his many limitations, is the most American of our
handful of dramatists who matter most: Williams, Miller, Wilder, Albee,
perhaps Mamet and Shepard. A national quality that is literary, yet has no
clear relation to our domestic literary traditions, is nearly always present in

O'Neill's strongest works. We can recognize Hawthorne in Henry James, and Whitman (however repressed) in T. S. Eliot, while the relation of Hemingway and Faulkner to Mark Twain is just as evident as their debt to Conrad. Besides the question of his genre (since there was no vital American drama before O'Neill), there would seem to be some hidden factor that governed O'Neill's ambiguous relation to our literary past. It was certainly not the lack of critical discernment on O'Neill's part. His admiration for Hart Crane's poetry, at its most difficult, was solely responsible for the publication of Crane's first volume, *White Buildings*, for which O'Neill initially offered to write the introduction, withdrawing in favor of Allen Tate when the impossibility of his writing a critical essay on Crane's complexities became clear to O'Neill. But to have recognized Hart Crane's genius, so early and so helpfully, testifies to O'Neill's profound insights into the American literary imagination at its strongest.

The dramatist whose masterpieces are *The Iceman Cometh* and *Long Day's Journey into Night*, and, in a class just short of those, *A Moon for the Misbegotten* and *A Touch of the Poet*, is not exactly to be regarded as a celebrator of the possibilities of American life. The central strain in our literature remains Emersonian, from Whitman to our contemporaries like Saul Bellow and John Ashbery. Even the tradition that reacted against Emerson—from Poe, Hawthorne, and Melville through Gnostics of the abyss like Nathanael West and Thomas Pynchon—remains always alert to transcendental and extraordinary American possibilities. The distinguished Robert Penn Warren must be the most overtly anti-Emersonian partisan in our history, yet even Warren seeks an American Sublime in his poetry. O'Neill would appear to be the most non-Emersonian author of any eminence in our literature. Irish-American through and through, with an heroic resentment of the New England Yankee tradition, O'Neill from the start seemed to know that his spiritual quest was to undermine Emerson's American religion of self-reliance.

O'Neill's own Irish Jansenism is curiously akin to the New England Puritanism he opposed, but that only increased the rancor of his powerful polemic in *Desire under the Elms*, *Mourning Becomes Electra*, and *More Stately Mansions*. The Will to Live is set against New England Puritanism in what O'Neill himself once called "the battle of moral forces in the New England scene" to which he said he felt closest as an artist. But since this is Schopenhauer's rapacious Will to Live, and not Bernard Shaw's genial revision of that Will into the Life Force of a benign Creative Evolution, O'Neill is in the terrible position of opposing one death-drive with another. Only the inescapable Strindberg comes to mind as a visionary quite as negative as O'Neill, so that *The Iceman Cometh* might as well have been called *The Dance of Death*, and

Long Day's Journey into Night could be retitled *The Ghost Sonata*. O'Neill's most powerful self-representations—as Edmund in *Long Day's Journey* and Larry Slade in *Iceman*—are astonishingly negative identifications, particularly in an American context.

Edmund and Slade do not long for death in the mode of Whitman and his descendants—Wallace Stevens, T. S. Eliot, Hart Crane, and Theodore Roethke—all of whom tend to incorporate the image of a desired death into the great, triple trope of night, the mother, and the sea. Edmund Tyrone and Larry Slade long to die because life without transcendence is impossible, and yet transcendence is totally unavailable. O'Neill's true polemic against his country and its spiritual tradition is not, as he insisted, that "its main idea is that everlasting game of trying to possess your own soul by the possession of something outside it." Though uttered in 1946, in remarks before the first performance of *The Iceman Cometh*, such a reflection is banal and represents a weak misreading of *The Iceman Cometh*. The play's true argument is that your own soul cannot be possessed, whether by possessing something or someone outside it, or by joining yourself to a transcendental possibility, to whatever version of an Emersonian Oversoul that you might prefer. The United States, in O'Neill's dark view, was uniquely the country that had refused to learn the truths of the spirit, which are that good and the means of good, love and the means of love, are irreconcilable.

Such a formulation is Shelleyan, and reminds one of O'Neill's High Romantic inheritance, which reached him through pre-Raphaelite poetry and literary speculation. O'Neill seems a strange instance of the Aestheticism of Rossetti and Pater, but his metaphysical nihilism, desperate faith in art, and phantasmagoric naturalism stem directly from them. When Jamie Tyrone quotes from Rossetti's "Willowwood" sonnets, he gives the epigraph not only to *Long Day's Journey* but to all of O'Neill: "Look into my face. My name is Might-Have-Been; / I am also called No More, Too Late, Farewell." In O'Neill's deepest polemic, the lines are quoted by, and for, all Americans of imagination whatsoever.

II

By common consent, *Long Day's Journey into Night* is Eugene O'Neill's masterpiece. The Yale paperback in which I have just reread the play lists itself as the fifty-sixth printing in the years since publication. Since O'Neill, rather than Williams or Miller, Wilder or Albee, is recognized as our leading dramatist, *Long Day's Journey* must be the best play in our more than two centuries as a nation. One rereads it therefore with awe and a certain apprehension, but with considerable puzzlement also. Strong work it certainly is, and twice I have been moved by watching it well directed and well performed. Yet how can this be the best stage play that an exuberantly dramatic people has produced? Is it equal to the best of our imaginative literature? Can we read it in the company of *The Scarlet Letter* and *Moby-Dick*, *Adventures of Huckleberry Finn* and *The Portrait of a Lady*, *As I Lay Dying* and *Gravity's Rainbow*? Does it have the aesthetic distinction of our greatest poets, of Whitman, Dickinson, Frost, Stevens, Eliot, Hart Crane, Elizabeth Bishop, and John Ashbery? Can it stand intellectually with the crucial essays of Emerson and of William James?

These questions, alas, are self-answering. O'Neill's limitations are obvious and need not be surveyed intensively. Perhaps no major dramatist has ever been so lacking in rhetorical exuberance, in what Yeats once praised Blake for having: "beautiful, laughing speech." O'Neill's convictions were deeply held, but were in no way remarkable, except for their incessant sullenness. It is embarrassing when O'Neill's exegetes attempt to expound his ideas, whether about his country, his own work, or the human condition. When one of them speaks of "two kinds of nonverbal, tangential poetry in *Long Day's Journey into Night*" as the characters' longing "for a mystical union of sorts," and the influence of the setting, I am compelled to reflect that insofar as O'Neill's art is nonverbal it must also be nonexistent.

My reflection however is inaccurate, and O'Neill's dramatic art is considerable, though it does make us revise our notions of just how strictly literary an art drama necessarily has to be. Sophocles, Shakespeare, and Molière are masters alike of language and of a mimetic force that works through gestures that supplement language, but O'Neill is mastered by language and relies instead upon a drive-towards-staging that he appears to have learned from Strindberg. Consider the close of *Long Day's Journey*. How much of the power here comes from what Tyrone and Mary say, and how much from the extraordinarily effective stage directions?

> TYRONE (*trying to shake off his hopeless stupor*). Oh, we're fools to pay any attention. It's the damned poison. But I've never known her to drown herself in it as deep as this. (*Gruffly.*) Pass me that bottle, Jamie. And stop reciting that damned morbid poetry. I won't have it in my house! (*Jamie pushes the bottle toward him. He pours a drink without disarranging the wedding gown he holds carefully over his other arm and on his lap, and shoves the bottle back. Jamie pours his and passes the bottle to Edmund, who, in turn, pours one. Tyrone lifts his glass and his sons follow suit mechanically, but before they can drink Mary speaks and they slowly lower their drinks to the table, forgetting them.*)

MARY (*staring dreamily before her. Her face looks extraordinarily youthful and innocent. The shyly eager, trusting smile is on her lips as she talks aloud to herself*). I had a talk with Mother Elizabeth. She is so sweet and good. A saint on earth. I love her dearly. It may be sinful of me but I love her better than my own mother. Because she always understands, even before you say a word. Her kind blue eyes look right into your heart. You can't keep any secrets from her. You couldn't deceive her, even if you were mean enough to want to. (*She gives a little rebellious toss of her head—with girlish pique.*) All the same, I don't think she was so understanding this time. I told her I wanted to be a nun. I explained how sure I was of my vocation, that I had prayed to the Blessed Virgin to make me sure, and to find me worthy. I told Mother I had had a true vision when I was praying in the shrine of Our Lady of Lourdes, on the little island in the lake. I said I knew, as surely as I knew I was kneeling there, that the Blessed Virgin had smiled and blessed me with her consent. But Mother Elizabeth told me I must be more sure than that, even, that I must prove it wasn't simply my imagination. She said, if I was so sure, then I wouldn't mind putting myself to a test by going home after I graduated, and living as other girls lived, going out to parties and dances and enjoying myself; and then if after a year or two I still felt sure, I could come back to see her and we would talk it over again. (*She tosses her head—indignantly.*) I never dreamed Holy Mother would give me such advice! I was really shocked. I said, of course, I would do anything she suggested, but I knew it was simply a waste of time. After I left her, I felt all mixed up, so I went to the shrine and prayed to the Blessed Virgin and found peace again because I knew she heard my prayer and would always love me and see no harm ever came to me so long as I never lost my faith in her. (*She pauses and a look of growing uneasiness comes over her face. She passes a hand over her forehead as if brushing cobwebs from her brain—vaguely.*) That was in the winter of senior year. Then in the spring something happened to me. Yes, I remember. I fell in love with James Tyrone and was so happy for a time. (*She stares before her in a sad dream. Tyrone stirs in his chair. Edmund and Jamie remain motionless.*)

CURTAIN

Critics have remarked on how fine it is that the three alcoholic Tyrone males slowly lower their drinks to the table, forgetting them, as the morphine-laden wife and mother begins to speak. One can go further; her banal if moving address to herself, and Tyrone's petulant outbursts, are considerably less eloquent than the stage directions. I had not remembered anything that was spoken, returning to the text after a decade, but I had held on to that grim family tableau of the three Tyrones slowly lowering their glasses. Again, I had remembered nothing actually said between Edmund and his mother at the end of act one, but the gestures and glances between them always abide with me, and Mary's reactions when she is left alone compel in me the Nietzschean realization that the truly memorable is always associated with what is most painful.

(*She puts her arms around him and hugs him with a frightened, protective tenderness.*)

EDMUND (*soothingly*). That's foolishness. You know it's only a bad cold.

MARY. Yes, of course, I know that!

EDMUND. But listen, Mama. I want you to promise me that even if it should turn out to be something worse, you'll know I'll soon be all right again, anyway, and you won't worry yourself sick, and you'll keep on taking care of yourself—

MARY (*frightenedly*). I won't listen when you're so silly! There's absolutely no reason to talk as if you expected something dreadful! Of course, I promise you. I give you my sacred word of honor! (*Then with a sad bitterness.*) But I suppose you're remembering I've promised before on my word of honor.

EDMUND. No!

MARY (*her bitterness receding into a resigned helplessness*). I'm not blaming you, dear. How can you help it? How can any one of us forget? (*Strangely.*) That's what makes it so hard—for all of us. We can't forget.

EDMUND (*grabs her shoulder*). Mama! Stop it!

MARY (*forcing a smile*). All right, dear. I didn't mean to be so gloomy. Don't mind me. Here. Let me feel your head. Why, it's nice and cool. You certainly haven't any fever now.

EDMUND. Forget! It's you—

MARY. But I'm quite all right, dear. (*With a quick, strange, calculating, almost sly glance at him.*) Except I naturally feel tired and nervous this morning, after such a bad night. I really ought to go upstairs and lie down until lunch time and take a nap. (*He gives her an instinctive look of suspicion—then, ashamed of himself, looks quickly away. She hurries on nervously.*) What are you going to do? Read here? It would be much better for you to go out in the fresh air and sunshine. But don't get overheated, remember. Be sure and wear a hat. (*She stops, looking straight at him now. He avoids her eyes. There is a tense pause. Then she speaks jeeringly.*) Or are you afraid to trust me alone?

EDMUND (*tormentedly*). No! Can't you stop talking like that! I think you ought to take a nap. (*He goes to the screen door—forcing a joking tone.*) I'll go down and help Jamie bear up. I love to lie in the shade and watch him work. (*He forces a laugh in which she makes herself join. Then he goes out on the porch and disappears down the steps. Her first reaction is one of relief. She appears to relax. She sinks down in one of the wicker armchairs at rear of table and leans her head back, closing her eyes. But suddenly she grows terribly tense again. Her eyes open and she strains forward, seized by a fit of nervous panic. She begins a desperate battle with herself. Her long fingers, warped and knotted by rheumatism, drum on the arms of the chair, driven by an insistent life of their own, without her consent.*)

CURTAIN

That grim ballet of looks between mother and son, followed by the terrible, compulsive drumming of her long fingers, has a lyric force that only the verse quotations from Baudelaire, Swinburne, and others in O'Neill's text are able to match. Certainly a singular dramatic genius is always at work in O'Neill's stage directions, and can be felt also, most fortunately, in the repressed intensities of inarticulateness in all of the Tyrones.

It seems to me a marvel that this can suffice, and in itself probably it could not. But there is also O'Neill's greatest gift, more strongly present in *Long Day's Journey* than it is even in *The Iceman Cometh*. Lionel Trilling, subtly and less equivocally than it seemed, once famously praised Theodore Dreiser for his mixed but imposing representation of "reality in America," in his best novels, *Sister Carrie* and *An American Tragedy*. One cannot deny the power of the mimetic art of *Long Day's Journey into Night*. No dramatist to this day, among us, has matched O'Neill in depicting the nightmare realities that can afflict American family life, indeed family life in the twentieth-century Western world. And yet that is the authentic subject of our dramatists who matter most after O'Neill: Williams, Miller, Albee, with the genial Thornton Wilder as the grand exception. It is a terrifying distinction that O'Neill earns, and more decisively in *Long Day's Journey into Night* than anywhere else. He is the elegist of the Freudian "family romance," of the domestic tragedy of which we all die daily, a little bit at a time. The helplessness of family love to sustain, let alone heal, the wounds of marriage, of parenthood, and of sonship, have never been so remorselessly and so pathetically portrayed, and with a force of gesture too painful ever to be forgotten by any of us.

III

Like its great precursor play, Strindberg's *The Dance of Death*, O'Neill's *The Iceman Cometh* must be one of the most remorseless of what purport to be tragic dramas since the Greeks and the Jacobeans. Whatever tragedy meant to the incredibly harsh Strindberg, to O'Neill it had to possess a "transfiguring nobility," presumably that of the artist like O'Neill himself in his relation to his time and his country, of which he observed that "we are tragedy, the most appalling yet written or unwritten." O'Neill's strength was never conceptual, and so we are not likely to render his stances into a single coherent view of tragedy.

Whitman could say that: "these States are themselves the greatest poem," and we know what he meant, but I do not know how to read O'Neill's "we are tragedy." When I suffer through *The New York Times* every morning, am I reading tragedy? Does *The Iceman Cometh* manifest a "transfiguring nobility?" How could it? Are Larry Slade in *Iceman* or Edmund Tyrone in *Long Day's Journey into Night*, both clearly O'Neill's surrogates, either of them tragic in relation to their time and country? Or to ask all this in a single question: are the crippling sorrows of what Freud called "family romances" tragic or are they not primarily instances of strong pathos, reductive processes that cannot, by definition, manifest an authentic "transfiguring nobility?"

I think that we need to ignore O'Neill on tragedy if we are to learn to watch and read *The Iceman Cometh* for the dramatic values it certainly possesses. Its principal limitation, I suspect, stems from its tendentious assumption that "we are tragedy," that "these States" have become the "most appalling" of tragedies. Had O'Neill survived into our Age of Reagan, and observed our Yuppies on the march, doubtless he would have been even more appalled. But societies are not dramas, and O'Neill was not Jeremiah the prophet. His strength was neither in stance nor style, but in the dramatic representation of illusions and despairs, in the persuasive imitation of human personality, particularly in its self-destructive weaknesses.

Critics have rightly emphasized how important O'Neill's lapsed Irish Catholicism was to him and to his plays. But "importance" is a perplexing notion in this context. Certainly the absence of the Roman Catholic faith is the given condition of *The Iceman Cometh*. Yet we would do O'Neill's play wrong if we retitled it *Waiting for the Iceman*, and tried to assimilate it to the Gnostic cosmos of Samuel Beckett, just as we would destroy *Long Day's Journey into Night* if we retitled it *Endgame in New London*. All that O'Neill and Beckett have in common is Schopenhauer, with whom they share a Gnostic sense that our world is a great emptiness, the *kenoma*, as the Gnostics of the second century of the common era called it. But Beckett's post-Protestant cosmos could not be redeemed by the descent of the alien god. O'Neill's post-Catholic world longs for the suffering Christ and is angry at him for not returning. Such a longing is by no means in itself dramatic, unlike Beckett's ironically emptied-out cosmos.

A comparison of O'Neill to Beckett is hardly fair, since Beckett is infinitely the better artist, subtler mind, and finer stylist. Beckett writes apocalyptic farce, or tragicomedy raised to its greatest eminence. O'Neill doggedly tells his one story and one story only, and his story turns out to be himself. *The Iceman Cometh*, being O'Neill at his most characteristic, raises the vexed question of whether and just how dramatic value can survive a paucity of eloquence, too much commonplace religiosity, and a thorough lack of understanding of the perverse complexities of human nature. Plainly *Iceman* does survive, and so does *Long Day's Journey*. They stage remarkably, and hold me in the audience, though they give neither aesthetic pleasure nor spiritually memorable pain when I reread them in the study.

For sheer bad writing, O'Neill's only rival among significant American authors is Theodore Dreiser, whose *Sister Carrie* and *An American Tragedy* demonstrate a similar ability to evade the consequences of rhetorical failure. Dreiser has some dramatic effectiveness, but his peculiar strength appears to be mythic. O'Neill, unquestionably a dramatist of genius, fails also on the mythic level; his anger against God, or the absence of God, remains petulant and personal, and his attempt to universalize that anger by turning it against his country's failure to achieve spiritual reality is simply misguided. No country, by definition, achieves anything spiritual anyway. We live and die, in the spirit, in solitude, and the true strength of *Iceman* is its intense dramatic exemplification of that somber reality.

Whether the confessional impulse in O'Neill's later plays ensued from Catholic *praxis* is beyond my surmise, though John Henry Raleigh and other critics have urged this view. I suspect that here too the influence of the non-Catholic Strindberg was decisive. A harsh expressionism dominates *Iceman* and *Long Day's Journey*, where the terrible confessions are not made to priestly surrogates but to fellow sinners, and with no hopes of absolution. Confession becomes another station on the way to death, whether by suicide, or by alcohol, or by other modes of slow decay.

Iceman's strength is in three of its figures, Hickman (Hickey), Slade, and Parritt, of whom only Slade is due to survive, though in a minimal sense.

Hickey, who preaches nihilism, is a desperate self-deceiver and so a deceiver of others, in his self-appointed role as evangelist of the abyss. Slade, evasive and solipsistic, works his way to a more authentic nihilism than Hickey's. Poor Parritt, young and self-haunted, cannot achieve the sense of nothingness that would save him from Puritanical self-condemnation.

Life, in *Iceman*, is what it is in Schopenhauer: illusion. Hickey, once a great sustainer of illusions, arrives in the company of "the Iceman of Death," hardly the "sane and sacred death" of Whitman, but insane and impious death, our death. One feels the refracted influence of Ibsen in Hickey's twisted deidealizings, but Hickey is an Ibsen protagonist in the last ditch. He does not destroy others in his quest to destroy illusions, but only himself. His judgments of Harry Hope's patrons are intended not to liberate them but to teach his old friends to accept and live with failure. Yet Hickey, though pragmatically wrong, means only to have done good. In an understanding strangely akin to Wordsworth's in the sublime *Tale of Margaret* (*The Ruined Cottage*), Hickey sees that we are destroyed by vain hope more inexorably than by the anguish of total despair. And that is where I would locate the authentic mode of tragedy in *Iceman*. It is Hickey's tragedy, rather than Slade's (O'Neill's), because Hickey is slain between right and right, as in the Hegelian theory of tragedy. To deprive the derelicts of hope is right, and to sustain them in their illusory "pipe dreams" is right also.

Caught between right and right, Hickey passes into phantasmagoria, and in that compulsive condition he makes the ghastly confession that he murdered his unhappy, dreadfully saintly wife. His motive, he asserts perversely, was love, but here too he is caught between antitheses, and we are not able to interpret with certainty whether he was more moved by love or hatred:

> HICKEY. (*Simply*) So I killed her. (*There is a moment of dead silence. Even the detectives are caught in it and stand motionless.*)
>
> PARRITT. (*Suddenly gives up and relaxes limply in his chair—in a low voice in which there is a strange exhausted relief.*) I may as well confess, Larry. There's no use lying any more. You know, anyway. I didn't give a damn about the money. It was because I hated her.
>
> HICKEY. (*Obliviously*) And then I saw I'd always known that was the only possible way to give her peace and free her from the misery of loving me. I saw it meant peace for me, too, knowing she was at peace. I felt as though a ton of guilt was lifted off my mind. I remember I stood by the bed and suddenly I had to laugh. I couldn't help it, and I knew Evelyn would forgive

me. I remember I heard myself speaking to her, as if it was something I'd always wanted to say: "Well, you know what you can do with your pipe dream now, you damned bitch!" (*He stops with a horrified start, as if shocked out of a nightmare, as if he couldn't believe he heard what he had just said. He stammers*) No! I never—!

PARRITT. (*To* LARRY *sneeringly*) Yes, that's it! Her and the damned old Movement pipe dream! Eh, Larry?

HICKEY. (*Bursts into frantic denial*) No! That's a lie! I never said—! Good God, I couldn't have said that! If I did, I'd gone insane! Why, I loved Evelyn better than anything in life! (*He appeals brokenly to the crowd*) Boys, you're all my old pals! You've known old Hickey for years! You know I'd never—(*His eyes fix on* HOPE) You've known me longer than anyone, Harry. You know I must have been insane, don't you, Governor?

Rather than a demystifier, whether of self or others, Hickey is revealed as a tragic enigma, who cannot sell himself a coherent account of the horror he has accomplished. Did he slay Evelyn because of a hope hers or his—or because of a mutual despair? He does not know, nor does O'Neill, nor do we. Nor does anyone know why Parritt betrayed his mother, the anarchist activist, and her comrades and his. Slade condemns Parritt to a suicide's death, but without persuading us that he has uncovered the motive for so hideous a betrayal. Caught in a moral dialectic of guilt and suffering, Parritt appears to be entirely a figure of pathos, without the weird idealism that makes Hickey an interesting instance of High Romantic tragedy.

Parritt at least provokes analysis; the drama's failure is Larry Slade, much against O'Neill's palpable intentions, which were to move his surrogate from contemplation to action. Slade ought to end poised on the threshold of a religious meditation on the vanity of life in a world from which God is absent. But his final speech, expressing a reaction to Parritt's suicide, is the weakest in the play:

LARRY. (*In a whisper of horrified pity*) Poor devil! (*A long-forgotten faith returns to him for a moment and he mumbles*) God rest his soul in peace. (*He opens his eyes—with a bitter self-derision*) Ah, the damned pity—the wrong kind, as Hickey said! Be God, there's no hope! I'll never be a success in the grandstand—or anywhere else! Life is too much for me! I'll be a weak fool looking with pity at the two sides of everything till the day I die! (*With an intense bitter sincerity*) May that day come soon!

> (*He pauses startledly, surprised at himself—then with a sardonic grin*) Be God, I'm the only real convert to death Hickey made here. From the bottom of my coward's heart I mean that now!

The momentary return of Catholicism is at variance with the despair of the death-drive here, and Slade does not understand that he has not been converted to any sense of death, at all. His only strength would be in emulating Hickey's tragic awareness between right and right, but of course without following Hickey into violence: "I'll be a weak fool looking with pity at the two sides of everything till the day I die!" That vision of the two sides, with compassion, is the only hope worthy of the dignity of any kind of tragic conception. O'Neill ended by exemplifying Yeats's great apothegm: he could embody the truth, but he could not know it.

LAURIN PORTER

The Iceman Cometh *and* Hughie:
Tomorrow Is Yesterday

Harry Hope's saloon in *The Iceman Cometh* is the land that time forgot.
A rundown bar and rooming house of the "last resort variety" on the West
Side of New York, it is inhabited by a curious collection of misfits and societal
outcasts who are living in the past. Appropriately, as the curtain rises, all but
two of them are asleep; the atmosphere that prevails for much of the play
is one of somnambulance, a deathlike calm. In one of the play's oft-quoted
passages, Larry Slade, the saloon's elder statesman, explains to a newcomer,
Don Parritt, that the "beautiful calm in the atmosphere" stems from the fact
that for this dozen-odd human beings, this is the last harbor, the "No Chance
Saloon ... The End of the Line Cafe, The Bottom of the Sea Rathskeller."
He adds, "No one here has to worry about where they're going next, because
there is no farther they can go."[1] The sea metaphor is apt: The atmosphere
in which these men exist is like the half-light that filters to the ocean depths.
Dreamlike, deathlike, they live, by common consent, in a world oblivious to
clock and calendar—that is, until the drummer Hickey arrives with time's
winged chariot at his back. *The Iceman Cometh* is a play about time, both the
desire to escape it and the impossibility of doing so.

As we have seen, *Iceman* shares this theme with the earlier cycle plays, *A
Touch of the Poet* and *More Stately Mansions*.[2] It recurs in the autobiographical
works which will follow: *Hughie*, *Long Day's Journey*, and *A Moon for the*

From *The Banished Prince: Time, Memory, and Ritual in the Late Plays of Eugene O'Neill*, pp. 63–77.
© 1988 by Laurin R. Porter.

13

Misbegotten, all of which, in various ways, focus upon some ideal or lost hope available only to memory. In many ways, *Iceman* stands squarely between these two sets of plays; the pipe-dreaming of this fulcrum play looks both backward to the historical cycle and forward to *Hughie* and the Tyrone saga.

Iceman also occupies a middle position in terms of O'Neill's use of autobiographical material. In his creation of the Melody-Harford family, he drew very obliquely upon his own family members as models. In *Iceman* he turns to his own past more directly for characters and situation, using not his biological family but acquaintances from his Hell Hole, Jimmy-the-Priest days as a young man.[3] His direct use of this autobiographical material seems to have freed him psychologically to tell at last in undisguised fashion the story to which his whole career had been building, that of his own family. *The Iceman Cometh* stands at the crossroad of the historical and biographical cycles, linking them together; the history of its composition reflects the common pathway along which these cycles travelled.[4] For approximately five years before writing *Iceman*, O'Neill's time and energy were consumed in the enormous undertaking of his eleven-play cycle. By the spring of 1939 he had completed first drafts of two of the plays and third drafts of *Poet* and *Mansions*, along with endless notes and outlines for other plays, and was working on *The Calms of Capricorn*, at that time the cycle's fifth play. Then, on June 5, having gone stale on the historical cycle, he decided to put it aside and turn to two plays which he describes in his *Work Diary* as having "nothing to do with" it. These two plays became *The Iceman Cometh* and *Long Day's Journey into Night*. Although he did not recognize it at the time, the two "families" that he limns in these plays are not unrelated to the Melody-Harford clan over which he had been agonizing for the past four-and-one-half years. Both sets of plays, the historical and the autobiographical, actually form a single network, sharing common themes and shaped by a recurring obsession: the need to conquer time. Is it possible, these dramas ask, to escape the bonds of history and move forward, transformed, into a new day, or is Mary Tyrone right when she says that the past is both present and future?

The Iceman Cometh and Linear Time

The action of *Iceman* takes place in 1912, a watershed year in O'Neill's own life (and, not coincidentally, also the time frame he chooses for *Long Day's Journey*, which he outlined in full before turning to the first draft of *Iceman*.)[5] But this is only nominally the era of the play, since all of the boarders at Harry Hope's saloon are living in the past. Larry, we are told, left the anarchist movement eleven years before (1901) and had been involved in it for thirty years (since 1871). Harry hasn't been out of the saloon since his wife Bessie's death twenty years earlier (1892); his favorite song, "She's the Sunshine of Paradise Alley," became popular in 1895. The Boer War, which looms so large in the memories of Piet Wetjoen and Cecil Lewis ("The Captain"), took place in 1899–1902. In fact, about the only specific references to the America of 1912 are the I.W.W. and "du Bull Moosers" in act 1 and the West Coast bombing in which Rosa Parritt was involved.

The New York that Joe Mott, Harry, and the others recall is that of the 1890s—rich, exciting, and openly corrupt. The framed photographs over the bar are those of Tammany giants Richard Croker and "Big Tim" Sullivan and prize fighters John L. Sullivan and Gentleman Jim Corbett. (The comparison is apt: both Croker and "Big Tim" were known for their prowess with their fists and were fighters in every sense of the word.) Richard Croker, the ruthless Tammany boss from 1886 to 1902, organized corruption on a hitherto unparalleled scale, and Sullivan was in charge of gambling and gambling houses during this era.[6] This is the gilded age when a word from the top and the appropriate payoff were all the insurance necessary. Pat McGloin, Larry tells us, also had his heyday as a police lieutenant "back in the flush times of graft when everything went" (*Iceman* 36).

Even Harry Hope's saloon was a thriving enterprise in the "good old days." "Dis was a first class hang-out for sports in dem days," Joe reminisces. "Good whiskey, fifteen cents, two for two bits" (*Iceman* 46). At that time many aspiring Tammany politicians got their start by running a saloon; hence the talk about running Harry for alderman of the ward. In addition to their individual memories, these characters share a collective nostalgia.

Thus, for this motley crew, the passing of time serves only to mark the increasing distance between the present moment and a past golden age. One of the functions of the paired refrains and stock phrases is to emphasize this point. Their pipe dreams, mutually reinforced, consist in their wan hope that "tomorrow" they will restore the glories of yesterday. Joe Mott will reopen his gambling house, Jimmy will get back his job in the publicity department, the Captain will return to England, and Wetjoen, to the veldt. The list goes on: every one of the boarders clings to a dream that involves the reinstatement of a past status at some point in the future. A possible exception is Larry Slade, whose pipe dream is his insistence that, disillusioned with life, he wants only to die. For him the past represents not an ideal, but its loss. But that, at bottom, is not unlike the dilemma of the others: while they cling to a sense of wholeness and purpose that they link with former life situations, Larry's sense of mourning, disguised as cynical indifference, stems from the fact that he has had to relinquish the political ideology that gave his life meaning. He tells himself that he longs for death, when really he longs for an ideal like the one lost long ago. Even Cora and Chuck are shaped by their histories. They want to get married and move to a farm, but Cora is afraid Chuck will think he was a sap for marrying a prostitute and use that as an excuse to resume his alcoholism. No one, it would seem, can escape the icy fingers of the past; fate becomes simply what has been.

At this point, the function of memory becomes key. If time has betrayed them, so, in a different way, does memory. Although they turn to it for solace in a world grown cold and indifferent, the passing years have distorted the facts and wishful thinking has done the rest, until their memories only vaguely resemble reality. Jimmy has forgotten that his drunkenness drove his wife into the arms of another man, not vice versa, and that he didn't resign, but was fired; Lewis, that he gambled away regiment money; and Wetjoen, that his family and fellow soldiers disowned him for cowardice when he advised Cronje to retreat; none are free to go home. Further, the changes that time has brought have precluded the simple resumption of past positions. New faces have replaced the old ones, contacts are no longer available, jobs have been given to others.

Before Hickey's arrival, however, the bums can hide from these painful truths with the help of two anodynes, booze and a chorus willing to pretend belief in their pipe dreams. The ultimate objective of both these remedies, of course, is to try to stop the clock. The bottom-of-the-sea calm that Larry speaks of stems from this effort to simply repeat the present moment, unchangingly, again and again. This accounts for the endless repetitions that characterize *Iceman*—the stock epithets and repeated phrases associated with virtually all of the characters, the ritualistic recitation of the various pipe dreams, even the endless iterations of the phrase "pipe dream" itself.[7] O'Neill reinforces these repetitions by pairing the characters. Lewis and Wetjoen reenact the Boer War, Mosher and McGloin join forces to wheedle a drink out of Harry, Margie and Pearl tease Rocky. It is clear from the outset that these exchanges have occurred before and will occur again. Their constant repetition has lulled the bums into a sleeplike state where "worst is best ... and East is West, and tomorrow is yesterday" (*Iceman* 44). Opposites cancel out and time stands still.

The overall action of *Iceman* underscores this cyclic sense of time. Egil Törnqvist is among several critics who have pointed to this fact:

> *Iceman* begins rather harmoniously; the denizens of Hope's saloon have passed out and even after they wake up they contentedly go on pipe-dreaming. With Hickey's entrance it radically changes into the somber bleakness that comes of a life without illusions— and liquor. But once Hickey has been judged insane and has left, back comes the initial mood: the play ends with a cacophonous

chorus, indicating that everyone is "just a few drinks ahead of the passing out state." The movement is thus from happy sleep (illusions) through a painful awakening to life's realities and back into happy sleep.[8]

All references to the past are not golden; O'Neill includes historical allusions to civilizations that fell and revolutions that failed—an instance of cyclic time in the classical sense. Hugo, for instance, is fond of referring to Babylon, the luxurious ancient capital of the Chaldean empire which supported its wealth by subjecting the Israelites to slave labor. Babylon is again suggested when Larry describes the birthday party as "a second feast of Belshazzar with Hickey to do the writing on the wall" (*Iceman* 120). The "Mene, Mene, Tekel, Upharsin" of Biblical history foretold the fall of Belshazzar's kingdom to the Medes and the Persians. The world of *Iceman*, it is implied, will also be weighed in the balance and found wanting.

Revolutions seem to promise little improvement in this scheme of things. The anarchist movement in which Larry and Parritt participated led only to bombings. The French Revolution, recalled by "Dansons la Carmagnole" and Lewis' reference to Hugo as "our little Robespierre," resulted in the Reign of Terror. Even the American Revolution, recalled by Parritt's mention of Washington and Jefferson, led in the end to Harry Hope's saloon.

The audience, of course, is acutely conscious that these efforts to escape linear time are doomed to failure. Though constant repetition may dull time's effect, it cannot banish time altogether, a fact which is demonstrated by Hickey's arrival. His message of salvation is threatening to the derelicts precisely because it pierces through to this truth. To achieve peace, he insists, they must give up their pipe dreams and acknowledge that they—and the world—have changed. They must, in short, reenter the world of the present. Hickey has the smell of reality on his breath rather than rot-gut whiskey.

Before the events of these two days, Hickey's relationship with the derelicts had been a part of their yearly cycle. As Larry explains to Parritt, Hickey "comes here twice a year regularly on a periodical drunk" (*Iceman* 24). Participation in these biannual binges helped the boarders as much as Hickey; for the moment, history was abolished, renewing their belief in their respective pipe dreams and reinvesting their experience with reality and value. Thus restored, they could make it "through time" until Hickey arrived again. But from the play's beginning, it is clear that something has changed. Hickey is late, and the cycle has been interrupted. "I wonder what's happened to him," Rocky says. "Yuh could set your watch by his periodicals before dis. Always got here a coupla days before Harry's birthday party, and now he's on'y got till tonight to make it" (*Iceman* 13).

Hickey's conversion, which becomes obvious upon his arrival, can be seen as a function of his newly acquired consciousness of time. As such, he is the only character in the drama associated with linear time. He is, for instance, the timekeeper at Harry's party. He glances down at his watch, timing Harry's entrance for exactly midnight. As Hope appears in the door Hickey looks up and shouts, "On the dot! It's twelve! ... Come on now, everybody, with a happy birthday, Harry!" (*Iceman* 135). His birthday gift to Harry is a wristwatch, engraved with the date as well as Hope's name. (A more ironic gift to Harry or any of the other boarders is hard to imagine.)[9] Hickey's sense of urgency stems from his consciousness that time is running out. "I had to make you help me with each other," he says. "I saw I couldn't do what I was after alone. Not in the time at my disposal. I knew when I came here I wouldn't be able to stay with you long. I'm slated to leave on a trip" (*Iceman* 147). Having alerted the police to his whereabouts, Hickey is acutely aware that time is running out on his last chance to convert his friends and thereby assuage his own sense of guilt. For unlike the others, Hickey's life has radically changed. His decision to murder his wife, Evelyn, has rendered impossible the pipe dream that he will reform "tomorrow" and all will be well. He is forced to acknowledge present reality, and he desperately wants the others to do likewise.

It is precisely at this juncture that the play employs ritual; actually, two religious rituals, holy communion and confession, both deeply rooted in O'Neill's Catholic upbringing.[10] Religious allusions appear repeatedly throughout the play; the title itself is a cross between the bawdy joke about the iceman "coming" and an allusion to the foolish virgins of Matthew 25:6, who are warned to trim their lamps because "the bridegroom cometh." Hickey, of course, is not the expected bridegroom, a bona fide savior. He is rather the iceman, and the iceman is death, as Larry aptly comments. Hickey is not Christ, but anti-Christ; his salvation offers not fulfillment but annihilation. His actions, then, are the reverse of the Savior's. Christ turned water into wine; Hickey's wine is watered down. "What did you do to the booze, Hickey?" is the constant refrain. "There's no damned life left in it" (*Iceman* 26). Jesus told his disciples, "My peace I give unto you"; Hickey says, "I couldn't give you my peace. You've got to find your own" (*Iceman* 112). Hickey wants to cure his friends, but by stripping away their illusions and sending them out into the sweltering August morning, he merely renders them pathetic and defenseless.

Hickey fails as priest, as well. He would like to hear his friends' confessions, and, indeed, seeks them out individually to do just that. "He's been hoppin' from room to room all night," Rocky complains to Larry. "Yuh can't stop him" (*Iceman* 157). His penance is that they act on their pipe dreams, assuming that, as the dreams failed to materialize, the boarders would be rid of them forever. But his mission is doomed from the outset. The confessions are coerced, not made sincerely as the ritual requires, and his gospel, based on a false premise, is fraudulent. Hickey thinks he wants to save his friends, but actually, he is in need of salvation himself.

Thus, as the play reaches its climax, the real confessions take place and O'Neill's use of ritual becomes more direct. The parallels to Christ's last supper establish the eucharistic ritual as a backdrop to the action of the play, but in Hickey and Parritt's dual confessions we actually see a ritual enacted before our eyes, although it first appears that neither man feels the need of expiating his crime. When, for instance, Parritt confesses to Larry that his motives for betraying his mother weren't patriotic, as he initially insisted, but financial, he seems to feel no remorse for what he has done. The stage directions point out that "he has the terrible grotesque air, in confessing his sordid baseness, of one who gives an excuse which exonerates him from any real guilt" (*Iceman* 160). He has been driven relentlessly, first to find Larry and then to make him his confessor, and he clearly wants Slade to discover his crime, but precisely what sin needs absolution is not yet apparent.

It is the same with Hickey, who for much of the play seems anything but the contrite sinner. His first revelation, that his wife is dead, is spoken in quiet tones. When they gasp, stunned, he quickly reassures them that there is no need for this to spoil Harry's party: "There's no reason—You see, I don't feel any grief.... I've got to feel glad, for her sake. Because she's at peace. She's rid of me at last." All this is said with "a simple, gentle frankness" (*Iceman* 151). Even his confession the next day that Evelyn has been murdered is made "quietly" and "matter-of-factly." His only concern at this point is that the peace he has promised Hope and the others is not taking hold. He "gazes with worried kindliness at Hope" and says, "You're beginning to worry me, Governor.... It's time you began to feel happy—" (*Iceman* 207). It is only at the end of the second day, when it is clear that Hickey's plan has failed, that his carefully composed facade begins to crumble. His sense of urgency, like Parritt's, reaches a point where a confession clearly must be made.

Both make one last desperate attempt to achieve the peace which has thus far eluded them. In this climactic scene, with Hickey's powerful sustained monologue and Parritt's contrapuntal interjections, both turn to the appropriate parties for forgiveness and understanding: Parritt, to Larry, who, if not his biological father, has come to fulfill that role; Hickey, to Hope and the other boarders, the family he has chosen over his own wife.[11] Parritt has insisted all along that Larry was the only one who could really understand his dilemma—not just because he serves as Don's father, but also because he too has known Rosa's rejection. Hickey instinctively knows he must convince Harry and the others of the necessity of his deed, though he is wrong about his motive. He rationalizes that they, understanding the reason for his peace, will relinquish their own pipe dreams and be equally at rest. Actually, however, he needs them to validate his decision to murder Evelyn, a decision that he has begun to question. Thus their choice of confessors is fitting in terms of the events and relationships of the play.

It is also appropriate in terms of the religious ritual that structures this scene. The Catholic rite of confession is designed to reincorporate the penitent sinner into the mystical body of the church. The priest is efficacious as confessor to the extent that he represents the spiritual community as a whole; this is the source of his power. In the joint confessions of Hickey and Parritt, both priest and community are represented. Larry Slade, who is described at the outset as having a face with "the quality of a pitying but weary old priest's" (*Iceman* 5), plays the part of confessor; Harry and his cronies represent the community.[12]

The question, then, becomes whether the confessions take hold. Thus far the efforts of both Parritt and Hickey have failed, since neither has been willing to admit his true sin. They need absolution, not so much for their crimes as for the motives which inspired them. Both have gradually revealed their secrets, one step at a time, throughout the course of the play, and now the moment of truth-telling is at hand. As Hickey tells his story to Hope and the boarders, and Parritt, in antiphonal fashion, echoes the drummer's confession point by point to Larry, we learn that the real sin, which both have refused to acknowledge, is their hatred.

Hickey insists, of course, that this is not the case. As he finally reveals the whole truth about Evelyn's death, he continually reiterates that his only motive was love. His search for "the one possible way to free poor Evelyn and give her the peace she's always dreamed about," he explains to the boarders, was complicated by the great love they felt for each other. The derelicts, however, remain unconvinced, and Hickey, to demonstrate his sincerity, goes back to the beginning. As his story unravels, however, in spite of his protestations to the contrary, Hickey's anger and resentment begin to surface. "If she'd only admitted once she didn't believe any more in her pipe dream that some day I'd behave!" he exclaims (*Iceman* 238). "Sometimes," he goes on, "I couldn't forgive her for forgiving me. I even caught myself hating her for making me hate myself so much" (*Iceman* 239). Thus when he reaches the climax of his confession, still insisting on his love for her, we are not surprised to hear him say: "I remember I stood by the bed and suddenly I had to laugh. I couldn't help it, and I knew Evelyn would forgive me. I remember I heard myself speaking to her, as if it was something I'd always wanted to say: 'Well, you know what you can do with your pipe dream now, you damned bitch!'" (*Iceman* 241).

The ritual has served one purpose; Hickey's true sin has been uncovered. It is his hatred that has driven him to make converts of his friends in order to assuage his own guilt. His anger in the face of Evelyn's pipe dream, his resentment at her attempt to make him over in her own image—these are the furies that have pursued Hickey to this moment of truth. But it is a truth he cannot abide. Rather than confront his deep hatred for Evelyn, he falls back on the comforting delusion of insanity, even when it means allowing Harry and the others to reclaim their own pipe dreams. Thus Hickey is led off in darkness, denying this blinding insight into his soul. The confession has not proved efficacious since Hickey denies what it has taught him.

Parritt, on the other hand, is able to face the truth about himself. Like Hickey, at first he insists that he loved his mother. But gradually the truth unfolds. When Hickey recalls that he tore up Evelyn's picture, Parritt confesses to burning Rosa's. When Hickey admits that he murdered Evelyn, Parritt "suddenly gives up and relaxes limply in his chair," saying "in a low voice in which there is a strange exhausted relief, 'I may as well confess, Larry. There's no use lying any more. You know, anyway. I didn't give a damn about the money. It was because I hated her'" (*Iceman* 241). Interestingly, Parritt's unmasking is completed before Hickey's. While the drummer is still confessing the deed itself, Parritt pierces through to its cause. This is the moment he has been waiting for, the moment of truth.

The crucial difference, however, is that Parritt refuses to deny what he has discovered. "I can't kid myself like Hickey, that she's at peace," he says. "And I'm not putting up any bluff, either, that I was crazy afterwards when I laughed to myself and thought, 'You know what you can do with your freedom pipe dream now, don't you, you damned old bitch!'" (*Iceman* 247). At this, Larry explodes with the judgment Parritt has sought all along: "Go! Get the hell out of life, God damn you, before I choke it out of you!" Parritt's manner, we are told, "is at once transformed. He seems suddenly at peace with himself." As he leaves, about to become his own executioner, his words to Larry are simple and grateful: "Jesus, Larry, thanks. That's kind. I knew you were the only one who could understand my side of it" (*Iceman* 248). Parritt's confession has brought him peace because he accepts the truth it revealed.

The epithet in Parritt's response is no accident, nor is Larry's curse, for the issues in this scene are ultimately spiritual in nature. Both Parritt and Hickey, and, insofar as they are identified with them, the other derelicts, as well, desperately desire the peace which has heretofore evaded them. One way to articulate the nature of their impasse at this point is in terms of time, a concern which unites them all. The past, as we have said, is forever past, and insofar as memory has made of it an Eden (for Parritt, before he betrayed his mother; for Hickey, before he murdered Evelyn; for the others, those periods with dreams still intact or in reach), the present holds only emptiness and the future, only death. They need a means of escaping into another dimension of time, where the virulence of linear time and the futility of cyclic repetition can for the moment be suspended. Thus it seems neither accidental nor insignificant that, at precisely this point, the play draws upon a religious ritual to structure the action. The confessional ritual is a key to the action at this climactic moment, and it is best explained in terms of time and memory.

Ritual, in allowing for the momentary suspension of time, the experience of sacral time, if you will, collapses past, present, and future into a single moment. One is reminded of Yahweh's injunction to Moses to tell the Israelites, held captive in Egypt, that "I am" has sent him. God makes no distinction between past, present, and future; all is subsumed in an eternal now, much like the time frame of Nietzsche's eternal return and Eliade's cosmogonic rituals. Thus, in the presence of faith, the participating believer who can, within the context of ritual, tap the dimension of the divine can experience a moment outside time. It is admittedly a mysterious experience, like all ecstatic or mystical phenomena, one that defies precise articulation and one that is not automatically attained by all participants in religious rituals. Nonetheless, it is the underlying source of power that rituals offer: the intersection of the human with the divine, the family of man transformed into the communion of saints.

Hickey's confession, we have said, proves inefficacious, since he denies the truth it reveals, and Parritt's, though it brings him solace, still exacts the penance of death. Time has run out for them both, though Parritt leaves life strangely renewed, if not forgiven.[13] The boarders still have time left, however, and they embrace this sudden realization with gusto in the play's closing moments. With Parritt and Hickey gone, they return to their pipe dreams, declaring Hickey insane and discovering that the booze has regained its kick. Although this is not sacramental wine they drink, it does derive its power from a communion of sorts, the earthly communion of Harry and his family. And although it does not offer salvation or any kind of ultimate regeneration, it does help them kill time, literally, as they wait for the iceman, death.

Even that solace is denied Larry, who calls himself "Hickey's one true convert." Left alone without even a pipe dream to warm him, Slade has now taken Hickey's place, a fact which is emphasized by Hugo's response to Larry as he listens agonizingly for sounds of Don's suicide. Sitting at Larry's table, Hugo eyes him uneasily and says, "What's matter, Larry? Why you keep eyes shut? You look dead. What you listen for in backyard?" (*Iceman* 254). When Larry, still transfixed, does not answer, he gets up hastily and joins the group around Harry, muttering with frightened anger, "Crazy fool! You vas crazy like Hickey! You give me bad dreams, too" (*Iceman* 254). Larry is now the outsider, watching and waiting, not just for Don's death, but also his own.

Thus the possibility of transcending the limitations of time ultimately fails to materialize. In the confession ritual O'Neill presents a strategy for experiencing the regenerative mythic moment, but it is one that ultimately fails. One cannot live without illusions, the play tells us; "the lie of a pipe dream is what gives life to the whole misbegotten mad lot of us, drunk or sober" (*Iceman* 10).[14]

O'Neill's play, then, refuses to provide a way out for Parritt and Hickey. Their well-hidden hatred is finally revealed and, although they respond differently to it, each must pay with his life. Insofar as both characters are reflections of the playwright's own life experience, this suggests that—at this point, at any rate—O'Neill is unable to resolve his own sense of guilt. The tension that is at the root of so much of his creativity is focused clearly in the fates of Parritt and Hickey. Through them, O'Neill pursues his own relentless search for salvation. It is a search that he will continue in his next play, *Long Day's Journey into Night*, where he will once again employ the confessional ritual to explore the possibility of transcending time.

HUGHIE

Hughie, O'Neill's one-act play from the *By Way of Obit* series, presents a condensed version of *The Iceman Cometh*.[15] Its themes, concerns, and anagogue replicate those of its longer predecessor; its characters, too, are fighting a losing battle with time.

O'Neill composed *Hughie* at the height of his creative powers. It is, in fact, excepting *A Touch of the Poet* and *A Moon for the Misbegotten*, the last play he was to complete, though he conceived the idea two years earlier. After completing *The Iceman Cometh* on December 20, 1939, referring to it in his *Work Diary* as "one of [the] best plays I've written," O'Neill turned immediately to *Long Day's Journey into Night*. He worked steadily on it from January 1940 through April of the following year, stopping occasionally to jot down notes or outlines for new plays or returning to the historical cycle. During this period, on November 29, 1940, O'Neill conceived *By Way of Obit*, a series of five short, monologue plays. A few days later he added notes for three more, bringing the total to eight.[16]

He outlined scenarios for several of the one-acts, but in the face of his encroaching illness and the prospect of further deterioration, O'Neill destroyed them on February 21, 1944; only *Hughie*, the sole completed play (finished June 23, 1942), was preserved.[17] It appears to be fairly representative of the venture as a whole. According to a letter to drama critic George Jean Nathan in July of 1942, "It [*Hughie*] give [sic] you an idea of how the others in the series will be done."[18]

In *Hughie*, O'Neill has created a small gem whose brilliance derives as much from its economy of characterization as from its poetic use of language. Like *Iceman*, *Hughie* deals with issues of time as well as the need for life-sustaining illusions. The plays thus have much in common. Though the particulars vary, both present a world in decline. *Iceman* focuses its attention on a seedy bar in New York's West Side in 1912; *Hughie*, on a run-down hotel near Times Square in 1928. While fifteen societal dropouts inhabit the world of *The Iceman Cometh*, in *Hughie* there are only two. In both cases, however, we are presented with failed communities. As the boarders at Harry Hope's have formed a family of their own to ward off the desperation that threatens to engulf them, Erie Smith, a small-time gambler, seeks a similar comfort in the companionship of the new night clerk at his hotel, Charlie Hughes. The common denominator in both cases is the need for a pipe dream, since life cannot be endured without a protective shield of illusion. The only obstacle to happiness in this scheme of things arises when someone refuses to play by the rules, challenging the validity of the dream and breaking its soporific spell. For Harry and his crew, this occurs when Hickey arrives, peddling a return to the present. For Smith, the game breaks down with the death of Hughie, the previous night clerk, who participated in his fantasies of excitement and glamour. Erie must find a replacement for his feckless pal, since the dream must be shared to be believed. Around this need the plot, such as it is, unfolds.

NIRVANA, THE BIG NIGHT OF NIGHTS

As the action opens, somewhere between 3:00 and 4:00 A.M. on a summer morning in 1928, both Charlie and Erie are losing their respective battles with time. Charlie, in his early forties, has been a night clerk so long, we are told, he has forgotten even how to be bored. His "blank brown eyes contain no discernible expression,"[19] and he has perfected the art of seeming to listen to endless patrons without actually hearing them. His primary objective is to get through the night, to pass the time, which he does by ticking off the various sounds of the city that parcel out the hours. We learn about him primarily through the stage directions, which describe his reactions to these street noises, his inner clock. Early in the play, for instance, as Smith is trying to strike up a conversation with him, the stage directions indicate that the clerk's mind remains in the street. The garbagemen have come and gone, and now he's listening for the El. Its approach is "pleasantly like a memory of hope," but as it roars by, then recedes into the distance it leaves a melancholy echo in the air. But still there is hope, Hughes thinks to himself: "Only so many El trains pass in one night, and each one passing leaves one less to pass, so the night recedes, too, until at last it must die and join all the other long nights in Nirvana, the Big Night of Nights. And that's life" (*Hughie* 19).

This passage sums up nicely Hughes's attitude toward time. He has long since given up hope of attaining meaning in his life, so that the future holds no promise and the present offers only boredom. Unlike the boarders at Harry Hope's, he doesn't even have the memory of a happier past, real or imagined, to warm him. We learn a little about Charlie's past in the course of the play. We know he came from Saginaw, Michigan to New York, ostensibly to make his fortune (like all the other suckers, Erie comments cynically). He is married and has three children, the oldest of whom is eleven, or maybe twelve, he can't remember. For all intents and purposes, emotionally and psychologically (and spiritually, one might add), Charlie died a long time ago. He has learned not to react to the predictable wisecracks of the endless, anonymous hotel guests ("That's what comes of being careless," Erie says of the clerk's three children) and can scarcely recall feeling any emotions at all. The last time he was able to feel despair, we are told, was when he was out of a job for three months some fifteen years ago.

His experience of time combines linear and cyclic modes. To kill time, he ticks off the night sounds: the garbagemen, the El, the cop on his beat. After years of experience, these have become as carefully calibrated as any clock; he doesn't need to consult the one hanging on the wall. Yet as each night joins the next, the overall effect is cyclic since, sooner or later, all nights must end. The nirvana he experiences now, a kind of mindless oblivion, is a precursor of the death he longs for. When he hears the ambulance in the street and imagines a conversation with the attending physician, he says, "Will he die, Doctor, or isn't he lucky?" (*Hughie* 26). It is no accident that he shares the name of a dead man.

Erie Smith, down on his luck and nearing desperation, is also associated with both modalities of time in the play. Like Charlie, he takes comfort in the cyclic nature of experience. He's hit losing streaks before, he tells the clerk, but he always bounces back; life has its ups and downs. "I've been in the big bucks," he says. "More'n once, and I will be again" (*Hughie* 15). This faith, we suspect, has helped him to survive.

Furthermore, the play implies that his experience is fairly typical. O'Neill assigns him the name "Smith" quite deliberately, then draws our attention to it by having Erie emphasize that it's his real name ("Ain't that a knockout!"). He insists that Charlie call him "Erie," since if there's a sucker (and a night clerk) born every minute, he says, there are *ten*

Smiths born during the same time, thousands of "Smiths" following the same cycle.

Erie is also associated with time as a continuum: one way, irreversible, and in his case—as in so many of O'Neill's characters of this period—downward. Even allowing for his tendency to exaggerate in his own favor (he is described in the list of characters as a teller of tales), we gather that life for Smith has been a steady, if gradual, decline. He tells of meeting Hughie for the first time just after returning from Tijuana where he'd made a "big killing." He returned all the way in a drawing room with a blond movie star. "I was lucky in them days," he says. "Used to follow the horses South every winter," he adds, but "I don't no more. Sick of traveling" (*Hughie* 23). He insists, arousing our suspicions, that he can still "make" the Follies dolls if he wants to; "I ain't slippin'" (*Hughie* 16). The hourglass keeps emptying, and even Erie can't deny it completely.

In some ways, he doesn't want to. Like Hickey before him, Erie is an apostle of change. What Hughie needed in his life was "interest," Erie insists. In the fantasies that the gambler would spin for the dead clerk, stories of glamour and excitement, horse racing and fancy cars and beautiful women (in that order), he brought vitality and zest to the dull routine of Hughie's life, one much like that of the present clerk. In this, he reminds us of the early Hickey, who, before the events of *Iceman*, used to join the bums in a binge twice yearly, blowing in like a breath of fresh air and relieving the stultifying boredom of their lives.[20] Like another predecessor, Con Melody, Erie relied on his imagination to create a persona that Hughie would find exciting. "The bigger I made myself the more he lapped it up," Erie says. "He thought gangsters was romantic. So I fed him some baloney about highjacking I'd done once. I told him I knew all the Big Shots.... Hughie wanted to think me and Legs Diamond was old pals. So I give him that too. I give him anything he cried for" (*Hughie* 28–29).

The difference between this self-creation and that of Con (aside from the fact that Con's is more solidly anchored in reality) is that Erie's tale-telling depends upon an audience. Melody bolsters his self-esteem in front of a mirror; he speaks only to himself, while Smith's self-creation, like the pipe dreams of Harry and company, is communitarian in nature.

Erie has managed to survive thus far by virtue of his relationship with Hughie. His nightly return to an admiring audience imposed some sense of meaning or purpose on the trivial events of the day. "Some nights I'd come back here without a buck, feeling lower than a snake's belly," he tells Charlie, "and first thing you know I'd be lousy with jack, bettin' a grand a race. Oh, I was wise I was kiddin' myself. I ain't a sap. But what the hell, Hughie loved it, and it didn't cost nobody nothin', and if every guy along Broadway who kids himself was to drop dead there wouldn't be nobody left" (*Hughie* 29). This is basically a cyclic experience of life. The mutual pipe dreams of the night give both men the strength to face the coming day. But reality intrudes with Hughie's death, and Erie's luck and confidence abruptly disappear. Time has caught up with him.

Charlie, too, is defeated by the passage of time. The usual comfort he derives from the routines of the night, the El trains and streetcars passing into oblivion one by one, is suddenly not enough. As he counts the slow hours, we are aware that his real battle is not with this guest who won't stop talking or his aching feet or even his humdrum existence, but with time itself. Director Bengt Ekerot of Stockholm's Royal Dramatic Theatre reflected this dimension when, at the play's world premiere, he had the clerk count silently on his fingers as each El train passed—a gesture which reviewer Henry Hewes called "the action most essential to the drama."[21]

At Erie's lowest point, when he is "too defeated even to twirl his room key" (*Hughie* 30), the symbolic fetish with which he wards off death,[22] Charlie also reaches his nadir. The stillness of the night closes in on him and reminds him of life's final silence, death: "The Clerk's mind still cannot make a getaway because the city remains silent, and the night vaguely reminds him of death ... 'I should have paid 492 more attention. After all, he is company. He is awake and alive. I should use him to help me live through the night.'" (*Hughie* 30). Thus he seizes upon Erie in the hope that his rambling chatter will bring him back to life. He recalls Smith's mention of gambling, and, as it occurs to him that Erie might know his hero, Arnold Rothstein, he "is now suddenly impervious to the threat of Night and Silence" (*Hughie* 32). The link between the two lonely, desperate men is forged and, as Charlie assumes the role of the dead clerk, the old cycle is once again resumed. If linear time has not been defeated, they have at least discovered a way to cheat it a little longer.

As such, the play ends on a positive note; life wins out over death, although it is hardly what one would call optimistic.[23] It is true that life prevails—at least for the moment, and that a bond is formed between two human beings that will strengthen and sustain them both. But the vision of life that O'Neill presents to us is attenuated at best. There is no possibility of transcendence, no viable means of breaking through the limitations of time and space, no discovery of ultimate meaning or value. O'Neill employs religious language at the point of the clerk's transformation ("Beatific vision swoons on the empty pools of [his] eyes. He resembles a holy saint, recently elected to Paradise"), but the images echo ironically. The "rapt hero worship [which] transfigure[s] his pimply face" (*Hughie* 32) is merely for Arnold Rothstein, a gambler associated with the New York underworld as well as Tammany Hall, hence a symbol of the city's corruption. The cycle of mutual self-deception is merely perpetuated, as Charlie takes Hughie's place and the pipe dream goes on.

It is interesting that O'Neill does not employ ritual in this play and that the few religious allusions that he selects are used ironically, especially when we consider the time of *Hughie*'s composition. O'Neill conceived the play as early as 1940 and worked on it intermittently through 1941 and 1942; the last notation of his "going over" this drama, as he puts it in his notebook, occurs in June of 1942. During this period he completed *Long Day's Journey into Night* and a first draft of *A Moon for the Misbegotten*, works in which, as chapters 5 and 6 will detail, O'Neill employs ritual precisely at that juncture when linear time and memory threaten to overwhelm the characters. This would suggest that there is no unwavering, tidy progression in O'Neill's thinking or, in psychological terms, in the resolution of his anguish over personal memories. While he composed the serene *Moon*, a play which puts to rest his dead brother Jamie (and by extension, deals with his own guilt), he worked on the much more cynical *Hughie*. But the central issues in all of the plays remain constant; the themes that obsessed O'Neill throughout the historical cycle continued to haunt him up through his final works. They are questions of the greatest import, dealing ultimately with free will in the face of the past and the prospect of the future, which only brings death with certainty. What are we to do if we live *By Way of Obit*?

NOTES

1. Eugene O'Neill, *The Iceman Cometh* (New York: Random House, 1940) 25. All future quotations will be taken from this edition, with page numbers included parenthetically in the text.

2. Earlier, that is, in terms of their conception and initial drafts, not necessarily their dates of completion. O'Neill continued to revise *Poet* up until 1942 and never finished *More Stately Mansions*.

3. For the most concise and thorough information on the autobiographical sources for the characters in *Iceman*, see Floyd, *At Work*, 260–68. With the possible exception of McGloin and the tarts, all the characters seem to be based partially or wholly on people O'Neill knew or knew of; interestingly, O'Neill says that "the most imaginary character in the play" is Hickey (Sheaffer, *Artist*, 498).

4. See Laurin R. Porter, "*The Iceman Cometh* as Crossroad in O'Neill's Long Journey," *Modern Drama*, 31 (March 1988): 56–62.

5. That was the winter of O'Neill's attempted suicide at Jimmy-the-Priest's, a New York waterfront dive where he had been living with the bums and outcasts he later immemorialized in *The Iceman Cometh*. That same summer saw him living with his family in a rare period of relative harmony at the New London Monte Cristo cottage; shortly thereafter he learned of his consumption and left for the sanitorium, where he made his famous resolution to become a playwright. Thus, both personally and artistically, O'Neill's life turned around that year; *Iceman* and *Long Day's Journey* tell the story of his two "families" at that critical juncture.

6. Sullivan's prototype is suggested in Joe Mott's interview with "de Big Chief." Although Harry refers to the chief as "Big Bill," it is likely that O'Neill's model was "Big Tim" Sullivan. For the most thorough analysis of the cultural milieu of *Iceman*, see John Henry Raleigh's *The Plays of Eugene O'Neill* (Carbondale: Southern Illinois University Press, 1965) 66–75.

7. A frequently quoted anecdote has it that when Laurence Langner suggested that O'Neill eliminate some of the references to "pipe dreams," noting that the phrase or its equivalent was expressed eighteen times, the playwright replied emphatically, "I *intended* it to have been repeated eighteen times!" (see, e.g., Sheaffer, *Artist*, 572).

8. Egil Törnqvist, *A Drama of Souls: Studies in O'Neill's Supernaturalistic Technique* (New Haven: Yale University Press, 1969) 249–50.

9. An interesting detail in this regard is the fact that Mosher has a heavy brass watch-chain but no watch (*Iceman* 7).

10. The communion motif has received its fullest treatment in Cyrus Day's classic article, "The Iceman and the Bridegroom," in which he points out the parallels between Leonardo da Vinci's painting of the last supper and O'Neill's careful staging of Harry's birthday party. Like Christ, Day points out, Hickey has twelve disciples. They all drink wine at the party, and Hickey leaves, again like Christ, aware that he goes to his execution. The three tarts correspond with the three Marys, while

> one of the derelicts, Parritt, resembles Judas Iscariot in several ways. He is the twelfth in the list of dramatis personae; Judas is twelfth disciple in the New Testament. He has betrayed his anarchist mother for a paltry $200; Judas betrayed Christ for thirty pieces of silver. He is from the far-away Pacific Coast; Judas was from far-away Judaea. Hickey reads his mind and motives; Christ reads Judas's. Parritt compares himself to Iscariot when he says that his mother would regard anyone who quit the "Movement" as a Judas who ought to be boiled in oil. He commits suicide by jumping off a fire escape; Judas fell from a high place (Acts 1:18) or "hanged himself" (Matthew 27:5).

See Cyrus Day, "The Iceman and the Bridegroom," *Modern Drama*, 1 (May 1958): 6–7.

11. Of the many commentators who point to the confessional elements of *Iceman*, Raleigh provides the most thorough history of the background and practice of confession, as well as its occurrence in Western literature. He distinguishes between two types: the private (auricular) confession made to a priest and the public one made to the community at large. Parritt's confession to Larry is of the former variety; Hickey's to Hope and the boarders, the latter. John Henry Raleigh, "The Last Confession: O'Neill and the Catholic Confessional," in Floyd, *World View*, 212–28.

12. The proprietor of Jimmy-the-Priest's, the model for Hope, "earned his name because he looked more like an ascetic than a saloonkeeper" (see Gelbs 161–62). To the extent that Harry partakes of this role, he parallels Slade not just as patriarch but also as father-confessor.

13. The confessional experience brings Parritt relief not because it cancels his sin, but because it allows him his punishment (note Slade's "God damn you" as he sends him to his death). If the ritual were fully efficacious, both penitents would be reincorporated into the community, but this is not the case. Hickey and Parritt remain intruders to the end.

14. Leonard Chabrowe, in *Ritual and Pathos: The Theater of O'Neill* (Lewisburg, Pa.: Bucknell University Press, 1976) sees O'Neill's aesthetics in terms of two primary thrusts:

the theater as a temple to Dionysus and drama as a ritualistic celebration of life, on the one hand, and the idea of life as inevitably tragic on the other. The former culminates for Chabrowe in *The Iceman Cometh*; the latter, in *Long Day's Journey*. Of *Iceman* he writes, "Life, with its manifold suffering, is accepted and renewed through a celebratory experience of it. For a celebratory experience, a participation in ritual, a singing and dancing about life, exorcises all pain and the fear of death, magically invoking more life" (97–98). I have difficulty reconciling the play's decidedly bleak conclusion about the necessity of illusions and life as a waiting for death with Chabrowe's notion of a "celebratory experience." One hardly experiences *Iceman* as "magically invoking more life."

15. For a more detailed treatment of this matter, see my "*Hughie*: Pipe Dream for Two" in James J. Martine, ed., *Critical Essays on Eugene O'Neill* (Boston: G. K. Hall, 1984) 178–88.

16. The following February, O'Neill refers in his notes to what may have been a ninth play in the series, the "Thompson-rat idea." See Floyd, *At Work*, 346n.

17. See Floyd, *At Work*, 349.

18. Gelbs, 844.

19. Eugene O'Neill, *Hughie* (New Haven: Yale University Press, 1959) 7. Subsequent citations in the text refer to this edition and will be indicated parenthetically.

20. Smith also resembles Hickey in that he is associated with chronological time in the play. If Hickey prides himself on never forgetting a face, Erie is a whiz at guessing ages. He accurately puts Charlie at forty-three or forty-four, though he looks over fifty; the clerk himself can't remember which it is.

21. Henry Hewes, "*Hughie*," *Saturday Review*, October 4, 1958; rpt. Oscar Cargill, N. Bryllion Fagin, William J. Fisher, eds., *O'Neill and His Plays: Four Decades of Criticism* (New York: New York University Press, 1961) 226.

22. Bogard notes in this regard:

> The use of the key is important stage business. It is the only non-verbal sound from within the lobby until the dice roll along the counter at the end of the play. O'Neill marks the turning point in the play, the moment when Erie hits the farthest ebb of his loneliness, with the stage direction, "*For a while he is too defeated even to twirl his room key*" (*Hughie* 30). The moment was underscored memorably in the Stockholm production when the actor, Bengt Eklund, dropped the key. In so bare a scene, the action, the loss of the fetish, assumed climactic proportions. (Bogard 420n)

23. There are those who disagree with me on this point. Raleigh, in *The Plays of Eugene O'Neill*, calls *Hughie* "one of the most optimistic plays that O'Neill ever wrote" (28). J. Dennis Rich also takes this position. Rich sees the late plays (*Iceman*, *Long Day's Journey*, and *Hughie*) as existential in their vision, dramatizing Camus's definition of the absurd: man's confrontation with a meaningless universe. See "Exile without Remedy: The Late Plays of Eugene O'Neill," in Floyd, *World View*, 257–76.

DORIS ALEXANDER

Mourning Becomes Electra

"Life is growth—or a joke one plays on oneself!" O'Neill decided. *Dynamo* had been a step back. He felt it wronged his love for Carlotta, and he told her that his next play would "make the world see how much you have done for me." He had battled the forces of hatred and death within himself, and he wanted a theme to fit that struggle. When he found and plunged into it, he exulted to Saxe Commins: "It's the sort of thing I needed to come to me—one that will *call* for everything I can give it—a glorious opportunity to grow and surpass everything I've ever done before!" He did not know whether he had the "stuff" to do it, but he did know "I'd rather fail at the Big Stuff and remain a success in my own spiritual eyes, than go on repeating, or simply equalling, work I've done before." It would be "the biggest and hardest I have ever tackled."

The first idea had come to him in the spring of 1926, when he thought of "a modern psychological drama using one of the old legend plots of Greek tragedy"—the Electra, or the Medea. The Electra story would set him in direct rivalry with the great Greek dramatists, for Aeschylus, Sophocles, and Euripides had all treated it. He would make it a real trilogy, like theirs, with three plays treating the same characters. Through it he could achieve—what he had always striven to arrive at—a sense, like the Greek sense, "of the Force

---

From *Eugene O'Neill's Creative Struggle: The Decisive Decade, 1924–1933*, pp. 149–169. © 1992 by Doris Alexander.

behind" life, whatever one called it, "Fate, God, our biological past creating our present." It was to be "primarily drama of hidden life forces."

On his voyage to China this play of hidden forces took life, and so the sea washes through it from beginning to end. His fated family became shipbuilders and shipowners, and he had them long for liberation by sea, just as he had felt on the *Charles Racine* that he could "at last be free, on the open sea, with the trade wind" in his hair. The sea chanty "Shenandoah" sounds throughout his play, for he thought that it "more than any other holds in it the brooding rhythm of the sea." Although he set the play in the family house, haunted by the family past, he put one act aboard the *Flying Trades* and very deliberately placed it at the "center of whole work" to emphasize "sea background of family and symbolic motive of sea as means of escape and release." In this act the two lovers, Adam and Christine, plot in vain to escape by sea after the chanty "Shenandoah" ("Way—ay, I'm bound away") has reached an ironic crescendo of longing.

The sea and O'Neill's recall of the white sails of the *Charles Racine* determined his choice of time. He wanted to make this play American, and so he needed an American war to match the Trojan War from which the Greek hero Agamemnon had triumphantly returned to be murdered by his wife and her lover. O'Neill thought World War I was too close; his audiences would not see beyond its surface to the real drama of hidden forces, and he was sure that the American Revolution would also blind them with its "romantic grammar-school-history associations." The "only possibility" was the fratricidal Civil War, which fit a "drama of murderous family love and hate" and provided a detached "mask" for the timeless struggle beneath. It allowed him to make the ships of his play Clippers and to use his old thrill at white sails and his old longing to reach China of his voyage out of Boston to Argentina, for the Clippers had all been bound for China by way of Argentina in the tea trade. He made a China voyage the heart of this play, which began to grow in him on the "Arabian Sea en route for China" and on the "China Sea."

He set his investigation of family fate where his own family's fate had worked itself out, in the small New England "seaport, shipbuilding town" of New London. He actually called it "N.L." in his notes. New England, with its "Puritan conviction of man born to sin and punishment," was the "best possible dramatically for Greek plot of crime and retribution," he thought, and he could reexamine his own guilts through all five members of his New England family. He called his Agamemnon "Ezra Mannon," and "Mannon," suggestive of "Man," became the name of his tragic family, whose struggle would reveal the larger struggle of life-and-death forces within the soul of man.

O'Neill hoped the play would have a "strange quality of unreal reality." He wanted to show that the surfaces of life—which are taken for reality—are meaningless and that the great realities, the "hidden life forces" beneath the surface, are so overwhelming when perceived, as to seem unreal. (He who sees Pan, dies.) So he built his penetration through surfaces into the three plays of his trilogy. Each one has the curtain rise to reveal a painted backdrop of the Mannon house as it looks to the townspeople from the street, set in a splendor of orchards and gardens behind a white picket fence. Then this obviously artificial surface lifts to bring the audience directly before the reality of the house and all the embattled forces within the family. O'Neill had seen at once that he could make his house "Greek temple front type that was rage" at the time and that it was "absolutely justifiable, not forced Greek similarity." He remembered the Greek Revival houses of his boyhood New London, but he took care to buy Howard Major's *Domestic Architecture of the Early American Republic: The Greek Revival*, in which he found just the severe tomblike house he wanted for Ezra Mannon's father, Abe, to have built as a "temple of Hate and Death" after expelling his brother David from the family, supposedly in outraged morality but actually in jealous revenge. O'Neill took for it Marshall House at Rodsman's Neck, New York, with its cold stone base, its pagan portico with six tall columns, its central doorway with a "squared transom and sidelights flanked by intermediate columns," and its arrangement of windows—only he changed its eight steps to four in mercy to the actors and added the shutters he needed for his final catastrophe. This house, like the house in *Desire Under the Elms*, was to participate in the drama. The family is torn between pagan joy in life, and Puritan condemnation of pleasure as sin, and their conflict appears in the facade of the house, where the pagan temple portico is stuck on "like an incongruous white mask" over the "sombre gray ugliness" of its stone walls. In the first play "Homecoming," all the windows of this outraged house reflect the sun "in a resentful glare," and as the murder is planned the inside of the house is stained with the crimson of the setting sun. Whether the columns are bathed in sunlight, haunted moonlight, or bloody sunset, they throw their shadows in black bars against the wall, suggesting the imprisonment of the fated family.

Each of the three plays moves from the embattled exterior of the house to its haunted interior, dominated by the family past in the portraits of the dead Puritan Mannons. Most of the indoor scenes take place at night, and in "the flickering candlelight" the eyes of the portraits take on "an intense bitter life." They glare so "accusingly" at the Electra character after all her crimes, that she justifies herself to them as if they were living judges. O'Neill knew that this haunted interior came out of his deepest self, "whom the past always haunts so persistently." As soon as he had written these plays and had returned to America, he went to New London with Carlotta to "revisit Pequot Ave. old time haunts," and right after that visit he got "Idea play—house-with-the-masked-dead and two living intruding strangers," so much had his own family past in the house at 325 Pequot Avenue haunted him when he designed the haunted interior of the Mannon house.

He even dared to give the same penetration through surfaces, the same sense of "unreal reality" to his characters. Each of the plays begins with a group of townspeople, looking upon the Mannons in a prying, gossiping way as the New Londoners of O'Neill's youth had once looked upon the O'Neills. O'Neill gave them purely "exterior characterization," each with a few emphatic mannerisms. He also made the two fiancés of the tragic young Mannons "almost characterless"—embodiments of simplicity, goodness, and health. All these external people set off the entirely "inner" characterization of the fated Mannons. He wanted to avoid for the Mannons, "as far as possible and consistent with living people, the easy superficial characterization of individual mannerisms." Because they speak directly out of the passions engendered in the family past, O'Neill found that any experiments with asides or stylized soliloquies—and he tried both in the course of rewritings—only got "in the way of the play's drive." His characters were already speaking out of the depths, out of the hidden forces within them, and no technique could cut deeper than that. He thought his play "needed great language to lift it beyond itself. I haven't got that." Instead, he created a prose with a "forceful repeating accent and rhythm" that expressed the "compulsion of passions engendered in family past." The rhythm was so intense that the actors found anything but a letter-perfect reading of their lines broke the headlong drive of the play. All O'Neill's poetry went into the living symbolism of color, light, sound, and action, composed for the theater.

He needed a tragic conflict from the previous generation of Mannons to weigh upon his characters and to motivate his Aegisthus to take revenge on the Agamemnon, Ezra Mannon. A modern audience would not accept the legendary revenge of Agamemnon's father on Aegisthus's father for seducing his wife: serving him up his own children's flesh at a banquet. The "general spirit," not the "details of legend," interested O'Neill, so he eliminated the cannibal banquet and used the rivalry in love of the brothers, but it took hold of him only when he thought to make it a rivalry over a nurse in the family, rather than a wife, and conceived of her as Irish among the Puritan Mannons. This fatal nurse girl came out of his memories of the nurse introduced into his own family, Sarah Sandy. She had been English in a family of Irish, and O'Neill suspected that his mother had chosen an Englishwoman because, as he wrote in his family history, "Husband hates English intensely. Always hostile to nurse secretly and she to him. Was M [Mother] actuated by revenge motives on husband in this choice—to get reliable ally in war with husband?" Sarah's introduction into his family, O'Neill knew, had had fatal repercussions for him, and he thought of putting its reverse—an Irish nurse among Puritans—into his fated family.

One of the striking ideas that came to him as he worked with the second draft of *Mourning Becomes Electra* was to make all the women in the play look alike, starting with the nurse. He had Ezra Mannon select a wife who resembles the nurse he adored as a boy, and had the Aegisthus character fall in love with her because she looks like his mother, that same fatal nurse. O'Neill had read the popular book his friend Kenneth Macgowan had written with Dr. G. V Hamilton, *What Is Wrong with Marriage*, with data from the research in marriage in which O'Neill had participated. They had pointed out that a man's "ideal of feminine beauty" usually "goes straight back to the mother of his boyhood." O'Neill saw that this idea would give him a chain of fatal attractions among his Mannons in line with modern psychological theory, and he used it because he had seen its truth in the power over his own love choices exercised by his second mother, his nurse Sarah Sandy.

He certainly knew that in Carlotta he had selected, for the first time, a wife with his own mother's beautiful dark eyes and his mother's "long and straight" nose (as described in *Long Day's Journey into Night*). He dedicated the first galley proofs of *Mourning Becomes Electra* to Carlotta "with a large kiss on her long nose." Agnes had been very beautiful in a totally different style, with ash-blonde hair and blue-green eyes and prominent cheekbones. The light hair, blue eyes, and high cheekbones all reflected Sarah Sandy. Moreover, with Agnes, O'Neill had brought another Englishwoman into his Irish family. In a loving note of thanks to her for pictures of herself and Shane (when he had left Provincetown to stay with his parents in New York for his first Broadway production, *Beyond the Horizon*), O'Neill gave her a message, supposedly for his infant son, in which she was to "tell him my advice as one Shin Fein to another: Never trust a woman, or depend on her, especially—as Shane the Proud will be sure to whisper out of the subconscious—a woman born in London, surely!" He told her of the pride and joy he and his parents took in the pictures of her and Shane; she looked so beautiful he feared that she could not really be his. His profound love for Agnes had roots in his attachment for his English nurse, and so in a way all the pain, passion, love, and hatred of his marriage had proceeded from her.

Even before Agnes he had been drawn to a woman who recalled his nurse rather than his own mother when he became caught up in Kathleen Jenkins, who was an Episcopalian, rather than Irish Catholic, with light hair, blue-gray eyes, and broad cheekbones. His involvement with Kathleen went into his story of rivalry between Abe and David Mannon over the nurse girl, for David Mannon, expelled from the family by his brother Abe, repeats the main outline of O'Neill's story. He gets the girl with child, marries her, then is filled with shame, takes to drink, and finally commits suicide—as O'Neill had tried to do. This old suicide hangs over all the action—as O'Neill's old suicide had been hanging over him—and it brings with it a chain of further suicides.

At first O'Neill pictured his Clytemnestra—Christine—in the image of his own mother. His Plot Notes give her "beautiful, large and dark" eyes like his mother's, and the "reddish brown" hair that his mother recalls having in *Long Day's Journey into Night*. After he had decided on a fatal Irish nurse girl for all his women to resemble, he made the appearance typically Irish with "hair black as night and great soft eyes as blue as the Caribbean Seas." Then he decided to erase his own intimate Irish-English conflict out of the nurse, and he made her French-Canadian. He was writing in a French château of the Loire Valley, and if a French nurse pushed her way inexorably into his mind she came probably as the ghost of his son Shane's nurse Fifine Clark, born in and married out of France. O'Neill had been pained by her separation from his children—coming as it did at the same time as his own—for he read his own loss in hers. News of her death came to him in a cable on July 13, 1929, just as he was working on the plot for *Mourning Becomes Electra*, and he wrote in his *Work Diary*: "Deeply grieved—real mother to Shane & Oona." So the "real" mother of his children combined with his own nurse-mother and really real mother, and although he kept the eyes blue as the Caribbean Sea, he gave the nurse girl hair that combined his mother's reddish brown with his nurse's blonde to make a color "partly a copper brown, partly a bronze gold." He also made Ezra's wife part French, as was Carlotta. His own mother ended by setting only one clear sign of her presence on the nurse-mother in his play; she gave her the name "Marie," French for her own name "Mary."

O'Neill wanted all the women of his play—Marie Brantôme, Christine Mannon, and her daughter Lavinia—to share an inner "psychic identity" shown by their physical resemblance. Marie, the Canuck nurse girl, and the French-origin Christine have the same pagan freedom. The family servant Seth recalls Marie to Lavinia as "frisky and full of life—with something free and wild about her like an animile." Christine also moves with a "flowing animal grace." Their postures stand in sharp contrast to the wooden military movements of the Puritan Mannons, who fall into the stiff stances of statues of eminent dead men in parks. O'Neill expressed the same conflict between pagan joy and Puritan life-denial in their dress. At first he thought the color for Christine should be the deep purplish crimson of Cybel's parlor and Tiberius's brothel-palace, but at last he chose green—the color of life—and had her appear first in green satin and then in green velvet. Her first defiant gesture is to carry a great bunch of flowers into the tomblike Mannon house. Her green is set against the black of the life-repressing Mannons, and black is the color of death. It is the color that becomes her daughter, as the title "Mourning Becomes Electra" declares. At the beginning of the play, Electra—called "Lavinia" after her other name in the legends, "Laodicea"—identifies with the Puritan Mannons, wears black, and echoes their wooden posture and military manner. She rejects any comparison with her mother, insisting, "I'm not a bit like her! Everybody knows I take after Father!" But Adam Brant sees at once: "Your face is the dead image of hers. And look at your hair." Lavinia has the same contrast between conscious identification with her parent of the opposite sex and real psychic identity with her parent of the same sex that O'Neill gave Eben of *Desire Under the Elms*—he who had insisted that he was "Maw—every drop o' blood!" although his brothers saw that he was "Like his Paw. Dead spit an' image!" O'Neill had seen just such a contrast in himself, with open hostility toward his father and inner identification with him, like the "strange, hidden psychic identity" between all the women of *Mourning Becomes Electra* and between all the men. In his "Diagram" for Dr. Hamilton he placed his "hatred and defiance" of his father as open and outward, while inwardly he lived in a world of "fantasy-father as hero." This self-knowledge went into all his fated Mannons. They really are quite unlike the orthodox Freudian Oedipus complex, in which the love for the father is outward, while the hostility is inner and repressed. No wonder O'Neill rejected the accusation of such critics as Barrett Clark that he was following psychoanalytic theory in this play, and tried to tell them—what was perfectly evident to him—that he could "have written *Mourning Becomes Electra* almost exactly as it is if I had never heard of Freud or Jung or the others." Out of the psychic identities, and out of the fated attraction of Puritan Mannon men for women with conflicting pagan life-strivings, O'Neill's "modern psychological approximation of Greek sense of fate" emerged.

"HOMECOMING"

Electra had fascinated O'Neill, and even in this first play—essentially the tragedy of her father Agamemnon—he made her his protagonist. So she became the most deeply imbued of all his characters with his own struggle against the forces of hatred and death, his own longing for life and love. He gave her his own profound loneliness, and the feeling of being shut out of love that had come with his exile to boarding school, and his resentment—in his case against his father—for sending him there. He found a way to have Lavinia rejected by her mother, so that she has a similar feeling of being shut out of love—and it served him also to motivate Christine's hatred for her husband—for the legendary reasons did not fit his play. In *What Is Wrong with Marriage*, Macgowan and Hamilton had pointed out that a major cause of sexual disability in married women was "a husband's ineptitude as a lover" and that it was "the husband's *initial* ineptitude that counts" rather than his later abilities in the act of love. Ezra Mannon's Puritan shame cripples his lovemaking into crude lust, so that his first relations with his wife change her love for him to "disgust." The disgust is so intense that she hates even the child born of it. She tells Lavinia, "You were always my wedding night to me—and my honeymoon!" Lavinia feels that her mother "stole all love from me when I was born!" She feels in her way what O'Neill himself felt and wrote into *Long Day's Journey into Night*, that he would "always be a stranger who never feels at home" and "who must always be a little in love with death!" Mourning—the color of death—becomes her, fits her destiny, and her tragic struggle for life and love was O'Neill's own.

As dominated by hatred as Lavinia is at the beginning of his play, O'Neill had been in the year preceding the writing of it. Into this story of betrayal went all his own sense of betrayal during the death throes of his marriage to Agnes, and as always, inextricably intertwined with it, came the crucial betrayal of his life, his mother's drug addiction. Both found their way into the plot he developed from the legends. He found a way to allow Lavinia to share in her father's tragedy, betrayed with his betrayal, and he did so by having Christine bring her lover to the house under the guise of courting Lavinia, and so awaken her love for him. Her love puts her in unsuccessful rivalry with her mother as she had been all her life before for the love of her father and brother. Her discovery that Adam Brant has been cuckolding her father brings discovery that Adam has been betraying her as well. Jealousy—more than protection of her father—moves her to divide her mother from Adam. By doing so she provokes the murder of her father that leaves her doubly bereft of love at the end of "Homecoming."

O'Neill easily put himself into her struggle, into that of her father, and even into that of his betrayer, Christine, whose struggle to free herself from a marriage poisoned by hatred echoes his own struggle to liberate himself from Agnes. The only character who did not immediately invite O'Neill's participation in his tragedy was that of his Aegisthus, Adam Brant, son of the nurse girl. When O'Neill read over his first draft, he found the character "hackneyed and thin" and decided "Must find new one." At that point a complete character walked into his play and blended so fully with his fated family that O'Neill himself never saw that his Captain Brant was really George Bernard Shaw's Captain Brassbound stepped intact out of *Captain Brassbound's Conversion*. (O'Neill had read Shaw's play years ago and had even seen it performed while a student at Harvard.) Once Captain

Brassbound had walked out of Morocco and out of Shaw's inquiry into the meaning of justice, he became entirely unrecognizable, for in O'Neill's play he immediately fell passionately in love, which he never would have done for Shaw. Still, he brought with him the same motive for revenge that he had against his uncle in Shaw's play, whom he charges "with the death of my mother and the theft of my inheritance." In *Mourning Becomes Electra* he accuses his cousin Ezra Mannon, and does so out of the same feeling of guilt he had in Shaw's play because he had not been "very fond" of his mother or "very good" to her. In Shaw, "she had unfortunately a very violent temper," and Brassbound confesses that his childhood had been "Hell." In O'Neill's play Brant confesses that his mother had been "very strict" with him, like Brassbound's, even beating him—although this confession conflicts with O'Neill's other picture of her as petting and spoiling the boy Ezra. In both plays the Captain Brassbound-Brant hides his own guilt by accusing his uncle-cousin of letting his mother die "of sickness and starvation," for he himself had fled from her. He is very touchy about her honor in both plays. In Shaw he springs at his uncle, crying, "He did not spare my mother—'that woman,' he calls her—because of her sex. I will not spare him because of his age." In O'Neill's play Brant springs up at Lavinia's taunt at her, crying, "Belay, damn you!—or I'll forget you're a woman—no Mannon can insult her while I—." Probably it was Brassbound who made Brant a "captain," and from there O'Neill went on to make him a Clipper captain and gave him the same romantic appearance, "more like a gambler or a poet than a ship captain," of a notorious Clipper captain who appeared, picture and all, in one of the many Clipper books O'Neill had bought for background. So closely did O'Neill associate Captain Robert H. Waterman with his Brant that he had a chantyman in the ship scene shout up at him, "I don't give a damn if ye air a skipper! Ye could be Bully Waterman himself an' I'd not let you insult me!" In dress, Brant was Bully Waterman. Otherwise, he kept his Brassbound origin, and even took from Shaw's character the irony of judging a judge. Before Brassbound took over Brant, Ezra Mannon had been only "town's leading citizen, Mayor before war." He became a former judge as well when Brassbound came into O'Neill's play. O'Neill had Ezra look down from his portrait in black judge's robes, as his wife and Brant sentence him to death, and the judge judging him looks so much like him, sitting sternly in his chair, that Christine is frightened and asks him to move. Adam says, when he sees the portrait, "It would be damned queer if you fell in love with me because I recalled Ezra Mannon to you!"

The whole plot became invested with O'Neill's mistrust of Agnes in the last year of their marriage. He had Christine cover her meetings with her lover under visits to a genuinely sick father in New York. Agnes's father had fallen ill with tuberculosis, and Agnes's departures from Bermuda to New York to see after him had aroused O'Neill's old distrust and all his uncertainty of her love. She had only to postpone her return to drive him frantic, and when she did so in April he sent her a telegram that even he realized was, he said, "harsh and unreasonable but I had been counting the days." He said that if she failed him Wednesday he would never trust her word again. Later, when his brains had become "wooly with hatred," he confided to Kenneth Macgowan his suspicion of what a private detective would discover about Agnes's infidelities once set to trace her past. His suspicions even found a vent in his first draft for his second God-trilogy play. In it his hero would be tortured when his wife visited her father by "imagining that she had lied to him about the purpose of her visit, that she was being unfaithful to him." In *Mourning Becomes Electra* Lavinia becomes the detective who spies out the infidelity, and she makes her first threatening hint of her discovery in a pointed question about her grandfather, who "seems to have been sick so much this past year."

Ezra's homecoming became fraught with O'Neill's two crucial homecomings, that of 1926, when he began the last struggle to preserve his marriage, and that of October 1927, when he made his final struggle, telling Agnes, "I'm simply eaten up by impatience and actually counting the days! ... It will be so marvelous to take you in my arms and kiss you again!" Instead of his imagined homecoming, he had seen the death of their love. In *Mourning Becomes Electra*, Ezra Mannon returns from the orgy of hatred and death of the Civil War, bent on a desperate struggle to save his marriage, to regain his wife's love, to break through his own barriers of silence and give voice to the truth of his feeling for her. He has been always "a strange, hidden man," and he confesses to his wife, "Something queer in me keeps me mum about the things I'd like most to say—keeps me hiding the things I'd like to show." The words were O'Neill's. He knew himself to be a quiet man "hiding within a crevice of the mind," with a voice that "begins and ends in silence." O'Neill went so fully into the "inexpressive" Ezra Mannon that he told the cast of this play on opening night, "Like Ezry Mannon I am a bit dumb when it comes to expressing the things I would like most to say." After years of silence Ezra pleads with his wife in front of the moonlit temple of Hate and Death that has been their home to help him save their marriage. His plea is O'Neill's to Agnes. O'Neill wrote Agnes during her April New York visit: "We must get away alone to beaches and places when you return." He thought they should have a private life together as well as a family life. His Ezra tells his wife they might win through "if we'd leave the children and go off" together. Ezra cries to her out of the silence and alienation since their beginning: "I love you. I loved you then, and all the years between, and I love you now."

O'Neill had told Agnes, "I love you! For our nine years I have loved you and you alone, loved *you* with my whole being." All the ironic futility of O'Neill's own struggle and all the horror of his final smash went into Ezra Mannon's homecoming to a wife who plans to murder him.

She does so in a way that shows how intimately O'Neill's distrust of Agnes was linked to the distrust of his mother because of her addiction. Both shape the murder in his play. Of course, O'Neill needed all his ingenuity to let his characters "commit murder without having to dodge detection, arrest, trial scenes," so that retribution would come directly out of the forces that swept them to their crimes. He had Christine murder her husband through a "medicine" that is actually "poison." She lets it be known that he has a heart condition, deliberately provokes a heart attack by taunting him with her infidelity, and then, instead of his medicine, gives him poison she has had Brant send her—and so he appears to have died of angina. The murder takes Agnes's weapon of deliberately provoking jealousy and joins it to O'Neill's mother's betrayal through a "medicine" that was really "poison." (In *Long Day's Journey into Night* he has his mother call the drug "medicine," and his father call it "poison.")

In dying, Ezra makes a commentary on O'Neill's old dream that his mother would rise out of death to reassure him with a message of life and love. For Lavinia, he had the father rise, and his message is the reverse of reassurance. He gasps, "She's guilty—not medicine!" The words bring suspicion of the murder to Lavinia, who enters in time to hear them, yet they apply equally to O'Neill's distrust of a mother who was "guilty"—in very different circumstances—because the drug she administered was "not medicine" but poison. So powerful was that indelible memory that O'Neill meant at first to have Christine commit suicide with the drug that killed her husband, so that the same "medicine" that was really "poison," destroys both, as it had poisoned the life of both his parents.

"THE HUNTED"

The same double betrayal—Agnes and his mother—shaped the second play of *Mourning Becomes Electra*, "The Hunted." In all the legends the son Orestes—whom O'Neill calls "Orin"—knows at once of his mother's guilt. In O'Neill's play it is the revelation, the realization, of his mother's guilt that is his particular tragedy, as it had been in his own case. As a matter of fact, O'Neill and his mother took over Orin and Christine. Christine has had the same "fierce" affection concentrated on her son, as O'Neill's mother, and she treats him exactly as O'Neill's mother treats him in *Long Day's Journey into Night*. Both call their grown son "my baby"; both promise to "nurse" him and both make him "comfortable" with the same gesture—placing a pillow behind his back. Both mothers play father against son by pointing out the father's jealousy. O'Neill's mother says in *Long Day's Journey into Night*, "He's been jealous of you most of all. He knew I loved you most because—." Except that the words are more cruel in *Mourning Becomes Electra*, they are the same. Christine tells Orin his father was "jealous of you. He hated you because he knew I loved you better than anything in the world!" Of course, Christine appears more treacherous because she is deliberately using her son's love in order to escape to her lover. She moves into O'Neill's old vision of the prostitute mother—and into her reincarnation in the Agnes of his distrust, redolent of betrayal. Certainly O'Neill had begun to see clearly the meaning of that old vision, for in less than two years after he finished *Mourning Becomes Electra* he noted in his *Work Diary* that he had "Idea M-harlot play." "M" was his usual abbreviation for "mother," so he had reached the point where he could write a "Mother-harlot" play, with his old vision made perfectly explicit.

"The Hunted" is largely Christine's tragedy, and O'Neill saw her guilt and horror through his remembrance of his mother's, and through his regret at the loss of innocence and trust which came from learning of her loss. Before the goodness of Hazel, Christine almost lets out the truth of her guilt, as she longs for her lost innocence. "If I could only have stayed as I was then! Why can't all of us remain innocent and loving and trusting? But God won't leave us alone. He twists and wrings and tortures our lives with other's lives until—we poison each other to death!" In *Long Day's Journey into Night* his mother's regret for the "poisoning" within her own family comes when she says, "None of us can help the things life has done to us. They're done before you realize it, and once they're done they make you do other things until at last everything comes between you and what you'd like to be, and you've lost your true self forever." The more acute agony in Christine's words was wrung from O'Neill by the last agony of his love for Agnes, by his regret for his own "poisoned" family life—the word was his—and regret for all the torture of their love.

O'Neill endowed Orin with his own nerves, the nerves he would have his father speak of in *Long Day's Journey into Night*, when he calls himself a "healthy hulk," whereas his son has "always been a bundle of nerves like his mother." In *Mourning Becomes Electra*, Ezra tells his wife of Orin's breakdown: "Nerves. I wouldn't notice nerves. He's always been restless. He gets that from you." In fact, O'Neill brought Orin home from the war two days after his father's murder with a head wound and had the horror of the revelation of his mother's guilt, and his own guilt over her suicide after he has killed her lover, complete the shattering of his mind—in line with Euripides' interpretation of the legend, in which Orestes goes mad from the matricide.

Through Orin's haunted war-shattered brain, O'Neill was able to fuse the hidden forces of hatred and death within the nation with those within his fated family, so that the battle of life-and-death forces within the souls of the Mannons shows itself to be a battle within the soul of man. Orin speaks of "murdering" two rebels in a fog. "It was like murdering the same man twice. I had a queer feeling that war meant murdering the same man over and over, and that in the end I would discover the man was myself! Their faces keep coming back in dreams—and they change to Father's face—or to mine—." When he returns to his family's whited "sepulchre" and to his father's corpse laid out within it, the horrors of war become one with the realities of his family. He looks down on the austere face of his dead father in his coffin and says, "Death sits so naturally on you! Death becomes the Mannons!" Orin looks just like the dead man he addresses, and both look like the black-robed judge in the portrait, so his dream becomes palpable. In the end, when he has murdered his mother's lover, he sees his dead father in him. "He looks like me, too! Maybe I've committed suicide!" Actually he has, because Brant's death causes his mother's suicide, and her suicide brings on his own. The family resemblances make the family destiny visible.

The final horror of this second play comes with Christine's realization that her son has killed her lover, and with her last look of mingled fear and hatred at the daughter who has brought him to do it. Inside the temple of Hate and Death, she shoots herself with a "pistol," like the pistol of Agnes's suicidal letter, sending Orin into an agony of remorse: "I drove her to it!" His cry releases all O'Neill's guilt over Agnes joined to all his guilt at bringing on his mother's trouble.

"THE HAUNTED"

At the beginning of the third play, the blood out of the family past shows in a crimson sunset bathing the portico. Seth, the family servant, has bet a townsman that he will be afraid to stay alone in the empty Mannon house from sundown to moonrise. Although Seth intends the bet to make a joke of the town talk that the house is haunted, it actually serves to accentuate the deeper truth of its saturation with the past. Seth himself admits to Hazel and Peter that there is such a thing as "evil spirit," and he himself feels it in the house "like somethin' rottin' in the walls." Even Hazel feels gripped by "something cold" the moment she steps under its portico. So O'Neill set the homecoming of Orin and Lavinia, the last of the Mannons, returned from their China voyage to make a stand for life in the temple of Hate and Death.

Euripides had sent Orestes on a long voyage to the land of the Tauri to recover from the madness brought on by the matricide, and O'Neill had Lavinia take Orin away on one of their own Clippers to China. O'Neill's own China voyage in flight from the hatred and bitterness of his smashed marriage found its way into theirs, even though he disguised the obvious parallel by sending them on from China to one of the South Sea Islands. Yet even this additional voyage came of intimate personal history. With his second draft, he thought to accentuate the sea-longing of the Mannons by giving them all a dream of finding love, innocence, and peace on an island. The island would be for them—so O'Neill told himself—a "mother symbol" charged with their "yearning for prenatal non-competitive freedom from fear." He put it first into Adam Brant, who, having once been shipwrecked on the islands, thinks that they are "as near the Garden of Paradise before sin was discovered as you'll find on this earth!" Indeed, as he is the first male Mannon to enter the play, O'Neill named him Adam after the biblical first man. Adam tells Christine that he wants to take her away on his own Clipper to China and then to the South Pacific Islands: "By God, there's the right place for love and a honeymoon!" Even Ezra Mannon, determined to regain love, thinks he might win through to happiness with his wife if only they could sail to the other side of the world and "find some island." Orin comes back sure that he will find his mother in an island, from having read Melville's book *Typee*, and then hallucinated a mother-island in the first days of his head wound. Orin's most bitter disillusion, as he spies on his mother through the cabin skylight of the *Flying Trades*, is that she is plotting to go with Adam to "my island I told her about—which was she and I—."

Of course, O'Neill was perfectly clear on the Jungian overtones of the island dream. He went out of his way to point out to Barrett Clark that the only book of the psychoanalysts that had really interested him had been Jung's *Psychology of the Unconscious*, but only "in the light of my own experience with hidden human motives." Long before he had read Jung he himself had had a dream-vision of love in which the woman, the mother, merged with the setting of his deepest joy in life, the sea and the sand. He had once written a poem, "On the Dunes," to Beatrice Ashe—to his "Soul Mother of Mine" as he called her. In it her body had been "warm and undulating" like "the sand dunes," and he had found her in the moods of the sea—in the "laughter of spray," in the "exultant wave-crests," and in the "tender smiling" of its calm. So O'Neill put his own old love into Orin's dream of an island where, he tells his mother, "The breaking of the waves was your voice" and "The warm sand was like your skin."

If O'Neill put this old dream into his fated Mannons, he did so because it was also the dream that had permeated his entire love for Agnes. Their first happiness had been spent by the sea, among the dunes of Peaked Hill Bar. They had always longed for an island of perpetual summer and had found it at last—so they thought—on Bermuda. O'Neill told Agnes that it was their "ultimate island where we may rest and live toward our dreams." The very postmarks on their letters declared Bermuda to be "The Isles of Rest." The futility of his Bermuda dream pervaded the island dreams of his doomed Mannons. Even after he finished *Mourning Becomes Electra*, O'Neill still longed for his island. When he returned to America he sought the blessed isles once again on Sea Island Beach, Georgia, where he built "Casa Genotta," the house of Gene and Carlotta.

Even the two images of health, life, love—Peter and Hazel—for whom Lavinia and Orin make their final struggle, came to O'Neill out of his most intimate dreams of love. The names he chose for them were quite transparent—although partly based on the first initials of Pylades and Hermione, the fiancés of the legendary Electra and Orestes. O'Neill first called Lavinia's lover "Peter Oldham," giving his woman the same love ideal as his old mother-identified self, for the "old ham" was, of course, the old actor, his father. His first idea for Hermione was just as transparent. He called her "Hester Sand"—with "Sand" just one letter off the name of his nurse "Sarah Sandy." The next name he found for her—and kept—was even more transparent: "Hazel." O'Neill knew that Carlotta's legal name before she went on stage had been "Hazel Tharsing." Certainly he saw in her the same goodness and purity he put into Hazel, for a letter of his calls her "my pure and unspoiled one." Once O'Neill decided to make Peter and Hazel brother and sister like Orin and Lavinia, he found the same last name for both, "Niles." At this point he and Carlotta were planning a trip down the Nile, where O'Neill expected to feel his spiritual oneness with the ancient Egyptian conviction of the eternal renewal of life as symbolized by the recurrent overflowing of the Nile, bringing fertility and new growth.

He made Lavinia's China voyage culminate in the South Sea Islands as he had originally meant his own to do, and he put all the meaning of his China voyage into hers. On it Lavinia discards the Mannon black for her mother's green, the color of life, and she takes over her mother's struggle for life and love. In the hospital at Shanghai, O'Neill had felt that "all the bitterness got burnt out of me." He had triumphed over the hatred for Agnes, and he had triumphed over the lure of death, the compulsion to repeat his old suicide attempt. China, he knew, had done "a lot for my soul. I live now. I *can* live."

Indeed, it was only after the China voyage that he could consciously identify with his father and so enter with him the world of life-enjoyment and love that had always radiated from him. Only after China did Eugene O'Neill begin openly calling himself "son of the Count of Monte Cristo," because of the "slumbering director in me" (his father had always directed his own company). After China he could scorn the critics of *Dynamo* because he had been born on Times Square, not in Greenwich Village, and had heard dramatic critics "called sons of bitches—and, speaking in general, believed it—ever since I was old enough to recognize the Count of Monte Cristo's voice!"

But en route to China, O'Neill had still been helplessly bedeviled by compulsions out of the past—the whole voyage repeating, as it did, his flight from his first marriage in a flight from his second. And in his rage, his frustration, he became imbued with that other ubiquitous ghost out of the past, his brother Jamie. To Harold DePolo, who had been as much Jamie's friend as his own, and who had been with Jamie during his last self-destructive year of life, O'Neill confessed: "And now comes a sad tale! Prepare to weep! Whether it was sun-wooziness or what, I was introduced by a Frenchman to a swell gambling joint in Saigon and I bucked the wheel—and the game suddenly got me. I must have that Jim strain in me after all." What O'Neill did not tell Harold DePolo was how fully he had taken on Jamie's identity. He had gone on to a "booze bust" in Shanghai as suicidal as Jamie's, and that catastrophe—part alcoholism, part influenza, part nervous breakdown—had come close to bereaving him of love and life together.

Certainly his third trilogy play was haunted by Jamie's despair after their mother died. Orin's guilt, horror, and flashes of perverse malignity took much from Jamie's agony of self-destruction then. Lavinia is torn by watching Orin's pain and by an exasperation like O'Neill's own as he watched his brother destroy himself. He had wanted to be liberated from that lacerating spectacle, and the remembrance went into Lavinia's desperate impulse to push the brother she loves out of life. O'Neill's old feeling of living with his brother's life, of repeating his tragic destiny, had possessed him as he neared China. Sometime during the third draft of *Mourning Becomes Electra* O'Neill grasped the meaning of it all in one vision of how he could make fate—destiny—compulsion out of the past—both visible and palpable to an audience.

He did it by having his characters repeat words and gestures and even scenes out of the family past. Orin and Lavinia in the third play are the image—even to clothing and posture—of their father and mother in the first. Orin repeats his father's furious jealousy at Brant in the first play, and his own repetition of it with his mother in the second. He explodes into suspicions of Lavinia with all of O'Neill's own expectation of betrayal during his marriage to Agnes, which had culminated in all the mad hatred of the divorce delays.

Agnes's way of deliberately provoking his jealousy had found its way into Christine's outbreaks of taunting in his earlier plays, and he had Lavinia repeat them by deliberately provoking her brother to believe his own baseless suspicions. Lavinia herself is bewildered by what she has done, saying, "Oh, Orin, something made me say that to you—against my will—something rose up in me—like an evil spirit!" He laughs: "Ghosts! You never seemed so much like Mother as you did just then!"

The weight of the past upon these two is made tangible by the weapon Orin holds over his sister to keep her from marrying Peter. He writes a family history, and in the earlier versions it goes back to the beginning and merges the history of the country with the history of the family, so that Orin says of it, "I've tried to show that the evil fate goes back to the murder of Indians to steal their lands, to witch burning as a pleasure!" In the published play, it starts with their grandfather Abe Mannon, and Orin tells Lavinia, "Most of what I've written is about you! I found you the most interesting criminal of us all!" This blackmailing weapon comes out of what O'Neill saw as Agnes's "legalized blackmail" in the divorce, and particularly out of the last long dispute between them. O'Neill told George Jean Nathan that it was Agnes's "refusal to accept a clause specifying that she should write no articles about me or our married life or thinly-disguised autobiographical fiction exploiting me. Can you beat it?" In *Mourning Becomes Electra* Orin uses his family history to force Lavinia to give up Peter, and then in his agony seeks safety in irreparable guilt that sums up all the family past. His father had caressed Christine's hair awkwardly, telling her, "Only your hair is the same—your strange beautiful hair I always—," and she had shrunk from his touch. Orin himself had repeated the caress and his father's words, causing his mother to shudder. In the last play he turns incestuously to Lavinia, caressing her hair and saying, "There are times now when you don't seem to be my sister, nor Mother, but some stranger with the same beautiful hair—." As she pulls away violently, he cries, "Perhaps you're Marie Brantôme, eh? And you say there are no ghosts in this house?" Her struggle against him repeats their mother's against their father, and like her mother she sentences him to death.

O'Neill's most difficult problem from the beginning had been to find a tragic ending "worthy" of his Electra. Back in 1926, when his "Greek plot idea" first came, he had been struck by R. W. Livingstone's idea in *Pageant of Greece* that Sophocles showed "moral insensitiveness" in having the matricide Orestes live happily, instead of going mad as he does in Aeschylus and Euripides. O'Neill went him one further and decided that all the Greek plots were flawed because their Electra "peters out into undramatic married banality." O'Neill also had been intrigued by Livingstone's praise for the ending Sophocles found for *Oedipus*. "A lesser poet," Livingstone declared, "would have made him either kill himself, or drag out his life in obscurity," but Sophocles found a climax "more worthy" of his greatness. His Oedipus blinds himself, thus shutting himself off "from the world of sense," because his offense has "set him apart from men and in a sense, above them, in a world of his own." Sophocles had even given him a desolate world of his own, appropriate to his fate, on "the mountain of Cithaeron where his parents cast him forth as a child to die."

O'Neill found a "worthy" tragic ending for his Electra. She—like all the Mannons—is already set apart from men, for their faces in repose look like "life-like death masks," so that she and all the Mannons bear the stamp of their ultimate fate even while they struggle for life. When she gives herself over to retribution she says, "I'm the last Mannon. I've got to punish myself! Living alone here with the dead is a worse act of justice than death or prison! I'll never go out or see anyone! I'll have the shutters nailed closed so no sunlight can ever get in. I'll live alone with the dead, and keep their secrets, and let them hound me, until the curse is paid out and the last Mannon is let die!" She turns and enters the house—as the first shutter slams to—to inhabit a desolate world of her own, set apart from mankind by the grandeur of her suffering.

In this tragedy of the damned the Mannons have been defeated by the forces of hatred and death out of the family past. But O'Neill had won through to a "new era" of life with "my inner self freed from the dead, consciously alive in the new, liberated and reborn!" His triumphant struggle for life and love had been the heart impulse of *Mourning Becomes Electra*. His characters were defeated, but their struggle passionately affirmed life and love, and so they achieved the exaltation of the original Greek tragedies in celebration of Dionysus—of Life. Christine with her flowers and her green dress is struggling for life and love. Ezra returns from the murder of the war, declaring, "I'm sick of death! I want life!" Adam Brant reaches love out of revenge and achieves his own spiritual victory by sacrificing his beloved ship and the sea for love. He tells Christine, "You've brought love—and the rest is only the price." His very words echo those of O'Neill, who had given up his whole past for love. He had said then: "For everything real one gets in the vale of beefs one pays on the nail! And I have got something real!" His Orin achieves affirmation at the very brink of death, able to say, "I'm glad you found love, Mother! I'll wish you happiness—you and Adam!" And Lavinia's is the most passionate affirmation of all. In her last desperate struggle she cries, "I want to feel love! Love is all beautiful! I never used to know that!" She wants to "have children and love them and teach them to love life so that they can never be possessed by hate and death!" She is tragically defeated by her own past, doomed by her crimes to the "darkness of death in life." But the exaltation of her affirmation came from O'Neill's own. When he dedicated *Mourning Becomes Electra* to Carlotta, he told her that it represented for him "a victory of love-in-life."

O'Neill had plunged into *Mourning Becomes Electra* in May 1929 and did not come out of it until he had done five drafts and sent the fifth to the Theatre Guild on April 7, 1931. It had been "harrowing labor" all the way. By the third draft he exclaimed to Manuel Komroff "And the wear and tear of it—it's an intense business from start to finish—leaves me sick with writing at the end of each day." When the Guild wired back enthusiastically accepting it, O'Neill and Carlotta sailed at once for the United States. He wanted to watch over this play's production every inch of the way. The Guild suggested Alla Nazimova for Christine, and O'Neill agreed. It had been the sight of Alla Nazimova as Ibsen's Hedda Gabler—seen during an Easter recess in March 1907, when he was a Princeton freshman—that had, he said, "discovered an entire new world of the drama for me. It gave me my first conception of a modern theatre where truth might live." He told the Guild that Nazimova "would be grand in spite of accent if can be directed to act as she did first Ibsen productions and cut out ham mannerisms acquired later." (She became so "grand" as O'Neill's Christine that Gerhart Hauptmann declared her "the greatest actress I have seen since Duse.") Alice Brady became Lavinia. Earle Larimore became Orin, and O'Neill thought he did "the finest work of them all." Philip Moeller again directed for O'Neill, and his old colleague Robert Edmond Jones did the sets.

After the first complete rehearsal, they saw that the headlong tempo would let them do all three plays on one night with a dinner break, as they had with *Strange Interlude*. O'Neill immediately did an entire sixth draft, cutting to the bone. (He was sorry that he published this acting version, for the fifth draft, he thought, made a better reading play.) All through rehearsals he changed and sharpened lines, so that Alice Brady said she would "wonder with horror" at every utterance whether she had the old words or the new ones. O'Neill saw to it that Brady let no pathos weaken the grandeur of Lavinia's tragic destiny. Particularly at the finale, he told her again and again that "no one should feel sorry for her." He participated completely in bringing his play to life in the theater. At the dress rehearsal he could only think, "Farewell (for me) to the Mannons!" *Mourning Becomes Electra* became a glorious success from its opening on October 26, 1931, but O'Neill felt suddenly "worn out—depressed—sad that the Mannons exist no more—for me!"

He thought this had been "a great Guild achievement against great odds" and "a high example of the combined acting, producing, and writing art of the American theatre." Not one critic grasped the battle of life-and-death forces in the play, but all the critics were deeply moved by it. The more intelligent ones, such as Krutch, were content to say that *Mourning Becomes Electra* meant only in the sense that "*Oedipus* and *Hamlet* and *Macbeth* mean— namely that human beings are great and terrible creatures when they are in the grip of great passions." The rest called it "melodrama" but confessed that it had thrilled them inexplicably. O'Neill was glad that a play beginning at 5:30 with a dinner break played to packed houses in the darkest years of the Depression. Indeed, it was so successful that the Guild added a road company by January 4, 1932, with Judith Anderson as Lavinia, and O'Neill thought that she was often better than Brady.

Almost at once, negotiations were under way for production throughout the world. When the British made an offer, O'Neill responded as his father's son. He said that he wanted "a substantial advance" or it was "no go," and he added, "Tell Bright I've sworn off giving plays to the British for nothing. (If James O'Neill of Monte Cristo fame heard that I ever gave the cursed Sassenach the slightest break he'd come back from the grave and bean me with a blackthorn! My, but didn't he love them!)" Almost every capital in Europe did *Mourning Becomes Electra* in the following years. Even ten years later O'Neill was still following new triumphs in Portugal, Switzerland, and Spain. At first he had been all for a film, but after he saw what Hollywood did to his *Hairy Ape* he shrank from the thought. He told Terry Helburn: "I so deeply regret having sold that play, need or no need, to be boy-and-girled by the Amusement Racket." He could not bear to see Hollywood desecrate *Mourning Becomes Electra* as well. He was right too, for when Dudley Nichols produced it quite faithfully, R.K.O. cut it to ribbons after its premiere, to get it down to standard feature length, and sent it out mutilated.

Later O'Neill was sure that it was largely for *Mourning Becomes Electra* that he received the Nobel Prize. He always loved *The Hairy Ape* and *The Great God Brown* best of his early plays, but he had gotten "the most personal satisfaction" from *Mourning Becomes Electra*, he said, adding, "You know that is Carlotta's play." Later still, he declared it the best of all his old plays—but by that time he had written *Long Day's Journey into Night*, and that, he knew, was "the best of all."

Notes

page 31:
> "Life is growth." O'Neill said so in a letter to Saxe Commins of August 4, 1929 (Princeton).
>
> "Make the world." From a letter to Carlotta of December 4, 1929 (*Inscriptions*).
>
> "It's the sort of." Letter of August 4, 1929 (Princeton).

"THE BIGGEST AND HARDEST." Letter from O'Neill to Shane of May 27, 1930 (Virginia).

"A MODERN PSYCHOLOGICAL." *MBE Notes*, 530.

pages 31–32:

"OF THE FORCE." "FATE, GOD." From a letter to Arthur Hobson Quinn, April 3, 1925 (Cargill, 125–26; *SL*, 195), which declares: "Where the theatre is concerned, one must have a dream, and the Greek dream in tragedy is the noblest ever!" Among some plays O'Neill thought should be included in a National Theatre repertory, he listed Aeschylus's *Agamemnon*, *Choephoroe*, and *Eumenides*; Sophocles' *Antigone*; and Euripides' *Medea*. "What Shall We Play?" *Theatre Arts*, February 1941, p. 147.

page 32:

"PRIMARILY DRAMA OF." *MBE Notes*, "April, 1929," 531.

"AT LAST BE FREE." From O'Neill's poem "Free," written on the *Charles Racine* and first published in the *Pleiades Club Year Book* for 1912 (*Poems*, 1).

"CENTER OF WHOLE." "SEA BACKGROUND OF." *MBE Notes*, "March 27, 1930," 533.

"ROMANTIC GRAMMAR-SCHOOL-." *MBE Notes*, "April, 1929," 531.

"ONLY POSSIBILITY." "DRAMA OF MURDEROUS." "MASK." *MBE Notes*, "April, 1929," 531.

"ARABIAN SEA EN." *MBE Notes*, "October, 1928," 530.

"CHINA SEA." *MBE Notes*, "November, 1928," 530.

"SEAPORT, SHIPBUILDING TOWN." *MBE Notes*, "April, 1929," 531.

"N.L." In his Plot Notes (Yale), O'Neill said that his first Clytemnestra, like his own mother, "has always hated the town of N.L. and felt superior disdain for its inhabitants" (Floyd, 188, reads "felt a superior disdain"). O'Neill called these notes his "first fruits (very unripe!)."

"PURITAN CONVICTION OF." *MBE Notes*, "April, 1929," 531.

"*MANNON*," SUGGESTIVE OF "*MAN*." Sheaffer thinks that O'Neill chose *Mannon* to suggest "Mammon" (Sheaffer II, 338). Because their wealth is largely extraneous to their tragedy, this is not likely. Even in *The Great God Brown* O'Neill had suggested the universal significance of his hero's struggle by having Cybel answer, when the policeman asks his name, "Man" (323).

page 33:

"STRANGE QUALITY OF UNREAL." *MBE Notes*, "August, 1931," 536. The *MBE Notes* show that O'Neill finished his first draft on February 21, 1930. When he picked it up again on "March 27 (533), he noted that he wanted "more sense of the unreal behind what we call reality which is the real reality!—The unrealistic truth wearing the mask of lying reality, that is the right feeling for this trilogy, if I can only catch it!"

EACH ONE HAS THE CURTAIN. Sean O'Casey was so struck with this idea of penetrating a curtain to a deeper dimension of reality that he borrowed it for his play *Within the Gates*, noting that it came "from Eugene O'Neill's suggestion of a front curtain for his great play, *Mourning Becomes Electra*." See O'Casey's *Collected Plays* (London: Macmillan, 1950), 2:114.

"GREEK TEMPLE FRONT." "ABSOLUTELY JUSTIFIABLE." *MBE Notes*, "April, 1929," 531.

HOWARD MAJOR's *DOMESTIC*. O'Neill's copy of Major's book (Philadelphia: Lippincott, 1926) is in the Post Collection; Marshall House appears on plate 23. O'Neill probably lent his copy to Robert Edmond Jones when he designed the settings for *Mourning Becomes Electra*, and Jones followed the plaster walls of the plate, rather than O'Neill's extension of the stone base all the way up the facade.

"WHOM THE PAST." So O'Neill told Harold DePolo in a letter [postmarked May 9, 1928] (*SL*, 299).

page 34:

"REVISIT PEQUOT AVE. OLD." *Work Diary*, 1:104, July 1, 1931.

"IDEA PLAY—HOUSE-." *Work Diary*, 1:105, July 17, 1931.

"EXTERIOR CHARACTERIZATION." *MBE Notes*, "March 27, 1930," 533.

"ALMOST CHARACTERLESS." *MBE Notes*, "March 27, 1930," 533.

"INNER." "AS FAR AS POSSIBLE." *MBE Notes*, "March 27, 1930," 533.

"IN THE *WAY* OF." *MBE Notes*, "July 18, 1930," 534.

"NEEDED GREAT LANGUAGE." So O'Neill told Arthur Hobson Quinn in a letter of 1932 reprinted in Quinn's *History of American Drama* (New York: Crofts, 1936), 2:165, 206.

"FORCEFUL REPEATING ACCENT." "COMPULSION OF PASSIONS." *MBE Notes*, "July 19, 1930," 534.

THE RHYTHM WAS SO: Alla Nazimova declared that she and the others could not "substitute words or phrases" as they usually did "without throwing the entire passage out of rhythm and spoiling the effect. We have to be letter perfect in our parts, and that's hard work." (Lucius Beebe, "Nazimova Regrets Her Vamping Days," unlabeled clipping in the Theatre Guild Press Book, No. 125 [Yale].)

"GENERAL SPIRIT." "DETAILS OF LEGEND." *MBE Notes*, "April, 1929," 531. O'Neill had a copy of Aeschylus with the Greek on one page and the English translation by Herbert Weir Smyth in the Loeb Classical Library (London: 1926), vol. 2 (Post Collection). He also bought *A Classical Dictionary of Greek and Roman Biography* by Sir William Smith (London: Murray, 1925). His copy inscribed "Villa Les Mimosas '29" is at Yale.

"HUSBAND HATES ENGLISH." Sheaffer II, 511–12.

page 35:

WHAT IS WRONG WITH MARRIAGE (New York: Boni, 1929). Kenneth Macgowan told me in a letter of October 22, 1948: "I believe O'Neill read the joint book and probably some of the articles which appeared in magazines."

"IDEAL OF FEMININE BEAUTY." *What Is Wrong with Marriage*, 124.

"WITH A LARGE KISS." *Inscriptions*. The dedication is dated by O'Neill "Beacon Farm August 1931."

ALL REFLECTED SARAH SANDY. Sheaffer produces a dim photograph of Sarah, squinting in the sun, which has these features, and he declares that she had "reddish-blond" hair and "grayish-blue" eyes" (Sheaffer II, 53 and 23, respectively).

"TELL HIM MY ADVICE." Letter to Agnes of January 29, 1920 (*SL*, 111).

KATHLEEN JENKINS. The May 11, 1910, *New York World* printed a large photograph of Kathleen.

page 36:

"HAIR BLACK AS NIGHT." First draft of *Mourning Becomes Electra* (Yale).

SHANE'S NURSE FIFINE CLARK. Part of a letter to Shane from O'Neill in the spring of 1928 (Correspondence) tells him: "You remember how Gaga could speak French? Well, she would be right at home here because that is the language all the people around here speak." A letter to Agnes [April 8, 1928] (*SL*, 284) pleads with her to take Mrs. Clark back, for they had both loved her; their children had loved her; and she had loved and stood by them from the day of Shane's birth.

"PSYCHIC IDENTITY." *MBE Notes*, "March 27, 1930," 533.

DEEP PURPLISH CRIMSON. So it is described in the first typescript of *Mourning Becomes Electra* (Yale). In the third play, Lavinia wears a "copy of her mother's dress with the deep crimson color predominating."

page 37:

"STRANGE, HIDDEN PSYCHIC." *MBE Notes*, "March 27, 1930," 533.

"HAVE WRITTEN *MOURNING*." Apparently Clark read the play before production and made what O'Neill called a "Freudian objection." O'Neill told him, "Authors were psychologists, you know, and profound ones, before psychology was invented" (Clark, 136).

"MODERN PSYCHOLOGICAL APPROXIMATION." His very first note of "Spring–1926" asks if he can get such an approximation (*MBE Notes*, 530).

page 38:

THE LEGENDARY REASONS. For a while, O'Neill thought of including a Cassandra character, but she demanded straight Greek characters, as he noted in his *Work Diary*, 1:75, on September 25, 1929. By September 27 he had become "disgusted" with the idea and abandoned it.

A HUSBAND'S INEPTITUDE. P. 207.

"HACKNEYED AND THIN." *MBE Notes*, "March 27, 1930," 532.

CAPTAIN BRASSBOUND'S CONVERSION. In a letter to Beatrice Ashe dated "Wednesday" of May 13, 1915 (Berg), O'Neill tells her that his friend Felton Elkins has invited him to see this play of Shaw's in a box at the Toy Theatre and that he would wear evening clothes. He had been reading Shaw ever since his prep school days.

page 39:

"WITH THE DEATH OF." *Selected Plays of Bernard Shaw* (New York: Dodd, Mead, 1948), 1:640.

"VERY FOND." "VERY GOOD." "SHE HAD." *Selected Plays of Shaw*, 646–47.

"HE DID NOT SPARE." *Selected Plays of Shaw*, 640. In "Captain Brant and Captain Brassbound: The Origin of an O'Neill Character," *Modern Language Notes*, April 1959, 306–10, I have listed all the similarities between the two.

CLIPPER BOOKS O'NEILL. O'Neill's large, lifelong collection of Clipper books has been preserved in the Post Collection. Among those he probably bought for *Mourning Becomes Electra* are Arthur Clark's *Clipper Ship Era*, Carl Cutler's *Greyhounds of the Sea*, Alfred Lubbock's first two volumes of *Sail: The Romance of the Clipper Ships*, Howe and Matthews's *American Clipper Ships*, and Richard McKay's *Some Famous Sailing Ships and Their Builder Donald McKay*. All O'Neill's Clipper details are authentic, from the black hull of Brant's ship below the waterline to its name, *The Flying Trades*, after such genuine ships as the *Flying Cloud*, the *Flying Dragon*, the *Flying Fish*, the *Flying Scud*, and the *Flying Dutchman*.

CAPTAIN ROBERT H. WATERMAN. I have corrected the erroneous "Watermann" in Random House, 2:105, to the correct "Waterman," which O'Neill certainly used, for he was very exact about all the Clipper lore in *Mourning Becomes Electra*. The picture of Waterman he saw is in Clark's *The Clipper Ship Era* (New York, 1910) opposite page 152, and the Captain's romantic outfit stands in sharp contrast to the sober suits of other skippers. "Bully" Waterman's reputation as a bully reached a climax on his ship the *Challenge*, New York to San Francisco, when so many of the crew died on the way (including some mutineers he slew with a belaying pin) that a mob gathered to lynch him.

"TOWN'S LEADING CITIZEN." *MBE Notes*, "April, 1929," 531.

page 40:

"HARSH AND UNREASONABLE." Letter to Agnes dated "Friday" [April 22, 19271 (*SL*, 242).

CONFIDED TO KENNETH MACGOWAN. The letter, with what he confided suppressed, is in Bryer, 184–86. The nature of the confidence was reported in Gelb, 679.

"IMAGINING THAT SHE HAD." First longhand draft of *Days Without End* (Yale).

"I'M SIMPLY EATEN UP." Letter dated "Thursday" [September 29?, 1927] (*SL*, 261).

"HIDING WITHIN A." "BEGINS AND ENDS." These words come from an intimate poem that O'Neill wrote about himself, apparently on August 17, 1942 (*Poems*, 103, 102).

"INEXPRESSIVE." This was a word that O'Neill used to describe himself when telling Agnes that he loved his children as much as she did, maybe more, in his "oblique, inexpressive fashion," in a letter [ca. April 8, 1928] (*SL*, 284).

"LIKE EZRY MANNON." From a telegram addressed to "The Mourning Becomes Electra Company," October 26, 1931 (Moeller Collection).

"WE MUST GET AWAY." Letter to Agnes of April 16, 1927 (*SL*, 241).

page 41:

"I LOVE YOU!" Letter to Agnes of April 16, 1927 (*SL*, 240).

"COMMIT MURDER WITHOUT." *MBE Notes*, "July 11, 1929," 532. O'Neill also managed to make the murder of Adam Brant in his second play appear to be a ship robbery.

"MEDICINE." "POISON." See, for example, pp. 74, 78, 103, 116, 123, 139.

"O'NEILL MEANT AT FIRST." See the first drafts of *Mourning Becomes Electra* (Yale).

"FIERCE" AFFECTION. In his family history (Sheaffer II, 512) O'Neill's words are "fierce concentration of affection."

"MY BABY." "NURSE." "COMFORTABLE." Compare *Mourning Becomes Electra*, 76, with *Long Day's Journey into Night*, 118; and *Mourning Becomes Electra*, 80–81, with *Long Day's Journey into Night*, 42–43.

page 42:

"IDEA M-HARLOT PLAY." The *Work Diary*, 1:159, dates this for April 24, 1933. It came from a "dream."

OWN "POISONED" FAMILY LIFE. O'Neill connected his mother's poison with the unhappiness of his marriage to Agnes. He talked (for instance, in his [December 26?, 1927] letter to Agnes) of the "poisonous bitterness and resentment" in the marriage (*SL*, 271). In his letter to Harold DePolo [postmarked May 9, 1928] (*SL*, 299) he spoke of his "home poisoned" by barely concealed hostility.

page 44:

ONE OF THE SOUTH SEA. In the first typescript (Yale), O'Neill specified the islands that Orin and Lavinia stop at as "the Marquesas" of Melville, but in the later versions, he left the islands vague, partly to enhance their dream-unconscious origins and partly because he realized from his Clipper readings that the

Sandwich (Hawaiian) Islands would be the logical stop for a Clipper after a China voyage.

"MOTHER SYMBOL." "YEARNING FOR PRE-NATAL." *MBE Notes*, "March 27, 1930," 533.

"IN THE LIGHT OF." Clark, 136.

"ON THE DUNES." This was one of the poems O'Neill left with John Reed in 1916. The Yale copy must have been without title, for it appears in *Poems*, 71, without one.

"SOUL MOTHER OF MINE." From a letter to Beatrice Ashe dated "Friday night," of February 5, 1915 (Berg). He tells her, in the words of Kipling's British soldier yearning for Mandalay, that he would like to wake up in a "cleaner, greener," land with her beside him.

page 45:

"ULTIMATE ISLAND." Letter of April 16, 1927 (*SL*, 239).

"THE ISLES OF REST." The envelopes in the letters sent from Bermuda in Correspondence are stamped "Come to Bermuda/The Isles of Rest."

"PETER OLDHAM." Plot Notes (Yale). O'Neill's father, in *Long Day's Journey into Night*, calls himself the "poor old ham" (128). "Peter," I suspect, came by association with O'Neill's idea that Electra "peters out into undramatic married banality" in the legends (*MBE Notes*, "November, 1928," 530). Who better to peter out with than Peter?

"HESTER SAND." Plot Notes (Yale).

"MY PURE AND UNSPOILED." Letter to Carlotta of May 25, 1932 (Inscriptions; *SL*, 399).

DOWN THE NILE. O'Neill talks of this prospective trip in a letter to Manuel Komroff of August 23, 1930 (Columbia). He tells Komroff that he has "a greater intuitive hunch for their feeling about life and death than for any other culture."

"ALL THE BITTERNESS." Undated letter from O'Neill to Shane and Oona [ca. January 31, 1929] (*SL*, 323).

"A LOT FOR MY." Letter to Eleanor Fitzgerald, May 13, 1929 (*SL*, 339).

page 46:

"SON OF THE COUNT." Letter to Barrett Clark, June 21, [1929] (*SL*, 344).

"CALLED SONS OF BITCHES." Letter to Robert Sisk, March 17, 1929 (*SL*, 330).

"AND NOW COMES." Letter of May 11, 1929 (*SL*, 336–37).

HIS CHARACTERS REPEAT. O'Neill made a note to aim for such repetition on September 21, 1930, in *MBE Notes*, 535.

O'NEILL'S OWN EXPECTATION. Orin suspects Lavinia with the first mate of the ship on which they voyage to China. During rehearsals O'Neill shortened his name to Wilkins, but until then he had been called "Wilkinson." Wilkinson was the name of Agnes's obstetrician for the birth of Oona (O'Neill speaks of him in a letter to Dr. William Maloney of February 18, 1925, Maloney Papers, Manuscript Division, New York Public Library). The name was associated with Agnes, even if O'Neill's distrust of Agnes was not actually directed at Dr. Wilkinson. Of course, O'Neill had other associations with the name, such as Keefe and Wilkinson's store in New London, mentioned in a letter to Beatrice Ashe of "Monday evening," January 14, 1915 (Berg).

page 47:

"GHOSTS!" O'Neill was thoroughly familiar with Ibsen's play Ghosts, and knew the moments when the past suddenly repeats itself in that play. He probably realized that he was taking up Ibsen's idea and giving it a new application.

"I've tried to show." First typescript of *Mourning Becomes Electra* (Yale).

"legalized blackmail." One of several places in which O'Neill speaks of Agnes's divorce demands as legalized blackmail is his letter to Harold DePolo, postmarked May 9, 1928 (*SL*, 300).

"refusal to accept." Letter of February 14, 1929 (Cornell). O'Neill told Nathan that he thought the clause was necessary because "even before we separated I knew she was dickering with an agent about an article of that nature."

Pageant of Greece. Manuel Komroff had sent O'Neill some books, and O'Neill told him in a letter of March 22, 1926 (*SL*, 200) that Livingstone's book looked like just what he wanted.

"Moral insensitiveness." *Pageant of Greece* (Oxford: Clarendon Press, 1924), 118.

"peters out into." *MBE Notes*, "November, 1928," 530.

page 48:

"a lesser poet." "more worthy." "from the world." *Pageant of Greece*, 119–20.

"worthy" tragic ending. It is probably significant that O'Neill, so sensitive to words, repeats Livingstone's "worthy," in his note telling himself he must "give modern Electra figure in play tragic ending worthy of character" (*MBE Notes*, "November, 1928," 530).

"life-like death masks." *MBE Notes*, "September 21, 1930," 535.

"new era." "my inner self." So O'Neill told Bio De Casseres in a letter of May 10, [1929] (*SL*, 335).

"for everything real." Letter from O'Neill to Harold DePolo [postmarked May 9, 1928], (*SL*, 299).

page 49:

"a victory of love-." O'Neill dedicated *Mourning Becomes Electra* to Carlotta on April 23, 1931, *Inscriptions*.

sent the fifth. In a letter to Terry Helburn of April 7, 1931, O'Neill says; "I am sending the script of *Mourning Becomes Electra* by this same mail—two scripts—so that the committee can get quick action on it" (*A Wayward Quest*, 262).

"And the wear and." Letter of August 23, 1930 (Columbia).

Alla Nazimova as Ibsen's. *Hedda Gabler* had thirty-two performances, opening March 11, 1907, at the Bijou Theatre in New York with Alla Nazimova in the title role. See *Best Plays of 1899–1909: And The Yearbook of the Drama in America*, ed. Burns Mantle and Garrison P. Sherwood (New York: Dodd, Mead, 1944), 439.

"discovered an entire." Letter from O'Neill to Mr. Olav of May 13, 1938, paying "tribute to Ibsen's memory" (published in *Nordisk Tidende*, "America's Leading Norwegian Newspaper," June 2, 1938 [*SL*, 477]).

"would be grand." The Guild had suggested Nazimova in their cable of acceptance, and O'Neill cabled this message back from Paris, April 28, 1931 (*SL*, 382).

"the greatest actress." "Dr. Hauptmann Hails U.S. Idea of 'Be Yourself,'" *New York Herald Tribune*, March 17, 1932. Hauptmann said the "two high spots" of his visit to the United States "were my meeting with Eugene O'Neill and attendance of 'Mourning Becomes Electra' last evening."

Alice Brady. O'Neill's friend George Jean Nathan had interested him in Lillian Gish, and he gave her the play first, but when she read it for O'Neill and the Guild they all found her too fragile. O'Neill reported to Terry Helburn on August 20, 1931 (*SL*, 392) that he had told Lillian the truth and she took it like a good sport; but he had hated having to do it. They also thought of Ann Harding, but she was tied up with cinema contracts.

"THE FINEST WORK OF." Letter from O'Neill to Dudley Nichols of May 29, 1932 (*SL*, 400).

HE WAS SORRY. O'Neill told Barrett Clark in a letter of December 15, 1944: "I trade too many cuts in *Mourning Becomes Electra* and let too many of them (but not all) stay in the book. It was a fuller, better play in its final written version, I think" (Clark, 149; *SL*, 567). The book was published on November 2, 1931.

"WONDER WITH HORROR." "NO ONE SHOULD." Morton Eustis, "Backstage with Alice Brady, the Guild's Modern Electra," *New York Evening Post*, October 31, 1931.

"FAREWELL (FOR ME)." *Work Diary*, 1:111, October 25, 1931.

"WORN OUT—DEPRESSED." *Work Diary*, 1:111, October 28, 1931. He started work on his other Greek plot idea, Medea, at once, but for December 30 his *Work Diary*, 1:116, says that he read a description of Lenormand's "Medea" in a *Paris Herald* clipping and that it had "great similarity to way I'd worked it out in my tentative outline—so guess I must abandon idea—too bad!"

"A GREAT GUILD." Letter from O'Neill to Terry Helburn of May 16, 1944 (*A Wayward Quest*, 278–79; *SL*, 558). O'Neill always resented the fact that the Guild left *Mourning Becomes Electra* off the list of achievements at the bottom of their letter paper, particularly as some of the plays on the list were "merely things to hang on a hook in a backwoods privy!"

page 50:

"*OEDIPUS* AND *HAMLET*." "Our Electra," *The Nation*, November 18, 1931.

PLAYED TO PACKED. See letter to Terry Helburn, May 16, 1944 (*SL*, 558).

SHE WAS OFTEN BETTER. Letter to Dudley Nichols, May 29, 1932 (*SL*, 400).

"A SUBSTANTIAL ADVANCE." "NO GO." "TELL BRIGHT." Letter to Richard Madden of September 24, 1932 (Dartmouth).

NEW TRIUMPHS IN PORTUGAL. O'Neill speaks of these productions in his letter to Terry Helburn of May 16, 1944 (*SL*, 558).

ALL FOR A FILM. In a letter to Terry Helburn of July 29, 1941 (*SL*, 520) O'Neill tells her he is very much for her idea of a film with Katharine Hepburn and Bette Davis With Pascal as director.

"I SO DEEPLY REGRET." From the May 16, 1944 letter to Terry Helburn (*SL*, 558).

DUDLEY NICHOLS PRODUCED IT. Katina Paxinou was Christine and Rosalind Russell was Lavinia. O'Neill saw the stills and telegraphed Nichols on June 12, 1947 (Yale) that Rosalind Russell "continues to grow and grow" and that Michael Redgrave was an "ideal Orin."

R.K.O. CUT IT. O'Neill told Dudley Nichols in a letter of December 4, 1948 (*SL*, 582) that he had no intention of ever seeing the mutilated *Mourning Becomes Electra*. It was just one more sign that culture had been banished from the world in favor of mob negative destiny.

LARGELY FOR *MOURNING*. O'Neill said so in his letter to Terry Helburn of May 16, 1944 (*SL*, 558).

"THE MOST PERSONAL." "Eugene O'Neill Undramatic Over Honor of Nobel Prize," *Seattle Daily Times*, November 12, 1936.

"THE BEST OF ALL." Letter from O'Neill to Professor Frederic Ives Carpenter of March 24, 1945 (in Carpenter's *Eugene O'Neill* [New York: Twayne, 1964], 75).

KURT EISEN

Melodrama, Novelization, and the Modern Stage

If *Anna Christie* proved to be more or less an artistic dead end for O'Neill, *The Great God Brown* turned out to be highly productive, perhaps his most important experiment in intersubjective dramatic characterization. O'Neill creates in *Brown* a bold and uncompromising amalgam of novelistic theme and dramatic form, partly through a more energetic plotting but chiefly through the complex use of masks. In certain key respects these masks function as the play's focus of consciousness, through which O'Neill tries to make legible the otherwise obscure gap between appearance and reality and between reality and desire. The masks allow O'Neill to explore "the collapse of the autonomous self" that Girard distinguishes as the starting place of the novel. The masks articulate distinct and unstable psychological levels, most strikingly when they cross the usual boundaries of character as they are exchanged from one to another. Though this technique gave way in later plays to the verbalized masking of the thought asides in *Strange Interlude* and to the doppelgänger technique of *Days Without End*, and even though O'Neill eventually repudiated masks altogether, as late as 1943 he still felt that the eight-month run of *The Great God Brown* in 1926 was "the one miracle that ever happened in the New York theatre" (*SL* 549). If the masks could not ultimately sustain the narrative function O'Neill intended for them, they did help him to drive another important wedge into the illusory unity of

From *The Inner Strength of Opposites: O'Neill's Novelistic Drama and the Melodramatic Imagination*, pp. 38–47. ©1994 by the University of Georgia Press.

character and thus to open new possibilities for representing a more complex self on stage.

In the "Memoranda on Masks," written in three parts several years after the premiere of *Brown*, O'Neill makes clear that he considered masks "the freest solution of the modern dramatist's problem as to how—with the greatest possible economy of means—he can express those profound hidden conflicts of the mind which the probings of psychology continue to disclose to us." "A comprehensive expression is demanded here," he continues, "a chance for eloquent presentation, a new form of drama projected from a fresh insight into the inner forces motivating the actions and reactions of men and women ..." (*UO* 406).[14] The masks are a theatrical sign system that designates a multilevel drama between different characters as well as an interior drama within individual characters. As they are donned, removed, and transferred throughout the play, O'Neill achieves a "splitting of the protagonist ... into two separate characters" (Valgemae 28). Thus O'Neill approximates theatrically what Brooks calls "the semiotic precondition" of the novel, the "desire to express all." The "comprehensive expression" that O'Neill seeks to realize through his use of masks is consistent with the melodramatic impulse that remains strong in the more diegetical structures of the novel.

On a narratological level the masks function somewhat like a narrator's mediating point of view in prose fiction, allowing a theater audience to see a character's hidden self below the surface behavior but also the psychic intimacy—or its absence—that binds different characters together. In the "Memoranda" O'Neill remarks that Goethe's Mephistopheles should be made to wear "the Mephistophelean mask of Faust": "For is not the whole of Goethe's truth *for our time* just that Mephistopheles and Faust are one and the same—are Faust?" (*UO* 407–408; O'Neill's emphasis). When O'Neill makes William Brown assume the mask of his counterpart Dion Anthony, he is proposing in effect that the concept of the isolated self is illusory and is dissolving the Manichean distinctions of melodrama—victim and villain, self and other—to create the kind of novelistic drama in which self and other become mutually interpenetrating categories. In place of the narrator of fiction, the masks allow the dramatist to make plain how completely Dion and Brown mediate each other's identity. The postmelodramatic subject who emerges in Brown is therefore far from unified or autonomous. The very ambitious but marginally talented Brown does not finally merge with the tortured, creative Dion to become a kind of Nietzschean *Übermensch* endowed with both poetic imagination and worldly acumen. Rather, the death of the man whom the prostitute Cybel calls "Dion Brown" in the play's final scene (*CP* 2:530) demonstrates that the self without the other—Brown without Dion—is self-consuming. The levels of discourse that would later remain clear and distinct throughout *Strange Interlude* become obscure in *Brown* as soon as Brown dons the mask of Dion: "O'Neill seemed to be changing the ground rules of the play without explaining them," Ronald Wainscott observes in his study of the original 1926 production (192). In any case, the melodramatic elements that linger in *Brown* are thus reformulated, and the questions that melodrama had effectively closed are decisively reopened.

O'Neill transforms one of these elements, the conflict between two antithetically drawn men over their mutual love of a woman, according to the novelistic paradigm Girard calls "triangular desire." One character's ambitions and desires are mediated by those of a second character, usually a rival but often an ego ideal such as Napoleon or Christ who looms in the play's mythic background (see Girard 1–52). The mediations in *Brown* are multiple and fluid, but in its most fundamental triangular structures Billy Brown defines his desires through Dion Anthony, and Dion in turn defines his through various religious, mythic, and artist figures, including Shelley, St. Anthony, Dionysus, Pan, and Christ. Dion's wife Margaret, whom Brown loves, stands at the center of the first triangle, which should be wholly melodramatic. Because Margaret is not at the center of the second triangle, however—Dion's deepest aspiration is to be not Margaret's husband but "life's lover" (*CP* 2:507)—the interest quickly veers from the question of who will win Margaret to how O'Neill will bring together and resolve the play's two patterns of triangular desire; that is, how Dion will consummate his ascetic passion for life and how Brown can manage to win Margaret along with the creative powers he believes will also become his own.

Dion's particular need for Margaret is established in the play's prologue. Discovering that he loves her is a preliminary act of self-definition: "She is my armor!" he declares. "Now I am born—I—the I!—one and indivisible—I who love Margaret" (*CP* 2:481). The metaphor Dion has chosen—"my armor"—is revealing because, like a mask, marriage provides him an external shield. Accordingly, Margaret (whose name derives from the Margarete of Goethe's *Faust*) refuses or is unable to recognize Dion whenever he has removed his mask: she desires only the outward self that the mask signifies. Dion thus realizes he can love her only "by proxy" (*CP* 2:483)—that is, by means of this masked, outward self. By contrast, the *I* beneath the mask is the Dion Anthony who reads *The Imitation of Christ* and who seeks his metaphysical comfort in Cybel, an earth mother as well as a prostitute. As the divergence between Dion's mask and the face beneath the mask becomes increasingly pronounced, so too does the discrepancy between his domestic and his spiritual needs. The fact that his children resemble Brown more than they do their own father reinforces this effect. Moreover, the ironic stance that Dion cultivates toward fatherhood is conditioned largely by

melodramatic categories: when lack of money and his poor prospects as an
artist compel him to ask for a job in Brown's architectural firm, Dion declares
it an occasion for Brown "to be a generous hero and save the woman and her
children" from poverty (*CP* 2:488). The masks thus permit the playwright to
distinguish a level of melodramatic symbology from a deeper level of critical
self-perception, from which one can view the melodrama of one's own life
with an ironic detachment.

On his side, Brown longs to have Dion's creativity, his mistress Cybel,
and above all his wife Margaret—an order of priority more or less the
reverse of Dion's, yet all of Brown's desires are mediated wholly through
this determining Other. In the course of the play Brown appropriates his
friend's architectural talents for the glory and profit of his own firm; then he
takes Cybel as his own mistress; finally with Dion's death at the end of act 2,
he assumes Dion's very identity and becomes Margaret's husband. O'Neill
depends on the masks to make this complete expropriation clear to the theater
audience, to demonstrate how utterly Brown's identity depends on Dion. But
just as Margaret can love only the masked Dion, Brown's desires are likewise
based only on the image of a mask; Dion's internal spiritual torment is closed
to him. Dion understands this point and sees where Brown's blind aspiration
will lead him: "When I die," Dion declares, Brown "goes to hell" (*CP* 2:507).
Dion observes further that after his own death, "Brown will still need me—to
reassure him he's alive" (*CP* 2:507). Even Brown's love for Margaret, Dion
insists, "is merely the appearance, not the truth! Brown loves me!" The scene
climaxes when Dion says, "I leave Dion Anthony to William Brown—for him
to love and obey—for him to become me—" (*CP* 2:510). Later, in a moment
recalling Dion's act of self-definition in the Prologue, Brown completes his
act of appropriation by addressing the mask through which he assumes Dion's
identity: "Then you—the I in you—*I* will live with Margaret happily ever
after" (*CP* 2:518). Brown clings to the hope that Margaret will come to love
the Brown beneath the mask, a hope in fact precluded by Margaret's ardent
devotion to the mask of Dion—that is, to the mask *as* Dion.

The masks in *Brown* allow O'Neill to dramatize the condition that
Girard observes in the novel, "the collapse of the 'autonomous' self," and
the emergence of "a truer Self than that which each of us displays." This
merging of Brown's and Dion's identities is decidedly different from the
psychic intimacy of characters one finds in such melodramas as Boucicault's
The Corsican Brothers (1852) and Augustus Thomas's *The Witching Hour*
(1907).[15] In Boucicault's play the brothers Fabien and Louis dei Franchi are
virtually interchangeable; indeed, they were often played by the same actor.[16]
Although Fabien prefers the outdoor life of hunting and exploring in his native
Corsica—what he calls "the theatre of nature" (37)—to his twin Louis's more

worldly life in Paris, Boucicault does not stress this difference as a conflict between opposing aspects of the human psyche, nor does he place them in a mediating relation of triangular desire. Together Fabien and Louis affirm the indestructibility of virtue and plain dealing: prompted by an amazingly strong telepathy, one brother rallies to avenge the other's death at the hands of the aristocratic villain Château-Renaud. Confronting the murderer and speaking the incontrovertible logic of melodrama, Fabien declares: "Know you not that the Corsican race is like the fabled Hydra—kill one, another supplies his place? You have shed my brother's blood—I am here to demand yours" (68). As in *Monte Cristo* (likewise based on a work by Dumas père), the avenging hero's virtue is never in doubt: his homicidal fury is always driven by noble moral principle, not selfish passion, and the upshot of retribution is a social, familial healing rather than a bloody cycle of revenge.

In *The Witching Hour* this moral clarity is threatened when the uncanny telepathic powers of the hero Jack Brookfield place him in a strange position of responsibility for a murder committed by Hardmuth, the ostensible villain. Because Hardmuth performed the murder precisely as Brookfield had dreamed it, Brookfield sees himself as complicit in the crime. "Every thought," explains Justice Prentice, the play's raisonneur, "is active—that is, born of a desire—and travels from us—or it is born of the desire of some one else and comes to us. We send them out—or we take them in—that is all" (747). Finally, however, instead of developing the implications of this potentially revolutionary psychology, Thomas diverts interest wholly into plot—that is, how evil will be punished and good rewarded. Still, Thomas's play reflects the imminent passing of the traditional moral antitheses, also evident in Belasco's *The Girl of the Golden West* (1905), which Daniel Gerould has called "one of the new villainless melodramas" of the early twentieth century (25). In *The Witching Hour* the hero is a gambler; in *The Girl of the Golden West* the villain and the hero—the outlaw Ramerrez and the noble stranger Dick Johnson—are revealed to be one and the same man. Gerould notes that in Belasco's play "the old polarity of good and evil has been replaced by more modern psychological and social discriminations" and a new "divided hero with a dual name and identity assumes the functions of villain and generates the conflict" (25). In both plays a woman's love reclaims the hero from his amoral life and thus melodrama's absolute moral categories and its inherent feminine-domestic center are preserved.

Margaret Anthony personifies what David Grimsted has called melodrama's "religion of domesticity" (228)—the irreducible values of wife, home, and family. Yet O'Neill makes her position in the play highly ambiguous. Marriage for O'Neill is in some respects the consummate instance of the relationship of self and other, in *The Great God Brown* and all his other major works. For Margaret marriage signifies everything Dion longs to transcend—banal domesticity, responsibility, bourgeois materialism—and all that Brown aspires to: prosperity, love, procreation. Marriage for this reason is central to the play's ideological debate. In getting married and settling into a job at Brown's firm Dion has taken on much of Brown's own persona; later, after Brown has reversed the exchange by taking on Dion's mask and in effect his identity, Margaret begins to feel that her husband has "become quite human" (*CP* 2:520); in a formulation that anticipates Nina Leeds describing her three men in *Strange Interlude*, Margaret also feels that her marriage is now whole: "You're my long-lost lover, and my husband, and my big boy, too!" (*CP* 2:521). All the aspects of melodramatic felicity are in place for her. Yet along with Dion's creative energies Brown also inherits Dion's inability to enjoy domestic happiness, an outcome he could not foresee.

This is the condition that Cybel names in calling him "Man" at the end of the play (*CP* 2:533): if he seems to Margaret "quite human"—that is, domesticated—Cybel realizes that "Dion Brown" can no longer be at peace, in a home or anywhere else. In some respects the play's clearest, most consistent line of interpretation may be located in this ideological debate between Margaret, who personifies melodramatic values, and Cybel, who, despite her deeply maternal nature, stands outside the circle of home and family and thus beyond the need for masks except the one she presents to the world generally. Of all the characters in the play Cybel sees most clearly how character reflects melodramatic modes of consciousness, how melodrama functions as a play of masks: in this she anticipates the more fully realized central consciousness that O'Neill achieves in *Iceman* and *Long Day's Journey*. Cybel understands the melodramatic roles that all the characters, including herself, are forced to play. "I gave them a Tart," she tells Dion. "They understood her and knew their parts and acted naturally. And on both sides we were able to keep our real virtue, if you get me" (*CP* 2:497).

Because Cybel understands the heuristic value of melodramatic forms she comes closest to functioning as the play's narrator, though she is too peripheral to the play's tragic structure to be more than an occasional, if highly instructive, raisonneur: "I love those rotten old sob tunes. They make me wise to people. That's what's inside them—what makes them love and murder their neighbor—crying jags set to music!" (*CP* 2:497). What had been a flaw in the characterization of *Anna Christie*—that is, its melodramatic sensibility—becomes an explicit mode of consciousness in *Brown*. Cybel perceives that people often see their lives as melodramas, with themselves as champions of virtue, victims of oppression or injustice, or, especially in moments of ironic self-consciousness, as villains. When O'Neill later treated his own family's history through the Tyrones of *Long Day's Journey* or examined what drives a man to murder his wife in *The Iceman Cometh* he is relying essentially on Cybel's observations in *The Great God Brown* on the power of "crying jags set to music" or constructed as theatrical recitatives.

Cybel sees that contriving life into a self–other duality can be emotionally purgative and morally reassuring, the melodramatic counterpart to tragic catharsis. Brown, pursued by the police as his own murderer, must stand as a communal scapegoat. Cybel offers what could be taken as a scathing summation of the dubious gratifications that unadulterated melodrama offers an audience: "They must find a victim! They've got to quiet their fears, to cast out their devils, or they'll never sleep soundly again! They've got to absolve themselves by finding a guilty one! They've got to kill someone now, to live! You're naked! You must be Satan!" (*CP* 2: 530). By annihilating the division between Dion and Brown, and creating in their place one "Dion Brown," O'Neill fashions a self-punishing hero who internalizes the melodramatic moral conflict; when Cybel designates this protagonist simply "Man," O'Neill's expressionistic transformation of melodramatic categories is complete.

This is the moral retribution that melodrama must inflict on its villains: no resolution is possible if the villain goes unchecked and unpunished, an aspect of melodrama's Aristotelian emphasis on action instead of character. O'Neill's renunciation of Aristotelian "purging," as made clear in a 1931 letter to Brooks Atkinson, emphasizes his own attempts to displace melodramatic resolutions with the kind of internal drama of character he tried to create in *The Great God Brown*:

> As for Aristotle's "purging," I think it is about time we purged
> his purging out of modern criticism, candidly speaking! What
> modern audience was ever purged by pity and terror by witnessing
> a Greek tragedy or what modern mind by reading one? It can't
> be done! We are too far away, we are in a world of different
> values! ... If we had Gods or a God, if we had a Faith, if we had
> some healing subterfuge by which to conquer Death, then the
> Aristotelian criterion might apply in part to our Tragedy. But our
> tragedy is just that we have only ourselves, that there is nothing
> to be purged into except a belief in the guts of man, good or evil,
> who faces unflinchingly the black mystery of his own soul! (*SL*
> 390)

O'Neill's criticism of "purging" here seems directed less toward Aristotle and more toward the deficiencies of the melodramatic stage in relation to the grandeur and cohesive mythic order of Greek tragedy. In the absence of such an order, O'Neill argues, in the modern postsacral world we turn instead to the kind of "healing subterfuge" offered by the moral clarity and comforting domestic affirmations of melodrama; when we recognize these as masks that shield us from the "black mystery" of the soul we begin to revive a true sense of the tragic.

In *The Great God Brown* O'Neill devised a sometimes effective, often confusing, but inherently theatrical means of expressing the interpenetration of self and other that Girard and Bakhtin have shown to be essential to novelistic representations of character while also exploiting the semiotic of melodrama outlined by Brooks and Heilman. In *Strange Interlude, Days Without End, The Iceman Cometh*, and *Long Day's Journey into Night*, O'Neill would continue to pursue his ambition in writing *Beyond the Horizon*, to find innovative means of realizing novelistic themes on the stage. Yet O'Neill explicitly denied having any desire to write novels as such. "I have no ambition to go out of my field and become a novelist," he told an interviewer in 1925, the year he wrote *The Great God Brown*. "In my opinion, the drama is a darn sight harder medium than the novel because it is concentrated. The only way I would want to write a novel would be if I had seven or eight years to devote to doing ten, all of which I would throw away before I should think I could possibly write one decent book" (*Comments* 48).

As late as 1932, even as O'Neill was pleading his incapacity for anything but drama he could still entertain the idea of trying a novel: "A play, can do. Might even do a short play still, although I have no idea for one. A novel, given the next ten years to learning how to use that form, maybe. But short stories or articles, no. Things appear too complicated and involved to me" (*AEG* 133). In fact, this is precisely the sort of lengthy apprenticeship that O'Neill undertook in composing his novelistic American history cycle, an epic series of plays that has been compared in conception to Balzac's *Comédie humaine*. After laboring for nearly the entire "seven or eight years" he had specified in 1925 as the minimum for producing a good novel, O'Neill destroyed all but two of its plays, including a sprawling, clearly unfinished draft of *More Stately Mansions*, preserved apparently by mistake.

Like other of O'Neill's epic failures, the labor he spent writing this cycle seems in retrospect a needed preliminary to better things: if it led him into certain artistic blind alleys it also forced him to look hard at the course of modern history. As the threat of world war grew increasingly real in the late 1930s, O'Neill shelved his eleven-play cycle and returned to the seminal, transitional experiences from his earlier years that had so decisively shaped not only his vision of life but also his artistic ambitions to transform the modern stage. In writing the American history cycle O'Neill would reexamine the period that began with revolutions in America and France, the period in which melodrama emerged as a coherent theatrical aesthetic and the realistic novel as practiced by Balzac, Stendhal, and others came into its own as a dominant literary form. In *The Iceman Cometh* and *Long Day's Journey* O'Neill's use of melodrama as a self-defining mode of sensibility would seem a necessary mirror of the modern world, a world moving irreversibly—as it seemed then to O'Neill—into perhaps its darkest, most violent era of moral and military polarization.[17]

NOTES

14. O'Neill appears to be citing the authority of modern psychology as a rhetorical convenience, a way of expressing his argument in terms readily intelligible to any literate audience. In fact, O'Neill elsewhere persistently and vehemently denied making direct use of the theories of Freud or Jung and claimed that he got his education in psychology from nineteenth-century novelists such as Stendhal and Dostoevsky. The truth seems to lie somewhere between direct incorporation and complete disregard. For a discussion of this issue, see the analysis of *Strange Interlude* in chapter 3.

15. For O'Neill, especially during the apprenticeship that included his brief stint in George Pierce Baker's course at Harvard, Augustus Thomas (whom Baker invited to address his students) was a name synonymous with "everything that was shoddy and dishonest" in successful American drama (see *SP* 306–307).

16. In the original 1852 production both Louis and Fabien were played by Charles Kean; see the cast list in Michael R. Booth, ed., *English Plays of the Nineteenth Century*, vol. 2 (25).

17. "To tell the truth," he wrote Langner in 1940, "like anyone else with any imagination, I have been absolutely sunk by this damned world debacle. The Cycle is on the shelf, and God knows if I can ever take it up again because I cannot foresee any future in this country or anywhere else to which it could spiritually belong" (*SL* 510), a sentiment that dominates his letters of the period. Even in letters to his children Oona and Shane he tries to convey a sense of impending world tragedy (see *SL* 508, 495).

EDWARD L. SHAUGHNESSY

Long Day's Journey into Night

T ragedy, whose arch theme is loss, summarizes the terrible cost of human experience. This classic form teaches the message of fate: We will be defeated in *time*. Whatever is precious becomes all the more cherished as we perceive its vulnerability. In time our very lives will become museum pieces. Thus it is that memory itself constitutes both a benison and a curse, since it permits us to keep alive essences even as it galls us with the knowledge of death. By these certainties the strong as well as the timid are chastened, the wise as well as the foolish. If we scold ourselves for having squandered opportunities, we recognize that not even the greatest husbandry could have preserved what has been lost. One concedes but can never quite fathom the inevitability of this law. These lessons haunt us. Yet we know that tragedy also celebrates the privilege of human experience. Some, the O'Neills and Quinlans perhaps, saw themselves as members of a pilgrim church. To the pilgrim the end of the journey meant the harbor, salvation. Others, less certain about the end, may have seen themselves as waifs in the cosmos. In any case, one was not given a choice whether to make the journey. Thus fated, the traveler embarks with the resources at hand—faith and hope, a brave toast to "sunny days and starry nights," or even the shaky supports of tomorrowism.[17]

Long Day's Journey confirms the timeless mystery of loss. How perfect the play's fundamental image, the dying of the light. It compares with

From *Down the Nights and Down the Days: Eugene O'Neill's Catholic Sensibility*, pp. 151–162. © 1996 by University of Notre Dame Press.

Shakespeare's sonnet 73 ("That time of year thou mays't in me behold") or Milton's "Sonnet on Blindness." The very metaphor suggests the theme of loss: loss of energy, illumination, creativity, warmth, love. As O'Neill's play begins in the light and promise of a new day, the audience cannot be criticized if it builds hopeful expectations. The stage directions indicate the day and season, *a morning in August*, just after breakfast. It could just as easily be the morning of July Fourth in the Miller household (*Ah, Wilderness!*). But in the tragedy the hope of this new day quickly fades, and the progressive decay of light brings to mind the coming on of death.

The setting in the family is also classic in its simplicity. But again the first promise is blighted. The Tyrones founder in malaise: sickness of soul and body, each member equally the victim of his and her own lost chances, each equally the plaything of heartless powers that devastate fair expectations. The natural grace of the family is at every moment strained, its vitality constantly threatened by warring tensions. "Here is a family living in a close symbiotic relationship, a single organism with four branches, where a twitch in one creates a spasm in another. [They are] chained together by resentment, guilt, recrimination; yet, the chains that hold [them] are those of love as well as hate."[18] If the characters bear little responsibility for the givens of their condition (*fate*), as partners in relationship they fulfill the other requirements of tragedy (*complicity*). Each fails the other, just as all have failed themselves. A burden of guilt is thereby incurred, the partial cost of sin. As always, however, paradox confounds us. For in wounding each other, all have become candidates for redemption.

O'Neill had not closed accounts with his parents and brother before they died. His father succumbed in 1920, his mother less than two years later, and his brother Jamie in 1923. In this undeniably autobiographical play, Eugene was paying his debt of love to "all *the four haunted Tyrones*." Here he registered "pity and understanding" for what he had done to them and they to him. He had found himself in the situation of many who survive parents and siblings but realize that necessary closure had never occurred. Such a dilemma is common enough, of course, and is addressed in various ways. Some seek the help of the analyst in coming to terms and working through guilt; others invoke the assistance of the clergy or a grief therapist. Most difficult are the cases where women and men simply carry on, but with the sense that things will remain forever unfinished.[19]

The Tyrones, like any other family, have been shaped in great part by historical forces and events. In this case the contributing impulses have been Ireland and the plague of famine and the attendant homesickness: Catholicism, ambitions, love, and marriage.[20] These givens, having produced the unit, account for common loyalties as well as conflicts within the group.

Differences in personality both strengthen and undermine the members' interdependence. Thus the sins of the father, and mother, have been visited upon their sons. And by some law of reciprocity the sons, in their very existence, constitute both the reward and punishment the parents have earned. The conditions are classic in their ubiquity. For, as the father and mother recall their own parents with combined fondness and bitterness, so do their children respond to them with a mixture of generosity and anger. In *Long Day's Journey*, then, we have the ancient story of the family as its own savior and tormentor. The organism has considerable potential for mending its own wounds. In its most hopeful self-management, it may function as one philosopher has envisioned:

> ... it is in the nature of things that the vitality and virtues of love develop first in the family. Not only the examples of the parents, and the rules of conduct which they inculcate, and the religious habits and inspiration which they further, and the memories of their own lineage which they convey, in short the educational work which they directly perform, but also, in a more general way, the common experiences and common trials, endeavors, sufferings, and hopes, and the daily labor of family life, and the daily love which grows up in the midst of cuffs and kisses, constitute the normal fabric where the feelings and the will of the child are naturally shaped.[21]

It is also possible, of course, that the family can be overwhelmed by these same dynamics. Even if its destiny could evolve propitiously, the family would remain locked together in their individual fates (Brustein's point). All is organic. The health or sickness of the body affects the members; the health or sickness of the member affects the body. It becomes us to grant this measure of determinism.

Long Day's Journey offers a splendid vehicle for testing these assumptions. Its simple plot hinges on two threats to individual, and therefore to family, health: Mary's regression into morphine addiction, and Edmund's developing case of tuberculosis. Before the harrowing day's end, each of the four Tyrones will be unmasked and his connections with the others severely tested.

* * *

The Tyrones have taken to their summer retreat on the [Long Island] Sound. James, immensely popular and a veteran actor, has accumulated a considerable fortune. Recalling the racking poverty of his youth, he has invested much of his wealth in the land. With immigrant parents and siblings, he had been driven to America by the mid-century famines of Ireland. By a most admirable dedication to craft, James had risen to the highest stratum of his profession. He married his beloved Mary, whose convent-bred innocence and piety he had hoped above all things to shield. But a shadow has long since fallen over the house of Tyrone. In giving birth to her third son, Mary was given morphine to diminish the pain of labor. Since that day she has been cruelly addicted and has suffered not only the addict's torment but also the humiliation of many confinements for cure. Although she loves James deeply, Mary blames him for bringing this curse upon them all by his unholy devotion to thrift. Indeed, his parsimony had caused him to seek out a physician who charged lesser fees. This lifelong habit has by now disaffected his sons. Not only do they blame him for their mother's agony, but they resent him for the constraints his frugality imposes on their pursuit of pleasure.

On his side James does not lack for complaints against his ingrate sons. Ever and always does he chide them for their profligate ways. Tyrone charges them with infidelity to their traditions and heritage: Ireland and Catholicism. He abhors their cynicism, their lack of filial respect, and their having both been "fired" from college. Especially does he condemn Jamie's pernicious influence on Edmund, ten years his junior.

> You've been the worst influence for him. He grew up admiring you as a hero! A fine example you set him! If you ever gave him advice except in the ways of rottenness, I've never heard of it! You made him old before his time, pumping him full of what you consider worldly wisdom, when he was too young to see that your mind was so poisoned by your own failure in life, you wanted to believe every man was a knave with his soul for sale, and every woman who wasn't a whore was a fool! (*LDJ*, 34)

Now Edmund, like Mary, feels the cold fingers of sickness on him, a sickness that can destroy his life. On this day he will learn whether he has consumption and, if he has, what will be done about it. The tensions mount as the morning and afternoon wear on. It soon becomes clear that Mary Tyrone has reentered the fog of her addiction. By evening, the men know well from experience, she will have slipped into a zone where they have no access to her. That terror is compounded by the suspense in waiting for the diagnosis of Edmund's condition. As the hours pass, father and sons spit fire at each other. At the same time each is moving more deeply into himself, is sinking under the influence of whisky and under the threat of collective disaster. The logic of this progression is brilliant in its persuasive power. After their earlier testiness, each Tyrone falls further into sad reverie and the recognition that he has lost the good life his talents might have earned. The terror suffered by each nearly crushes the figures we see on the stage.

* * *

Four sets of relationships operate in the Tyrone family. Of course, isolating any one for examination constitutes a somewhat artificial maneuver. As Brustein noted, each member acts and reacts as she or he is connected with the other three. All is organic. Even so, we can derive useful insights by focusing for a moment on the relationships in arbitrary sequence: mother–sons, father–sons, brother–brother, husband–wife.

That Mary Tyrone loves both her sons is a truth beyond dispute. But she does not love them without conflicting elements of ambivalence and guilt. Nor is the sons' love for her an affection without alloy. Indeed, this complexity of relationship is often magnified in Irish-Catholic families, where sons are trained to associate the mother with the Blessed Virgin Mary herself, the very ideal of purity. Irishman-litterateur Noel O'Hara offers an exceptionally helpful insight into this phenomenon.

The portrait of Ella, and indeed her children's attitudes to her, reminded me in one way of my own time growing up in Ireland. I have often thought since that, technically, the Irish Church, in its attitude to the Blessed Virgin, was idolatrous. We were much closer to her, and she was much more important in our lives, than the Man himself. There was no devotion more widespread or passionate than the rosary. Novenas were a grand opportunity for a girl to ask her to help find her a husband, and the young fellows would try and soft talk her into getting them a good job in the Civil Service.... Anyhow I often thought how in those bleak years in Ireland, very large families and little money, and no thought of a woman going out to work, that the Virgin Mary must have been the surrogate romantic mother for the untold thousands of offsprings of mothers too overburdened to have any softness left over. So perhaps there was a deep psychological factor in the Irish devotion to her, which no doubt carried over into America. No doubt too it was a factor in Irish sexuality, in generations of convent educated wives up to this day, to say nothing of priest or brother educated husbands and fathers, inhibitions that are manifest in a variety of ways. Ella O'Neill is partially a product of the same influence. And Eugene's own dichotomous attitude

to women, the double standard, can no doubt be traced back to
Irish Catholic puritanism.[22]

That she is not virginal greatly complicates the sons' view of the father,
of course. If the Oedipal complex operates more or less universally, in this
cultural milieu what is normally difficult can become positively baroque. One
has no reason to wonder, then, about O'Neill's having chosen Mary for the
mother's name, particularly since his own mother had been so profoundly
dedicated to the Virgin. Because she feels she has betrayed the Lady of
Sorrows, Mary Tyrone also feels guilt for having betrayed her sons. (She
does not seem to hold herself responsible for a similar betrayal of James.
Why?) But she does not see Jamie and Edmund as equally deserving of her
affection.

Jamie's words to and about his mother are harsher and more
cynical than Edmund's. The older son's conflicts suggest the first set of
complications. He has known about Mary's addiction for ten years longer
than Edmund. He resents that Edmund is "Mama's baby, Papa's pet."
Furthermore, outrageous as it seems, Jamie sees his father as "competitor"
for Mary's affection. He feels, moreover, apparently with good reason, that
he himself was long ago found guilty for having infected baby Eugene with a
fatal case of measles. As Mary says to Tyrone, "*her face hardening*: I've always
believed Jamie did it on purpose. He was jealous of the baby. He hated
him.... He knew. I've never been able to forgive him for that" (87). At the
same time she recognizes that she should not have left Jamie and Eugene
in her mother's care in order to be with James on the road. The brilliant
and poison-tongued Jamie, sensing her guilt, viciously cuts through her
denials as she retreats to her room for "another shot in the arm" (75). The
sins of anger, of lashing out against another's weakness, are always terrible
in their effect. The venom he releases cuts scars deeper into the soul of the
viper than into his victim's. His mask of Mephistopheles hides his otherwise
naked and terrifying vulnerability.

The acid that runs through Jamie's veins has corroded his heart. His
violations of those he loves most, sins of cruelty (*words, words, words*), have
intensified his: own pain almost beyond bearing. Since early childhood he
has lived with fear and guilt; now he needs his mother more than ever, since
he has not been able to grow up. One of the greatest questions in *Long Day's
Journey into Night* is this: Who will redeem Jamie? It may be that in this play
he is not, cannot be, saved by love. It may be that he is the object of love but
cannot summon the courage to accept the gift.

Mary seeks to give comfort to Edmund by caressing him. She speaks
with him tête-à-tête, as once she must have spoken with Jamie. She is solicitous

about his "summer cold." As it is often the case in O'Neill, however, outward appearance is deceiving. Mary has a heart's grudge against Edmund too, just as she has against James and Jamie. To Tyrone she makes known that his birth stands as a kind of reproof to her, a punishment: "I was afraid all the time I carried Edmund. I knew something terrible would happen. I knew I'd proved by the way I'd left Eugene that I wasn't worthy to have another baby, and that God would punish me if I did. I never should have borne Edmund" (88). One wonders if any child can ever come unscathed through the dark maze of childhood.

We should always be open to a fresh view of things, however. O'Hara sees the background a bit differently.

> O'Neill [Edmund] had a lot going for him really, when I think of his young man's head on his mother's lap and the consoling him for his marriage to poor old Kathleen [Jenkins]. Of course we read novels and lives from our own childhoods, and many a boy I knew would have envied him such love from a mother, absent or not. And James, the Count, doesn't seem to have been such a bad old stick.[23]

In the family one suffers much from all the pushing and tearing that takes place. But the kisses come as frequently as the cuffs, a truth that makes the deliberate injuries such a burden to bear in the after-years. What Edmund wants most is that Mary not take the drug that day. And she wants desperately to provide that succor to him; she nearly promises the impossible, inspired by her vision of the Virgin.

> Now I have to lie, especially to myself. But how can you understand, when I don't myself. I've never understood anything about it, except that one day long ago I found I could no longer call my soul my own.
> *She pauses—then lowering her voice to a strange tone of whispered confidence.*
> But some day, dear, I will find it again—some day when you're all well, and I see you healthy and happy and successful, and I don't have to feel guilty any more—some day when the Blessed Virgin Mary forgives me and gives me back the faith in Her love and pity I used to have in my convent days, and I can pray to Her again—when She sees no one in the world can believe in me even for a moment any more, then She will believe in me, and with Her help it will be so easy. I will hear myself scream with

agony, and at the same time I will laugh because I will be so sure
of myself. (93–94)

When he sees that she has begun once more, he is willing to jolt her by
pointing out that her habit has made "life seem rotten." Finally, driven by
fear, anger, and frustration, he lashes out: "It's pretty hard to take at times,
having a dope fiend for a mother!" (120).

The internecine character of these relationships fairly shreds the soul.
Once we understand this situation, we need not wonder why it took O'Neill
many years to "forgive" himself and the other "Tyrones." He knew how much
Ella loved her Catholic faith. Agnes Boulton tells how, after her recovery
from morphine addiction, Ella slipped away from the sleeping James each
morning to attend Mass at a church close by the Prince George Hotel where
they lived in the winters. And, when we know this, we know that O'Neill
must have retained some affection for the Church: because his mother loved
it, and his father did. If Ella O'Neill conquered her addiction, however, Mary
Tyrone cannot be saved. *Long Day's Journey* does not permit such an inference.
Indeed, all four characters are locked into the logic of the play. It will always
come out the same, just as *Antigone* does, and *Hamlet* and *Lear* Jamie will not
reform; no words will call Mary back.

James Tyrone's grudges against Jamie are long standing. He has been
repeatedly offended by his son's disregard for good taste and nearly all that
James holds sacred, by his "loafing" and waste of talent, and by the bad
example the older brother has set for Edmund. Tyrone describes Jamie's chief
fault in Shakespearean imagery: "Ingratitude, the vilest weed that grows" and
"How sharper than a serpent's tooth to have a thankless child." James wants
credit for supporting his son and giving him endless chances. (How difficult it
is to rise above our "good deeds.") Jamie, on the other hand, hates his father's
stinginess and his insistence on taking the moral high ground: "I wouldn't
give a damn if you ever displayed the slightest sign of gratitude" (32). But
these two men fight it out in the open, each knowing precisely what the other
thinks. Each knows, moreover, where the other is most vulnerable and strikes
there unfailingly. For the most part their complaints against one another are
real enough but are not especially complicated. In just one area does Jamie
tread on sacred ground: his assertion that Tyrone loves his money more than
he loves Mary. His proof is that James nearly sacrificed "Mama's" health in
order to save a few dollars on the doctor bill. To Jamie such frugality was
more an outrage than a sign of virtue.

James's relations with Edmund are subtler. He sees in Edmund not only
Mary's finer sensibilities but her greater susceptibility to illness. The family
knows that its youngest member lives under the threat of consumption. To

survivors of the Irish famine, like James Tyrone, tuberculosis struck fear into the heart, for it was remembered as an almost certain sentence of death. Again he feels the pangs of guilt, for he had talked Mary into having this third child to take the place of stricken Eugene. Nor will Edmund let him off the hook. Like Jamie, he knows that his father will not send him to a private hospital: "Don't lie, Papa! You know damned well Hilltown Sanatorium is a state institution. Jamie suspected you'd cry poorhouse to [Doctor] Hardy and he wormed the truth out of him" (144). Even so, James and Edmund have a deep rapport because "I'm like Mama, I can't help liking you, in spite of everything" (142).

One of the greatest moments in O'Neillian drama takes place in the act 4 exchange between these two. It occurs when both are a little drunk and therefore even less inhibited than usual. Under the double stress of this terrible day, they have somehow made contact. The moment begins in lightness: the humor Edmund finds in Tyrone's claim that Shakespeare was an Irish Catholic. This levity is followed by their shared sorrow over Mary's addiction and Edmund's present danger. Their masks drop and each man sees the other briefly in a moment of unguarded truth. Each sees the human being who is his son or father. James's long *apologia*—about the paralyzing poverty of his youth, the suffering of his own beloved mother, abandonment by his father, and a confession that he betrayed his own talent for security—all touch Edmund: "It was at home I first learned the value of a dollar and the fear of the poorhouse. I've never been able to believe in my luck since" (146). Thus the son is moved to give his father the gift of his poetry.

Edmund begins by thanking James for sharing his sorrow. Because the usual distance between them has been bridged for once, he invites his father into his most intimate memory chamber. Such an act places one at great risk, of course; he lays himself open as he normally would not. It is not drink that has liberated his tongue, however; it is that variety of love that mends all the broken moments of the past: "I'm glad you've told me this, Papa. I know you a lot better now" (151). In language piercingly lyrical, O'Neill relates the story of Edmund's mystical experiences at sea. He tells of lying on the bowsprit, fusing into the spume and rhythms of the sea, "every sail white in the moonlight." Here, he says, he experienced a transport such as no drug can give, guilt-free and, for once, belonging to something outside time: "To God, if you want to put it that way." He tells his father that once the "veil of things" has been lifted, for a moment one becomes perfectly phased into the divine being at the heart of creation. But when the veil drops again and one becomes aware of his own awareness, one knows that he has been reclaimed by time and the misery of cosmic orphanhood. One will not share such moments, or try to, unless he trusts the other totally. For he permits his soul, his truest self, to become exposed to the other. James acknowledges the gesture by making an equally generous gift: "Yes, there's the makings of a poet in you all right" (154). In this miraculous instant of connection, father and son have been briefly redeemed, each blessed by the other's love.

No such moment can be shared between James and Jamie; the layers of defense are by now impenetrable. Again we wonder who will redeem Jamie. It will not be Mary, as the older son knows very well: "I suppose I can't forgive her—yet. I'd begun to hope, if she'd beaten the game, I could too" (162). She loves him, yes, but with such deep reservation that she reminds him, even without intending to do so, of his failures, his sins. Her natural affection for Jamie has been blighted by his inveterate negligence and thousand assaults on her sensibilities. Deepest wound: she can neither forget nor forgive his infecting baby Eugene so many years before. Every irresponsible act thereafter, his sins of omission and commission, merely reminds her of Jamie's selfishness. In her attitude toward this man, Mary Tyrone fails most glaringly to imitate her beloved model and namesake. Jamie, devoted to his mother in ways that cripple some men, has learned a bitter truth: her feelings for him can never be those of unalloyed grace. Her feelings for him are mixed: thus, something is forever held back.

If his redemption is to take place, it must be in connection with Edmund. But little time remains. Between Edmund's exchange with his father and Mary's coming in upon all three men in the play's final scene, Jamie has only brief minutes with Edmund. If he can muster courage to face the truth at all and confess his sins, it must be under these restricted conditions: "Not drunken bull, but in vino veritas stuff." Torn between self-hatred and a love for his brother, he confesses his envy in seeing Edmund succeed. He tells how he had set out "to make a bum of you.... Mama's baby, Papa's pet" (165). To make this gesture, even under the influence, has been agonizing. From the porch the old actor has also heard the confession. *"Edmund remains silent."* Now Tyrone, in mixed charity and despair, tries to ring down the curtain on the tragic farce of his son's life. To Edmund: "... don't take it too much to heart, lad. He loves to exaggerate the worst of himself when he's drunk. He's devoted to you. It's the one good thing left in him" (167). Then it's over. James and Jamie are back at each other's throats. Edmund tries fumblingly to mediate but to no good.

Enter Mary Tyrone.

* * *

In certain ways Mary is blessed in the very nature of her situation. For she lives with three adult men, each riveted to her in passionate devotion: her husband, a very model of fidelity; her sons, proud of her fragile beauty, aware that through her some gentleness attaches to their otherwise unlovely lives. In even the most prosaic cluster of mortals, a woman in such circumstances might come into her glory. But in the Catholic family, this veneration for her can border on idolatry. She is the vessel of honor: in the beginning the virgin lover and lifelong partner to husband; later the nonpareil feminine model to her sons. For these men, the sacrament of matrimony has sealed the conjugal union in holiness. (Of all the barbs delivered by his "ingrate" sons, none throws doubt on Tyrone's love for their mother.) In the Irish-Catholic family all characteristics of this beatification were intensified. The culture had nearly deified the wife-mother and equated her station with that of the Blessed Virgin Mary. This is why, when Edmund tells Mary what he felt on first learning of her addiction, his words carry such terrible resonance: "God, it made everything in life seem rotten" (118). All three Tyrone men had been brought up in the cult of Mariolatry. (It is worth recalling that James O'Neill's own mother was named Mary, a fact surely not lost on his playwright son.) At its least attractive, such veneration was made sentimental in portraits like those rendered in "Mother Machree." But the virtues praised were of constancy and compassion. In any case, Irish motherhood has been a powerful myth: the Sorrowful Mother becomes the Suffering Mother.

* * *

The union of James and Mary reminds all who have known them that love means fidelity. James, handsome and popular, had no doubt experienced many temptations to his virtue in the tawdry world of backstage romances. In a marriage of thirty-five years, moreover, indiscretions could never have been hidden. Mary loves him all the more for this, as she says to the second girl: "... there has never been a breath of scandal about him. I mean, with any other woman. Never since he met me. That has made me very happy, Cathleen. It has made me forgive so many other things" (105). Of course, the "other things" were real enough. Mary came to know very early that life with the matinee idol was not at all glamorous. Although she liked being with him, even on the road, the endless hours on rickety trains, the long nights in second- and third-rate hotels, the nearly inedible food all greatly lessened the pleasure of his company. She thought his background had prevented him from knowing how to make a fine home. But Mary recalls with greatest bitterness his having enlisted the services of the quack whose incompetence had led her into addiction. "I hate doctors! They'll sell their souls! What's worse, they'll sell yours, and you never know it till one day you find yourself in hell" (74).

The play records one day that represents hundreds, perhaps thousands, of others. Devoted to her as he is, James must chafe under Mary's constant reminders, often in front of their sons, of his lack of refinement and his inveterate miserliness. In their exchange James informs Edmund that her father's home wasn't quite what she liked to recall: "Her wonderful home was ordinary enough. Her father wasn't the great, generous, noble Irish gentleman she makes out.... [b]ut he had his weakness.... He became a steady champagne drinker, the worst kind. That was his grand pose, to drink only champagne. Well, it finished him quick—that and the consumption—" (137).

After so many years both have grievances. Yet in remaining faithful to their vow, Mary and James have found comfort. Their relationship has been tested endlessly by visitations of unfriendly fate and by their own imperfections, but in their tradition and culture they have found what alone redeems human frailty: the forgiving love of one for another. The power of this mystery deeply moved Eugene O'Neill. In creating the story of the Tyrones, he conquered his own ancient hostilities in an act of pity and forgiveness. He seemed, as it were, to become one with his family. As Travis Bogard wonderfully says, "In the agony of the others, it is possible, the playwright's identity was at last to be found."[24]

In the final, crushing scene all three men are paralyzed with a fear whose meaning we can infer: that they may not be able to recover Mary this time. She has come down to them and, in what she says and does, she pierces their hearts with the memory of what she has been to them: bride and lover, mother and confidante, gentle and wistful presence. So great has been her love for James Tyrone, so deeply has her soul entered his, that even in her remove from him Mary utters his name in the play's final phrase. As his private memories of her are stirred, each man recalls a Mary that is his alone. Yet, because she is one person whom they share, their memory is also collective. In the end each knows that he is forever trapped with her in the tragedy of time.

Notes

17. Biographers and literary critics claim to revere nothing so much as detached and objective commentary. Yet the critic occasionally does well to abandon the role of unbiased commentator. In the case at hand, the author's claimed detachment would constitute hypocrisy.

18. Robert Brustein, *The Theatre of Revolt*, 350–351.

19. As artist, O'Neill had available an option most men and women cannot invoke: he could include himself in the dynamics of reliving one day with his parents and brother. He could represent them all by the power of his art and see them more clearly through the lens of his moral imagination. Like the other Tyrones, he would be neither better nor worse than he had been. But now, having been liberated from the anger and terror of the

moment, he could give them a new grace. The creation of this *day* could be defended on the grounds of "faithful realism." Into the day would be absorbed the distilled essence of each haunted Tyrone: a phenomenon "more real than reality."

20. The Tyrones' immersion in an Irish-Catholic ethos is, of course, a given in *Long Day's Journey into Night*. The evidence of this cultural presence is revealed at every turn. James, for example, confesses that he is "a bad Catholic in the observance...... Mary's many references to the Blessed Virgin provide another rivet to traditional belief, although she never speaks of her devotion except in soliloquy or in the ending moments of the play, when James and their sons have lost contact with her.

I am aware of no critic, however, who has pointed to the absence of religious objects among the furnishing and fixtures of the Tyrone household: a crucifix or a holy picture on the wall, the statue of a saint, a flickering votive light such as we might see in one of O'Casey's Dublin plays. Such iconography was ubiquitous in the pious Catholic household of the period. Considering O'Neill's meticulous attention to detail, this omission is striking. The stage directions are quite explicit, for example, about what volumes should be included in the small bookcase (whose authors James disapproved) and "*the large, glassed-in bookcase with set of Dumas, Victor Hugo, Charles Lever, three sets of Shakespeare, the World's Best Literature in fifty large volumes, Hume's History of England ... and several histories of Ireland*" (*LDJ*, 11). A picture of Shakespeare hangs on the wall.

One can only suppose that the Tyrones held it to be in dubious taste to flaunt their faith by such open displays of piety. These items were visible, if at all, only in the precincts of the bedroom. But such fastidiousness or reticence would not have been typical.

21. Jacques Maritain, *Education at the Crossroads*, 96–97.

22. Noel O'Hara, personal letter to the author, 14 October 1993.

23. Ibid.

24. Bogard, *Contour in Time*, 451.

MARGARET LOFTUS RANALD

From Trial to Triumph (1913–1924): The Early Plays

In 1912–13, while a tuberculosis patient in the Gaylord Sanitarium, Eugene O'Neill decided to become a dramatist. As a result American drama during the first half of the twentieth century was totally changed, and a new high seriousness came into the theatrical market place. Dissatisfied with the old histrionic romantic theatre of his father (James O'Neill, the perennial Count of Monte Cristo), Eugene O'Neill made profitable use of his three-month hospital stay by reading philosophy, drama, and absorbing the influence of new theatrical movements in Ireland, France, Sweden, and Germany, led by J. M. Synge, Eugène Brieux, August Strindberg and Gerhart Hauptmann.

On his release from Gaylord he started to write, using his own life experiences as creative matrix. Thus he set the autobiographical pattern that was to culminate in the great family plays of his last years: *Long Day's Journey Into Night* and *A Moon for the Misbegotten*, with a return to the dissipation of his youth in *The Iceman Cometh*.

His devotion to his own personal "drama of souls" never ceased, and hence writing exacted a tremendous physical and psychological toll. He was also self-taught in dramatic technique, educating himself by reading and closely observing stage performances. From the theatrical touring world of his childhood he had repeatedly observed *The Count of Monte Cristo*, and James O'Neill's sometimes distinguished attempts at classics like *Hamlet*. Also, after

From *The Cambridge Companion to Eugene O'Neill*, ed. Michael Manheim, pp. 51–68. © 1998 by Cambridge University Press.

his suicide attempt (1910),[1] Eugene toured with the entire family in *The White Sister*, in the "made" position of assistant manager. Consequently, he became aware of dramatic structure, the possibilities of stage effects and the intellectual limitations of the theatrical audiences of his day.

Like his father, O'Neill was an autodidact. His Princeton year (1906–07) was essentially one of self-directed study, because he despised his course assignments, being suspended for "poor scholarship." He learned from wide, undisciplined reading, rather than academic instruction, claiming that the only result of his year in George Pierce Baker's English 47 Workshop (1914–15) at Harvard was his practice of first writing a scenario and then the dialogue, which he did throughout his productive life.[2]

One cannot explain the workings of genius, and Eugene O'Neill must be so considered. He saw the theatre as an enlightening, quasi-religious experience, a place where serious matters were to be dramatized, and audiences would empathize with the intensely human problems put before them. His was also a nationalistic view. He took the United States as his major theme documenting its collision of old with new in its attempt to make a dynamic world out of the curse of the old. As a result, he created a new theatre with a sense of a shared past and present, even projecting the future in *Strange Interlude*. More importantly, he created a family mythology which ascends to universality, dramatizing experiences which tease the alert beholder into empathy.

His early experimental plays (1913–24) demonstrate the structural influence of his father's theatre of melodrama, in his instinctive ability to build a scene or action toward a sometimes explosive conclusion, skillfully varying the pace of a play. Just as his audience's emotion or body flags, he revivifies attention by means of a gunshot, a sudden revelation, or a death. Like Chekhov and Ibsen he also knew that a weapon or important object once displayed on stage must eventually be used, something surely learned from *Monte Cristo*.

The influence of the vaudeville skit is also obvious in his very first play, *A Wife for a Life* (1913) written during his post-sanitarium residence in New London. In this piece, based on O'Neill's miserable mining experiences in Honduras, The Older Man (unnamed) renounces his claim on Yvette, the wife he has abused and abandoned (yet still loves) in favor of Jack, his young mining-assistant and friend in a final, banal vaudeville-style line: "Greater love hath no man but this, that he giveth his wife for his friend." This playlet also marks the beginning of O'Neill's use of monologue, a device he later used with singular skill.

It also initiates another theme: Woman as the intruder who destroys masculine ambition, or disturbs an enclosed, companionable male universe.[3]

This theme recurs throughout his career, finding its final statement in two of his last plays, *The Iceman Cometh* and *Hughie*.

"Thirst" and Other One-Act Plays (1914), the first published collection of O'Neill's plays, is important as indicating his future development. Published by Gorham Press, Boston, and underwritten by a $450 subvention from his father, O'Neill was to receive 25 percent of the profits, which did not materialize.[4] These five plays are important both for what they are and what they prefigure. *Thirst* (1913), portrays a raft as a microcosm, with its three unnamed shipwreck survivors of Dancer, Gentleman, and West Indian Mulatto Sailor. While introducing the theme of woman as whore, along with interracial and class conflict, it also portrays the behavior of individuals pushed to their emotional and physical limits, even to proposed cannibalism, after the Dancer dances herself to death. The stage directions demonstrate O'Neill's visual and aural sense as he instructs both stage designer and actors to evoke suitable audience reactions.

In *Fog* (1914) a lifeboat serves as a microcosm, this time with a Poet, a Man of Business, a Polish Peasant Woman and her dead child. Now O'Neill makes a notable advance in the use of sound and scenic effects: steamer whistles, dripping water, and the fog, still endemic to New London, which will recur as late as *Long Day's Journey*. Fog is used to evoke mood, and also a sense of supernatural mystery, when a passing steamer turns aside from its course after the sailors hear the cry of the dead child over the noise of their engines. This is O'Neill's first foray into the eerie world of supernatural fantasy.

Also in this collection are three plays dealing with the relationship of man and woman, which will later become a major topic of the O'Neill canon. In *The Web* (1913), a one-act melodrama, he presents a sympathetic portrait of a tubercular prostitute exploited by her pimp. A neighbor, who attempts to save her, is shot by the pimp, and the prostitute is accused of murder. In *Recklessness* (1913), reminiscent of Strindberg's *Miss Julie*, O'Neill moves into another important theme—marriage. Here Baldwin, a wealthy man whose wife, Mildred, has been forced by her family into a loveless, money-based marriage, causes the death of the chauffeur with whom she has found consolation. This clumsy piece, ending with the sound of an automobile crash, is highly contrived, while the chauffeur, Fred Burgess, is too ineffectual to be a believable suitor.

With *Warnings* (1914), O'Neill embarks on his first play in which a woman is responsible for the death of her husband. This simplistic piece, loosely modeled after Joseph Conrad's *The End of the Tether*, portrays a radio operator who, despite his growing deafness, is forced back to sea because of financial worries, a nagging wife, and too many children. When he realizes that his deafness has caused the loss of his ship he shoots himself in despair.

With the exception of *A Wife for a Life* (1912), all O'Neill's plays up to and including the "*Thirst*" volume conclude with sometimes savage and shocking violence. In the title play the two survivors drown after a struggle. *Recklessness* ends with a constructive murder by automobile, *Warnings* with suicide, *The Web* with murder and wrongful accusation. *Fog*, though ending with rescue, includes proposed suicide and near cannibalism.

Perhaps as the result of his almost total early immersion in melodrama, suicide and death offer a frequent solution for O'Neill at this time. In *Abortion* (1914), a play outside the "*Thirst*" collection, the college-athlete hero shoots himself after being threatened by the brother of his girl friend, dead after a botched abortion financed by his own father. The final scene, with its noisy victory parade outside the room of the suicide victim, remains a clever piece of ironic theatre, arousing sympathy for the young man's blighted promise, rather than for the "townie" girl.

Also ending with a death, *Bound East for Cardiff* (1914), originally called "Children of the Sea," is an astonishing dramatic advance from the melodramatic clumsiness of *Abortion*. The first written of the *S.S. Glencairn* series, it repeats the supernatural theme of *Fog*, concentrating on the central figure of the dying sailor, with his dream deferred, a theme to which O'Neill will often return. "Yank" greets death as "a pretty lady in Black," and with his death the fog lifts. Notable here are O'Neill's ability to create a sustained mood and a sense of community in this forecastle populated by an international (though all-white) crew. Repetitive sound in the snoring of the sleeping men and the blast of the steamship's whistle maintain atmosphere.[5]

This play also has continuing fame as the first O'Neill work to be publicly staged, 28 July 1916, in Provincetown, Massachusetts. It figures prominently in the history of the Provincetown Players, who nurtured the author's talents until his successes on Broadway eventually undermined the "faith" with which they began. Susan Glaspell, wife of George Cram Cook, founder of the group, tells of hearing from Terry Carlin, a well-known Provincetown and Greenwich Village anarchist, that O'Neill had "a trunk full of plays," and when in mid-July 1916 he read *Bound East for Cardiff* to the assembled members, "Then we knew what we were for."[6] Despite its frequent repetition this account should be reconsidered, and Gary Jay Williams has persuasively argued that O'Neill had unsuccessfully offered *The Movie Man*, along with the *Thirst* volume, a month before the celebrated reading took place.[7] He agrees with Sheaffer that O'Neill had probably submitted *Cardiff* to George Pierce Baker's English 47 course at Harvard, revising it there.[8] The play was again presented in New York in November 1916 as part of the successful opening bill at the Playwrights' Theatre, attended by both O'Neill's parents.

The three other plays of this group were written in 1917–18. *In the Zone* is a conventional submarine-warfare potboiler, spiced with some violence, with Smitty as the alcoholic lover, a failure driven to sea by a woman's rejection, while *The Long Voyage Home* is a predictable Shanghai-ing drama, including the reappearance of the dream-forever-deferred theme in Olson's wish to retire to a farm.

The greatest advance, however, comes with *Moon of the Caribbees* (1918) where O'Neill, in addition to developing mood, also experiments with the impact of black culture upon whites, and this, his first truly multicultural play, foreshadows also his interest in "total theatre." Character, theme, and mood become interdependent, with the old donkey-man as wise observer, a *persona* who reappears in *The Iceman Cometh* as Larry Slade, "the old foolosopher." The clash of cultures leads to a bacchanal and consequent violence, reinforced by music and dance as the bumboat women bring liquor to the ship. Then the mood changes, and the play comes full circle to the moonlit mystery of the opening, the final stage direction identifying the "brooding music ... like the mood of the moonlight made audible." Here is a prophecy of future experimentation, and when the entire *"Glencairn"* series opens with *Moon of the Caribbees*, as is customary, that atmosphere gives spiritual form to the entire group. At the same time, it also prefigures O'Neill's later practice of frequently putting important details into stage directions to bring his readers also into emotional communion with text and staging—both aural and visual. John Ford's film of this series, entitled *The Long Voyage Home* (the only film of his plays O'Neill liked) offers a conflation of the individual plays and emphasizes the human conflicts.

O'Neill's evocation of mood to draw the audience into the action goes even further in *Where the Cross Is Made* (1918), where in a single act he attempts to seduce his audience into a collective hallucination as the ghosts of dead sailors return to the Captain's home with their chest of bogus treasure. Its reworking into the four-act drama *Gold* (1920) is less successful. Here the action is opened up to cover a number of years, from the discovery of the "treasure" through the captain's destruction of his familial relationships. The focus of this version is thus splintered and over-explication detracts from the mysterious supernaturalism when the drowned men reappear before the lunatic father and son.

Directly after *Gold*, O'Neill revised his previously unsuccessful sea play *Chris Christophersen* (1919), which offers insights into his revisionary techniques. Originally the emphasis is almost entirely on Chris the coal bargeman, while his daughter, Anna, is an unbelievable construct. Brought up by her mother's English family in Leeds, she descends upon Chris as a typist with a distinctly refined accent and a desire to gain a college degree. Nevertheless, there is a germ of what Anna will become as a character in the two later revisions, *"The Ole Davil"* and finally *"Anna Christie."* In *Chris* she is something of a salvific angel, the cause that Paul Andersen, second mate of the steamer that rescues them from Chris's drifting coal barge, discovers ambition (in order to become worthy of Anna), while Chris accepts the position of boatswain on the same vessel. His two tags of "the ole davil" (the sea) and the song "My Yosephine" appear in all three versions.

The intermediate draft, *"The Ole Davil"* (1920) is very close to the final version, *"Anna Christie"* (1921), which won O'Neill his second Pulitzer Prize. Anna is now from a Minnesota farm driven by familial sexual abuse to a life of prostitution, while Mat Burke, a sentimental and sexually radiant Irishman, sweeps her off her feet. He is a virile shipwrecked sailor, a savior who has risen from the sea to demonstrate the truth of love. But what really changes Anna is her discovery that the sea is in her spirit and in her veins, while the fog which leaves her in suspension from reality purifies her. Overemphasis on the baleful influence of "the Ole Davil sea" comes entirely from Chris, but the happiness of the young couple indicates his error, and the second version ends in laughter.

It remains doubtful which conclusion was used at the first performance of *"Anna Christie."* Reviewers generally thought it comic,[9] the published version looks like an ambivalent compromise and O'Neill steadfastly insisted that the play was incipiently tragic. There is a minor comedic flurry over the religious difference between Mat and Anna, then all three drink to their future, with Mat and Chris as shipmates, leaving Anna waiting at home for her men. Her defiant toast is "Here's to the sea, no matter what." But Chris with his complaints about losing one's way in the fog has the last word: "Only that ole davil sea—she knows."

O'Neill also disclaimed the drama, omitting it from his self-chosen selection *Nine Plays* (1932). Certainly it is creakily designed with somewhat predictable, even sentimental, stock characters. And if one looks closely at Mat's dialogue, one can see little beyond the stage Irishman. However, in performance, when the lines are rephrased by a strong Irish actor, sexual chemistry can make powerful drama.

Another dominant theme in O'Neill's work at this time is the masculine idealist, or artist destroyed by the predatory philistinism of woman or wife. *Bread and Butter* (1914) is the first of these, and its action culminates in the offstage suicide of the husband forced by his wife into the family hardware business, rather than developing his talent as a painter.

Before Breakfast (1916) is a bitter little monologue in which the wife, having tricked her honorable husband (the son of a millionaire) into marriage with an alleged pregnancy, finally drives him to offstage suicide, by refusing to divorce him so that he can marry the woman he loves.

In *Ile* (1917), Captain Keeney's gently stubborn, delicate wife, who has insisted on going to sea with him, has brought bad luck to his whaling expedition. When the vessel finally sights a school of whales, he breaks free, asserts his masculinity, follows his calling and will make the voyage a success. She, the intruder into his masculine world, pays with her sanity—frantically playing hymns on her harmonium as the curtain falls.

However, the most important treatment of this theme of woman as hindrance to man's self-expression, whether artistic or otherwise, came with O'Neill's first Broadway success and the first of his four Pulitzer Prize dramas. In *Beyond the Horizon* (written 1918, produced 1920) Ruth Mayo is a Strindbergian character who ruins the lives of two brothers as well as her own by her selfish romanticism. She wants to possess both Robert and Andrew Mayo, the romantic and the stolid farmer. Finally she is left alone, in total inanition, incapable of saving herself. With this play O'Neill first tasted prestige and satisfaction, even earning the reluctant approval of his father, who was to die within a few months. He, of all people, understood the extraordinary feat his son had achieved—though he still clung to his experientially validated and market-driven opinion that people came to the theatre to be entertained. "What are you trying to do—send them home to commit suicide?" he asked.[10]

For O'Neill, the life of the farmer was confining, while freedom would be found elsewhere. When at the conclusion the sun rises over the delimiting hills, and Robert Mayo follows into eternity that road not taken, one recalls the conclusion of Ibsen's *Ghosts* and looks ahead to the end of *Desire Under the Elms*. Those who live on in the light of full day have been beaten down, or have not followed their dreams.

With this play O'Neill singlehandedly started an intellectual and emotional revolution in Broadway theatre, to which he continued to contribute throughout his writing career. Yet there is still something simplistic in this undeniably moving play. Quite legitimately one can argue that Robert Mayo would either have been destroyed by the physical hardships of the sea, or have developed the same emotional carapace as the less sensitive Andrew, but the sincerity of O'Neill's realism and the colloquialism of his dialogue give strength to this ground-breaking play. The action also reaches mythic proportions and transcends specific locality.

But what did O'Neill expect from marriage both in life and in drama? *Servitude* (1914), often considered a satire, may well provide an answer. "Love means servitude; and my love is my happiness" (Act 2), says Alice Roylston, who is editor, housekeeper, mother, and lover to her writer-husband. When she finds Ethel Frazer in her house she immediately offers to step aside so that her husband's happiness will be completed, but fortunately the "other woman," amazed both by her self-abnegation and Roylston's selfishness, returns to her own husband.

Further, when one looks at *Now I Ask You* (1916), *The Straw* (1919), and *The First Man* (1921), the last two written during his second marriage, to Agnes Boulton, the "requirement" of servitude is again important. In all of these plays the necessity of the husband's self-fulfillment is paramount and the woman is expected to sacrifice herself for the career of her beloved. Even the appreciative dedication written by O'Neill in the printed copy of *Mourning Becomes Electra* (1933) which he presented to Carlotta Monterey O'Neill, his third wife, can be read as a statement of his continuing expectations: "... mother, and wife and mistress and friend, ... and collaborator, I love you."[11]

Now I Ask You (1916) is an unsuccessful attempt at comedy, a triple satire of Ibsen's *Hedda Gabler*, melodrama, and feminine self-expression, with roots in O'Neill's Greenwich Village period. The circular three-act structure, with Prologue and Epilogue, inverts Ibsen by opening with a young woman's onstage suicide by pistol shot to the temple. But then O'Neill dramatizes the foolish events which have led to this action. This still unperformed play offers a happy ending when the Epilogue reveals that the initial "gunshot" was the sound of a blownout tire.

With The Straw (1919), an autobiographical drama set in a tuberculosis sanatorium, O'Neill again celebrates feminine sacrifice. Stephen Murray, the author *manqué*, finds his courage and inspiration in Eileen Carmody, a young woman fellow patient who has spent her life serving her ungrateful family. She risks her health to bid him farewell and finally accepts the fact that he cannot love her. But then, as she lies dying, Stephen, now a successful, yet dissipated author, marries her in an ambiguous conclusion, admitting that without her self-sacrifice he would have been a failure. Through her he finds a kind of salvation—a theme that appears much later in *Days Without End* (1933), which celebrates his third wife, Carlotta Monterey. There, Elsa Loving, who survives near fatal pneumonia, is instrumental in the religious conversion of her husband, and lives to serve again.

Similarly, *The First Man* (1921) insists upon the necessity of a wife's duty as helpmeet, supporter of her husband's career, even at the expense of her biological imperative. A child will discommode Curtis Jayson's archeological expedition to China, by depriving him of his wife's assistance. He considers himself betrayed, but not as much as does his wife in the hostile and suspicious middle-class environment of his family. She dies in graphic childbirth agony and he sets out on his scientific expedition, planning that his work will be continued by his son. He has learned very little from the devotion of his wife, Martha.

Another theme here, recalling the earlier *Bread and Butter*, is the relentless hostility of middle-class values to anything creative, with the added suspicion of a woman who is more than a housewife. Jayson's family even doubts the paternity of the child. Money is usually the god of the families to which O'Neill's major characters of this period belong, or into which they marry. Artistic or intellectual creativity is despised as impractical. Overall, O'Neill reacted against this convention-ridden class—except in *Ah, Wilderness!* (1933), which depicts a happy, well-adjusted, bourgeois family with empathy, tolerance, and understanding.

Another, and earlier, destructive woman is the domineering character of *Diff'rent* (1920), where Emma Crosby, a sexually repressed and hyper-idealistic woman, given to the reading of romantic novels, falls so much under their influence that she cannot forgive her fiancé's single South Seas sexual peccadillo. The distraught whaling captain, Caleb Williams, waits thirty years to gain her forgiveness only to discover that she believes herself in love with his ne'er-do-well nephew. In despair he hangs himself in the offstage barn, and she follows him there as the curtain falls.

The psychology of both characters is rather clumsy, yet the play achieved considerable Broadway success at its opening. As is frequent in O'Neill's developing career, the play looks backward and forward. The hanging in the barn recalls the earlier one-acter, *The Rope* (1918), and the theme of sexual freedom in "The Blessed Isles," the typical subject of sailor yarns (found also in *Gold* and *Moon of the Caribbees*), is repeated as a tale told of Lavinia in the final play of the trilogy *Mourning Becomes Electra* (1929–31). Here, in Emma's expectations of chaste masculine behavior there may be an autobiographical reference to Ella Quinlan O'Neill's early disillusionment when her husband was the successful defendant in a marriage and paternity suit.[12]

Politics and political awareness also intrude upon O'Neill's consciousness in his early plays, as his treatment of the Pancho Villa expedition in *The Movie Man* (1914) indicates. However, this pedestrian, melodramatic piece is a major regression after "Children of the Sea" (in its later version *Bound East for Cardiff*). The central idea that the battles of the Mexican uprising be orchestrated at the behest of a film company is politically explosive and based on the frequent and thorough coverage appearing in North American papers. However, the treatment lacks verisimilitude while both dialogue and characterization are stereotypical and unconvincing. O'Neill had probably read the Mexican news dispatches of John Reed, though he may not have yet met him.[13] Certainly the play proves that O'Neill was not very successful when he was writing propagandistically. He soared highest when working out of, and transforming, his own personal experience.

His Harvard war play, *The Sniper* (1915, but begun earlier), is insightful in its pacifist questioning of the values epitomized by World War I. On a human level it indicates O'Neill's understanding of war's cost, as the French peasant tries to shoot Germans in revenge for their destruction of his family and farm. Predictably, he dies before an ad hoc firing squad, with a sympathetic priest having the last word, "Alas, the laws of men!" This play was submitted to George Pierce Baker's English 47 workshop at Harvard where it did not receive the first prize, much to O'Neill's chagrin. As he wrote to his then girl friend, Beatrice Ashe (Maher), Baker indicated that the reason was the unpopularity of the war topic, though he recognized the drama's emotional power.[14]

Again O'Neill returned to war with *In the Zone* (1917) and the unperformed one-acter *Shell Shock* (1928). Showing little psychological insight, the later play skims across the surface of the action, with affinities to a simplistic vaudeville skit. The central character's addiction to cigarettes, and the final revelation that his friend still lives are awkwardly contrived. In view of what O'Neill had already written in *Moon of the Caribbees* and *Beyond the Horizon*, *Shell Shock* disappoints.

Another forgettable unperformed play, *The Personal Equation* (1915) has a political topic drawn from O'Neill's Greenwich Village period. Even here, he is autobiographical. Notable is the absent mother (dead for a number of years, as in effect his drug addicted mother had been to him) and an obsessive father, a second engineer, more attached to his ship and its engines than anything else. When his anarchist son, Tom, is deputed to destroy these engines to further a labor dispute, the father shoots him, leaving him a vegetable. Then he and Olga, the young man's fiancee, dedicate themselves to Tom's care, renouncing politics for familial duty. Once again, the sea scenes have validity while the political ones smack of mere propaganda, and the conclusion is contrived.

In 1919 O'Neill moves into the politics of race relations with his one-act play *The Dreamy Kid* (1918) in which Gary Jay Williams detects an autobiographical resonance with Jamie as the prodigal son and O'Neill's "Darker Brother."[15] This interpretation gains probability when one recalls that James O'Neill, Sr. had recently played the role of Jesse, the father of that biblical wastrel, in *The Wanderer*. Dreamy, a black gangster, though warned by Irene, a black prostitute, that the white police are coming, stands his final watch over his grandmother's deathbed. For once there is no concluding shot as he crouches down, revolver cocked, while the police wait outside, and Mammy prays.

Though this small suspense drama engages in stereotypes, particularly in the figure of Dreamy and the matriarchal Mammy, it treats black people sympathetically as human beings, victims of society, with emotions and family ties. O'Neill was playing with fire here, and perhaps that is why he did not make the character of Irene a white prostitute, as he had once considered.[16] But even more important he broke new ground by seeing that the Provincetown Players engaged black actors for the roles, rather than having whites perform in blackface.

His much more significant African-American play, *The Emperor Jones*, came the following year (1921). This time the cast was integrated, with the white colonialist, Smithers, a distinctly unlikable character and Brutus Jones the first modern black hero to be played on Broadway by an African-American actor, Charles Gilpin. Essentially an expressionistic psychodrama, it goes beyond language into total theatrical experience. Not only does it give a reverse historical account of African-American history, but also draws the audience into sensory and emotional participation, aurally by the continually responsive sound of the tom-tom, and visually by the repeated action of disrobing, as Jones confronts the Little Formless Fears and his later adversaries.

Emperor Brutus Jones, the ex-Pullman porter, either throws off, or loses the trappings of white civilization as he moves through eight scenes back to his African origins, making a personal journey of internal discovery, reliving in reverse his own life and the Black Experience. He kills Jeff a former friend, then sequentially a prison guard, an auctioneer and a planter bidding at a slave auction, and re-imagines the slave ship. Finally, wearing only a breechcloth, he confronts the crocodile god and his witch doctor, calling on Jesus in his terror. Gradually mime takes the place of words, while lighting, projections, the evocative setting, and the ever-quickening beat of the drums combine to strip away the appurtenances of so-called civilization and evoke collective hallucination in the audience. Everything leads inexorably to the inevitable final pistol shot when Brutus Jones lies dead from a silver bullet cast by the hands of his own people. But since Jones has refused the ultimate return to his past by invoking Christianity before putting the witch doctor and crocodile god to flight with his own silver bullet, he has signed his death warrant. Perhaps O'Neill drew back at this last step, or perhaps he was condescending towards black culture by "redeeming" Jones through a return to the white man's religion.

Racism was covertly charged against this play by Charles Gilpin in his frequent changes in the text to avoid racist language. Consequently, O'Neill was happy to replace him in the London production with Paul Robeson, a graduate of Rutgers University and Columbia Law School, rather than a "mere" actor. The play was an astounding success and after a month in Greenwich Village it moved uptown and thereby helped hasten the demise of the idealistic Provincetown Players.

In *The Hairy Ape* (1921), another foray into expressionism, O'Neill combines a number of themes from his earlier sea plays, and also the symbiotic relationship of the second engineer with his engines in *The Personal Equation*. He develops further his interest in labor politics, and even more importantly, his commitment to expressionistic total theatre. This time he documents the downward spiral of a white man. The fellowship of the forecastle in the *S.S. "Glencairn"* series now becomes a dance of the damned, imprisoned in an inferno, sleeping in a crowded steel-barred space like a prison cage for Neanderthal man, dehumanized by the shipowners and big business. Much the same forecastle cast from the *Glencairn* is to be found here—the white human race in microcosm—but the unifying force is engines, steel, and coal. The filth of the stokehole has supplanted the sea's cleansing, uplifting power while the Irishman's romantic remembrance of sailing ships is ridiculed by these slaves to machines. The aptly named Yank is the leader of those who feed the engines in a repetitive, grotesque, infernal parody of brutal sexual intercourse.

Yank represents the unthinking, voiceless working class, unquestioning of their lot, perceiving themselves as the first moving principle, while Long, the typical labor agitator, spouts anarchistic clichés, but does nothing. It is Yank's demoralizing confrontation with the bored, bred-out young society woman, Mildred, that destroys him psychologically, leading him to question both himself and society.

O'Neill faced a difficult problem here: how to make an inarticulate character communicate ideas. As before with *The Emperor Jones*, he resorts to expressionistic techniques, especially in the Fifth Avenue scene, where the effetely oblivious members of the upper class are unaffected by Yank's superior strength. O'Neill here used masks for the first time—though they were an afterthought, suggested by Blanche Hays, the costume designer. The repeated image of the cage with Yank as the "beast," which the white-clad Mildred had called him, dominates the rest of the play, as the "hairy ape," who has lost his sense of "belonging," tries to find his place in a hostile universe which rejects him to the last. Like Emperor Brutus Jones he moves downward, rejected by Fifth Avenue and labor agitators, imprisoned briefly, and even rejected there, until he finds his death in a cage, whose gorilla occupant, like capitalist society, casually destroys him in an instant. Finally Yank considers himself no more than a grotesque beast in a sideshow where "perhaps, the Hairy Ape at last belongs." Once again, O'Neill had a major success, particularly in the performance of Louis Wolheim, with the production moving from Greenwich Village to Broadway.[17]

Returning to the theme of race relations in 1923 with *All God's Chillun Got Wings*, O'Neill met trouble. The only reason *The Emperor Jones* had been acceptable was that there was no question of miscegenation, but an interracial marriage was still anathema to the theatrical establishment. Howls of rage came from press and public alike when it was known that Paul Robeson would actually kiss a white woman onstage as his wife.[18] So, in a futile attempt to defuse audience hostility, and fill a hiatus caused by the illness of Mary Blair, the star of the new play, the Provincetown Playhouse presented Robeson in a limited run of *The Emperor Jones* to introduce this handsome, well-educated actor/singer to the New York audience.

O'Neill's choice of music is important in *Chillun* because he always tailors musical selections to fit the situation. The black music is warm and joyous, e.g. "I Guess I'll Have to Telegraph my Baby," while the white folk sing constrainedly of sentimental social limitation, "She's Only a Bird in a Gilded Cage." Expressionistic techniques are also used in the careful division of black and white in the scene of the doomed wedding underlined by contrasting lamentations of slavery—a spiritual, "Sometimes I feel Like a Mourning Dove," and Stephen Foster's banal "Old Black Joe." Then the disapproving church bell "clangs one more stroke, instantly dismissing."

Expressionism is repeatedly invoked in the growing dominance of the African mask, given to Jim by his Afrocentric sister, and through the physically contracting size of the room in which Jim and Ella live. As Brutus Jones strips off all his clothes, so Jim's attempts to succeed in a hostile white world diminish. Ella wishes him to fail, because she feels her own selfhood and power threatened by his intellect and potential upward mobility. Her attempt to kill Jim and her stabbing of the African mask signify both her assertion of white superiority, and her own insanity. With his last failure to complete his law examinations Jim regresses to his happy ignorant childhood, when the world seemed friendly and racism had neither tainted his ambition nor destroyed his love. Thus, they again become as little children in order to enter the kingdom of heaven, where "All God's Chillun Got Wings," as the spiritual says. Jim gives up his hopes and dreams to serve his now insane wife. And as with *Jones*, the conclusion can appear racist.

However, *Chillun* has more to it than simple race relations. Its real theme is the destruction of a good man by a selfish or inappropriate wife. Almost alone among reviewers, Heywood Broun understood that fact: "this tiresome play ... gives to a first rate Negro a third rate white woman," documenting her slide into insanity (*New York World*, 16 May 1924). There are also autobiographical overtones in the names James and Ella—like O'Neill's own parents. Indeed this play may point ahead to *Long Day's Journey into Night*, demonstrating O'Neill's continuing anger at his once drug-addicted mother.

Even more autobiographical is *Welded* (1923), O'Neill's tribute to his marriage with Agnes Boulton, the mother of his children Shane and Oona. Its subject is one evening of misunderstanding in the union of two artists, a playwright and his actress-muse—with a double attempted revenge. The wife tries to rekindle a relationship with an old flame, who brings her to understand her dependence on her husband, while he seeks out a prostitute, who cannot comprehend him. By the end of the third act, the pair, whose separateness has been defined by the use of individual spotlights, merge into one single illumination as they climb the stairs to their bedroom, pausing in an embrace that forms a cross, to signify an interdependence both sacrificial and redemptive. Unsuccessful at its first production and not revived in New York until 1981, the play does have some good moments, despite its depressing title. Yet O'Neill's attitude toward woman is unchanged. While ostensibly celebrating his own marriage, O'Neill has his playwright character dominate his wife, who as the interpreter of his roles is his puppet. Again he celebrates masculine creativity and feminine servitude to it.

A more affirmative attitude is found in *The Fountain* (1922, produced 1926) written just before *Welded*. This long experimental play embraces the total theatre espoused also by his designer/director, Robert Edmond Jones. Produced by the "Triumvirate" of O'Neill, Jones, and Kenneth McGowan ("The Experimental Theatre, Inc."), this successor to the earlier Provincetown Players was heavily influenced by the innovative dramatists and stage designers of Europe.

The Fountain deals with Juan Ponce de León and his search for emotional fulfillment. However much one may think that he seeks "the finer perfection of Love," the Fountain of Youth, or the eternal return, he initially looks for wealth, joining Columbus to pillage the New World. There, he exhibits the shabbiest qualities of Christianity, inflicting genocide, torture, and mayhem. Then in his old age he discovers the love he had denied in his youth, after the aptly named Beatriz, daughter of his once-beloved Maria, comes as his ward to Puerto Rico. She represents what he has lost by following an avaricious goal, and in her marriage to the young Luis, she becomes Juan's symbol of life. Her dream-appearance as the fountain spirit leads him to understand the conflict between emotions and cold intellect, demonstrating the inclusiveness of the world soul of Neo-platonic thinkers, and the oneness of all religions. Then, like her Dantean equivalent, Beatriz leads the dying hidalgo out of life into a new paradisal world. In marriage to her beloved she trusts love, where Juan did not.

Though this play tries to include too much, and suffers from O'Neill's lack of true poetic instinct, its importance lies in its experimentation, its circularity, and its attempt to go beyond the conventions of act division. The two-generation action is developed by symbolic scenes to evoke the cyclical quality of human existence, the power of love and the central mystery of human life.

O'Neill's next play, *Desire Under the Elms* (1924), established him as a dramatist of true genius and is the culmination of his first period of composition. The modern world is often thought hostile to tragedy, but in this play O'Neill discomfits the naysayers. He manipulates into an astonishingly successful tragic whole such different elements as the conflict between duty and joy, the Apollonian and the Dionysian (even more notable in *The Great God Brown*), the dysfunctional family, and a combination of Greek myth with the then current philosophical-psychological ideas of Friedrich Nietzsche and Sigmund Freud. These disparate ideas are melded together in a thoroughly American New England setting which carries with it the mythico-religious tradition of Puritanism, along with the dream of monetary success, the pioneering spirit of breaking new land, and the world of gold in the far West. In effect, within this single play O'Neill prefigures *Mourning Becomes Electra* and the totality of his uncompleted saga "A Tale of Possessors, Self-Dispossessed," demonstrating the dour and acquisitive quality of the Great American Myth, which he was to examine not only in the Mannon family, but also in the Harford and Melody families of *A Touch of the Poet* and the unfinished *More Stately Mansions*.

Desire also recalls the hardscrabble misery of *Beyond the Horizon* (1920), and *The Rope* (1918). Particularly important in *The Rope* is the second marriage of the old farmer Abraham Bentley, to a much younger woman (now dead), by whom he had a son, Luke. Bentley also has a secret hoard of gold pieces, keeping it for the son of his passionate old age. Also, like the later Ephraim Cabot of *Desire*, Bentley speaks in a biblical manner, especially when his prodigal son returns.

In *Desire*, everything falls into place. The gloomy farmhouse was presented in a much-praised set, superbly executed by Robert Edmond Jones from O'Neill's descriptions and drawings, its brooding trees reinforcing the sense of doom that pervades the play. In addition, O'Neill also solves the problem of the inarticulate central figure, which had been problematic in *The Hairy Ape*, by giving Ephraim Cabot the incantatory cadences of the Bible, particularly the *Song of Solomon*. But equally effective is Ephraim's long dialect-based monologue where he insists that "God's hard, not easy" (II.ii), in telling his new young wife of his earlier decision to return to his rocky farm rather than remain in the fertile Midwest.

The cycle of the seasons is also important for all these characters who are creatures of the soil. All members of this family are subject to it, none more than Ephraim, who rode out in an earlier spring to test himself in the Midwest, only to discover that his Puritan heritage was too strong, and happiness is not to be found in this world. Now in this later spring season the older brothers follow their father's example in seeking their freedom, departing for California after an act of betrayal that combines aspects of Jacob, Esau, and Judas Iscariot—selling their patrimony to their half-brother Eben for the thirty pieces of gold that Ephraim had hoarded.

But the newly aroused Ephraim has returned from his latest spring-wandering with a young bride through whom he hopes to restore his own fertility and that of the farm, bypassing all his sons. In so doing he unleashes on the family the mythic horrors of Oedipus, Phaedra, and Medea, in Greek tragedy. In the background are the sternly religious conflict between joy and duty, the familial psychology of Freud, and the racial unconscious of Jung. Thus Abbie seduces Eben in the front parlor that signifies his dead mother's personal space, claiming her son and the farm as her own. And here Eben also follows his father; just as all three sons had succeeded their father in their patronage of Min, the village prostitute, so Eben impregnates Abbie, in an Oedipal union, with Phaedrian overtones.

In the celebrations for the birth of "his" son, Ephraim becomes a capering satyr figure, ignorant of what all the world knows—the child is Eben's, and the instrument of his own disinheritance. So, in a rewriting of *Medea*, Abbie suffocates their child to keep Eben's love, driving the grief-stricken young father to report her to the sheriff. But the power of his passion calls him back to share her fate, and in a repetition of the ending of *Beyond the Horizon*, the two lovers walk forth into the sunrise to face their all too certain future. This conclusion seems more affirmative than in the earlier play, and O'Neill leaves the audience with a sense of love's eternity.

With this play, initially banned in Boston on moral grounds and refused a public performance in England until 1940, O'Neill reached true international status. This was not merely because of the steamy plot, but the extraordinary transmutation of mythology into modern garb. It also demonstrated one of O'Neill's greatest strengths—as myth user rather than myth maker. Here and in *Mourning Becomes Electra* he combined ancient myths with modern psychology to examine American emotional and cultural equivalents.

NOTES

1. He dramatized this attempt in "Exorcism," which he withdrew and destroyed after a single performance from the Provincetown Players (1920).

2. For discussion of O'Neill's intellectual background, see Egil Törnqvist's essay "O'Neill's Philosophical and Literary Paragons" in this collection.

3. See Ann C. Hall, "*A Kind of Alaska*": *Women in the Plays of O'Neill, Pinter, and Shepard* (Carbondale and Edwardsville: Southern Illinois University Press, 1993).

4. Louis Sheaffer, *O'Neill: Son and Playwright* (Boston: Little, Brown, 1968), p. 273.

5. Timo Tiusanen, *O'Neill's Scenic Images* (Princeton, NJ: Princeton University Press, 1968), p. 45, notes this idea of the "sound coulisse," described by Otto Kioischwitz, *O'Neill* (Berlin: Junket and Dünnhaupt, 1938), p. 73.

6. Susan Glaspell, *The Road to the Temple* (New York: Frederick Stokes, 1927), see pp. 253–54.

7. Gary Jay Williams, "Turned Down by Provincetown: O'Neill's Debut Reexamined," *Theatre Journal* 37 (1985): 155–66. Reprinted in *The Eugene O'Neill Newsletter*, 12, i (1988): 17–27. See also Williams's entry "The Provincetown Players" in Margaret Loftus Ranald, *The Eugene O'Neill Companion* (Westport, Connecticut: Greenwood Press, 1982).

8. Sheaffer, *O'Neill: Son and Playwright*, p. 242.

9. Travis Bogard, *Contour in Time: The Plays of Eugene O'Neill* (New York: Oxford University Press, 1972), p. 162n.

10. Sheaffer, *O'Neill: Son and Playwright*, p. 477.

11. See Eugene O'Neill, *Inscriptions: Eugene O'Neill to Carlotta Monterey*. Privately printed: New Haven: Yale University Press, 1960, n.p.

12. Though the accusations were not upheld in court, James O'Neill made at least two financial settlements on the young man, who later tried to claim against his estate.

13. John Reed, *Insurgent Mexico* (New York: D. Appleton, 1914), most of which comes from articles originally appearing in the *Metropolitan* magazine.

14. See undated letter in the Beatrice Ashe Maher correspondence, Berg Collection, New York Public Library, and a corroborative news item of 4 March 1915 in the *New London Morning Telegraph*.

15. Gary Jay Williams, "*The Dreamy Kid*: O'Neill's Darker Brother," *Theatre Annual* 43 (1988); 3–14.

16. Sheaffer, *O'Neill: Son and Playwright*, p. 430.

17. When the play moved uptown the role of Mildred was played by Carlotta Monterey, later O'Neill's third wife.

18. Attempts were made to abort the play, and child labor laws were invoked to prevent the first performance, forcing James Light, the stage director, to read the children's lines. Children appeared only in summer performances when school was not in session.

JAMES A. ROBINSON

The Middle Plays

By the time *Desire Under the Elms* closed in the fall of 1925, Eugene O'Neill was firmly established as the leading artistic playwright of the American theatre. The "Triumvirate" of O'Neill, Kenneth Macgowan and Robert Edmond Jones had successfully reorganized the Provincetown Players into The Experimental Theatre, an off-Broadway company ready to stage virtually anything which O'Neill could conceive. Guided by the tenets of the Art Theatre movement which Macgowan promoted, O'Neill indulged his imagination, composing the historical extravaganzas "*Marco Millions*" and *Lazarus Laughed* and the allegorical *The Great God Brown*, and sketching out two studies of modern bourgeois America, *Strange Interlude* and *Dynamo*, as well. But *Marco*, *Interlude* and *Dynamo* were not produced by the Triumvirate but the Theatre Guild, a prestigious Broadway company whose embrace of O'Neill signalled his arrival as a popular dramatist. The Guild also premiered O'Neill's Civil War trilogy *Mourning Becomes Electra*, and the autobiographical dramas *Ah, Wilderness!* (a domestic comedy) and *Days Without End* (a dogmatic miracle play). The artistic and commercial failure of the latter in early 1934 combined with the Great Depression to motivate O'Neill to compose an epic Cycle of historical plays exploring his country's greedy self-dispossession. No Cycle plays were to be staged until the series was complete. But he never finished it; so no new O'Neill play appeared until *The Iceman Cometh* in 1946,

From *The Cambridge Companion to Eugene O'Neill*, ed. Michael Manheim, pp. 69–81. © 1998 by Cambridge University Press.

ten years after his receipt of the Nobel Prize for Literature made official the worldwide recognition of his genius.

The international award seemed particularly appropriate for a playwright openly indebted to major European dramatists and thinkers, including Aeschylus, Sophocles, Henrik Ibsen, August Strindberg, Friedrich Nietzsche, Sigmund Freud and Carl Jung. During this middle period these foreign currents ebbed and flowed through his work, their influence sometimes challenged and sometimes fortified by mystical philosophy from Asia, and by techniques from medieval and Elizabethan theatre and the modern European novel. O'Neill thus continued to expose his audiences, critics and fellow playwrights to unfamiliar ideas and forms from abroad. But his emphasis on strong narratives and powerful feelings carried on an older American tradition of melodrama, as amended by more recent conventions of naturalism and realism that O'Neill himself had helped plant and nurture.

This combining of ancient and modern, foreign and native, pervades *Desire Under the Elms*, the 1924 play that foreshadows the works of O'Neill's middle decade. Its plot (like that of *Electra*) enacts ancient Greek myths in nineteenth-century New England; its characters, native folk-drama rustics, are viewed (like those of *Interlude*) through the filter of modern depth psychology; its vision betrays debts to Eastern mysticism (*Marco*), American Gothicism (*Electra*), and Dionysus via Nietzsche (*Lazarus* and *Brown*). Like *Interlude*, *Dynamo*, *Electra* and *Wilderness*, *Desire* pictures overt intrafamilial conflict; the more covert struggle within Eben Cabot between Jungian male and female principles assumes transcultural form in *Marco*, becomes theological in *Interlude* and *Dynamo*, and is exorcized in the Freudian family romance of *Electra*. Finally, the 1924 play's identification of transcendent forces in the land and in love reveals O'Neill's religious sensibility, his desire (expressed in a program note that year) to penetrate like his master, Strindberg, to a realm "behind life" where "our souls, maddened by loneliness and the ignoble inarticulateness of flesh, are slowly evolving their new language of kinship."[1] In the exalted speeches of *Brown* and *Lazarus*, the mysterious larger force controlling human destiny in *Interlude* and *Electra*, and the design for *Dynamo* and *Days* to compose two parts of a trilogy exploring the death of God, we witness O'Neill's consistent ambition during this phase for the restoration of theatre to its formerly sacred place in Western culture.

Indeed, the phase's three initial plays form an unintended trilogy on a theological theme: the spiritual emptiness of material desires. The first of the three to be composed (though not produced until 1928), *Marco* offers a protagonist who is part explorer, part tourist, part inventor, part local mayor, but mainly eager merchant: a variation on Sinclair Lewis's George Babbitt, without his redeeming moral sense. Blending history with romance, satire and tragedy, O'Neill creates from the famous Venetian's exploits a pageant worthy of David Belasco (the Broadway producer of dazzling theatre spectacles who in fact took out the first option on the play). The first act places Polo's entourage in a series of gorgeous, exotic Asian settings on their way to the Chinese emperor Kublai Khan's sumptuous court—the site of several subsequent scenes during Polo's fifteen-year residence in China and subsequent return to Venice, where he is nicknamed "Marco Millions" for the fabulous wealth he conspicuously displays. The nickname points up Marco's identity (in Kublai Khan's words) as "a shrewd and crafty greed" who "has not even a mortal soul," but only "an acquisitive instinct."[2] This vulgar materialism is underscored by a romantic story line involving the beautiful princess Kukachin, the Khan's granddaughter, who dies of her unrequited love for a man who fails to recognize a passion he is incapable of sharing or returning. As an emblem of the female, the intuitive and the spiritual (qualities O'Neill associated with the East), Kukachin offers the *yin* to the *yang* symbolized by Polo, whose male, rational and acquisitive attributes identify him as quintessentially Western (that is, modern American)—rich without, impoverished within.

The dualistic opposition between Kukachin and Marco Polo epitomizes a play that features vivid contrasts in its costumes, settings, characters and themes: West vs. East, matter vs. spirit, death vs. life, division vs. unity. A similar polar vision, prominent in the moral absolutism of American melodrama and reinforced by O'Neill's reading of Emerson, Jung, and Taoist texts, characterizes most of O'Neill's plays. It certainly informs *The Great God Brown*, a masked drama about the struggles between and within two architects. Externally, creative spirit battles obtuse matter in the conflict between the sensitive, artistic Dion Anthony and his rival Billy Brown, who employs and exploits Dion. Like Marco Millions, Brown is "inwardly empty and resourceless," O'Neill explained in a letter to New York newspapers shortly after the play opened in January 1926. He also outlined Dion's inner battle between "Dionysus and St. Anthony—the creative pagan acceptance of life, fighting eternal war with the masochistic, life-denying spirit of Christianity as represented by St. Anthony"; and he identified a "mystical pattern" of "conflicting tides in the soul of Man" as the play's central rhythm.[3]

A testimony to O'Neill's theatrical instinct, the play proved popular despite its mystical ambitions, despite the visual masks worn by Dion, Brown, Dion's wife Margaret, and Cybel (a prostitute who is mistress to both agonists), despite a bizarre plot spanning fourteen years that features two climaxes. At the first climax, the wealthy bachelor Brown—who envies Dion his wife, his mistress, and his talent—assumes Dion's cynical mask upon his rival's premature death, convincing even Dion's family that he is Dion.

A more elaborate (often comic) masquerade follows in scenes drenched in dramatic irony, as Brown manically alternates between the mask of Dion, a new mask of his former complacent self, and a face increasingly *"ravaged and haggard"* (II, 516) that is revealed only to Cybel upon Brown's death (the second climax) a few weeks after Dion's.

The play suffers from its implausible story, excessive rhetoric and stereotypical characterization—especially that of the gold-hearted, earth-mother prostitute Cybel. But it is among O'Neill's most intriguing plays, especially for biographical critics. Dion's Dionysian mask, "distorted by morality" (O'Neill's letter observes) "from Pan into Satan, into a Mephistopheles mocking himself in order to feel alive," strongly resembles O'Neill's self-contemptuous, cynical brother Jamie, prematurely dead from alcoholism in 1923.[4] Dion's hostility toward Brown, moreover, suggests O'Neill's intuition of the threat to his talent posed by his recent fame and success; he did not want to follow his father, whose fabulous popularity as *The Count of Monte Cristo* had led him to sacrifice his talent for wealth. Finally, Dion's inner battle between Dionysus and St. Anthony projects the playwright's own struggle between the Nietzschean doctrines of affirmation and tragic joy he repeatedly espoused in the mid-1920s, and Roman Catholic values that he could only half-repudiate. No doubt he regarded the Christian asceticism which tortures Dion as "masochistic"; but Dion's spiritual growth implies nonetheless the redemptive value of suffering, the central tenet of Christian faith. The same holds true for Brown, out of whose brief anguish (claims O'Neill's letter) "a soul is born, a tortured Christian soul such as the dying Dion's."[5]

If Dion is tormented by his deeper faith, Brown is murdered by Dion's superficial mask. The masking constitutes the play's most provocative feature. Presumably inspired by ancient Greek theatre, its implications are modern. It reveals the playwright's interest in contemporary depth psychology, which posited a private, authentic self beneath the personality presented to others. Only Cybel witnesses this sensitive, poetic, and vulnerable self; and this suppression of his genuine nature hastens Dion's self-destruction.[6] O'Neill himself, however, privately lamented that the play's production "suggested only the bromidic, hypocritical and defensive double-personality of people in their personal relationships" rather than the mystical "drama of the forces behind the people" that his public letter had stressed.[7] And from a third perspective, *Brown's* masks enunciate what W. B. Worthen terms O'Neill's deepest project, the "exfoliation of an unconscious, intensely private, and interior self in the public action of the theatre." The masking thus questions the identification of character and actor that modern realistic acting style asserts; moreover, the masked characters' painful awareness of audience implies that "'character' in this drama never escapes its subjection to and falsification by the coercion of the spectator, by the spectators in the audience, those on the stage, and those haunting the theatre of the self."[8] But on the deepest level, the suffering of the souls beneath the masks simply dramatizes the central theme of O'Neill's work, indeed of his life: the anguish of human loneliness.

The inability of Billy Brown to incorporate into himself the "Satan" which Dion's mask has become also reveals the influence of Jung, who argued that personal development required integration of one's hidden evil side, or shadow, into oneself. Jung's presence expands in *Lazarus Laughed*, the final drama of O'Neill's informal anti-materialist trilogy. The intricate masking schemes for its series of crowds follow the seven personality categories proposed by Jung's *Psychological Types* (1921), with each type divided into seven periods of life, then multiplied even further by race, gender, class, nationality and religious sect so that the play's production requires literally hundreds of masks. Not surprisingly, this most audacious of O'Neill's plays has never been produced on Broadway, and rarely elsewhere.[9] It follows the progress of the biblical Lazarus—the only unmasked character—from the days after his miraculous restoration to life by Jesus through a fictional journey with legions of followers to imperial Rome, where he is eventually executed by the old, decadent emperor Tiberius. But his true antagonist is the young, perverse Caligula, the self-proclaimed "Lord of fear, Caesar of death" (II, 627), who symbolizes corrupt and fallen mankind. Like all others, however, the Roman general responds to Lazarus' irresistibly contagious laughter, the consequence of the Jew's realization—proclaimed repeatedly—that "there is no death."

Lazarus' words echo Christ's, as do his charisma, radiance, loving nature and ultimate fate. But Lazarus' gospel of the ego's unreality draws more upon Hinduism, Buddhism and Gnostic faiths of the early Christian era; and his youthful personality and intoxicating effect resemble Nietzsche's Zarathustra and Dionysus. Most important, the God he worships offers not salvation but the enlightened insight that humans, like all material beings, participate in a process of "eternal change and everlasting growth, and a high note of laughter soaring through chaos from the deep heart of God!" (572). Jesus wept; Lazarus laughed. And the laughter, chanting and dancing of his mobs of followers (many of whom literally die laughing) is elaborately choreographed by a playwright who characteristically attends to rhythm, both in the texture and structure of this unique divine comedy. Perhaps only in *Lazarus* did O'Neill realize his middle period ambition (proclaimed in 1933) for a theatre that served as "a Temple where the religion of a poetical interpretation and symbolic celebration of life is communicated to human beings, starved in spirit by their soul-stifling daily struggle to exist as masks among the masks of living."[10] But the spectacle offered by this play (like religious theatre generally) has attracted few modern spectators.

The same cannot be said of *Strange Interlude*, which ran on Broadway from January 1928 to June 1929, sold 100,000 copies, and established O'Neill as a bankable playwright. It presents variations on another Nietzschean theme, the will to power, in the form of emotional possessiveness. "Forgive us our possessing as we forgive those who possessed before us" (II, 650), muses novelist Charles Marsden in one of this nine-act play's countless thought asides—a version of the Elizabethan soliloquy which exposes most of the spoken exchanges as verbal masks. Like Ibsen's Hedda Gabler, *Interlude*'s Nina Leeds seeks dominion over the men who love and surround her, including her family friend Marsden, husband Sam Evans, lover Ned Darrell, and son Gordon—named after her fiancé Gordon Shaw, who died in World War I before consummating their love. Gordon's ghost haunts Nina's mind, first prompting promiscuity, then marriage (promoted by Ned, her doctor) to Gordon's boyish admirer Sam, then intercourse with Ned to conceive Gordon II after her discovery of congenital insanity in Sam's family causes her to abort Sam's child. Their intermittent affair destroys Ned's promising scientific career over the following twenty years, while the blissfully unaware Sam prospers and young Gordon grows and marries in spite of his jealous mother's fierce covert resistance. Shortly after Sam's death in his late forties, Nina and Marsden plan a passionless marriage that signals her retreat from possessiveness.

A compelling character, Nina combines features of the Romantic eternal feminine (as in her *"unchangeably mysterious eyes"* [II, 675]), the Victorian *femme fatale*, Strindberg's castrating women, and Anne Whitefield of G. B. Shaw's *Man and Superman*. Embodying the instinctual Life Force (a version of Arthur Schopenhauer's Will), she deviously manipulates her male admirers, especially the scientist Ned who considers himself *"immune to love"* (661). Nina's cunning also aligns her with the predatory villains of melodrama, whose conventions *Interlude* both follows and critiques. As Kurt Eisen has observed, the play's two levels of dialogue (of speech and thoughts) strive to achieve the total emotional expressivity of melodrama. But that dialogue, modelled upon the conflicting discourses of the modern novel (as described by Mikhail Bakhtin), also ironically contrasts melodrama's sentimental values—celebrating home and motherhood—with the ideologies of business (Sam), psychoanalysis (Darrell), and fictional art (Marsden).[11]

Sam's discourse is the least complicated of the three, for this dense, complacent advertising executive has little inner life, hence rarely soliloquizes after little Gordon's birth confers (apparent) fatherhood upon him. His subtle power over others lies in the bourgeois honor code, associated with Gordon Shaw, that he carries on: a code honored by Nina and Ned, who protect Sam from knowledge of their adultery at heavy cost to the anguished Ned. The conflict between morality and sexuality, superego and id, points up the influence of Freud, whose popular psychoanalytical discourse shapes the words and thoughts of Dr. Darrell. Having himself briefly undergone psychoanalysis in 1926, O'Neill treats Ned with ambivalence. On the one hand, the neurologist offers acute insight into Marsden's Oedipal fixation and Nina's promiscuity; on the other, his Freudian ideas and language are often parodied. Thus, his promotion of Sam as a surrogate for Gordon Shaw and cure for Nina's neurosis backfires disastrously, with himself the primary victim. And his *"cold, emotionless, professional"* words as Nina seduces him at Act 4's conclusion satirically highlight the arrogant blindness of a theorist who succumbs to the sexual force to which he has claimed immunity (II, 709).

Not just Ned's language, but language itself is questioned by a work whose protagonist sees "how we poor monkeys hide from ourselves behind the sounds called words" (II, 667), hinting at mysterious depths of existence lurking beneath its characters' speeches and thoughts. Appropriately, the play also satirizes its language specialist as one who hides from himself. Charles Marsden's deep fear not just of sex but "of life" (II, 670), and the timid conventionality of his fiction, suggest O'Neill's mild contempt. Yet Marsden's *"indefinable feminine quality"* allows him penetrating intuitions about Nina's behavior (II, 633), and his numerous thought asides (which open and close the play) often provide a central consciousness to this novelistic drama. After all, the asides constitute a simplified, conventionally syntactical version of the stream-of-consciousness technique of the modern novel: Marsden's domain. And Marsden resembles Nina in a crucial respect. In a play structured around Nina's alternating moods of adjustment and alienation, Marsden's emotional life vacillates between a mild detached contentment and deep grief over the loss of loved ones. He moves symbolically between life and death: the deepest rhythm not just of this play, but of all O'Neill's drama.

In *Interlude*'s final scene, Nina declares their lives to be "merely strange dark interludes in the electrical display of God the Father" (II, 817), concluding a series of allusions to a distant, punishing father god who competes with an immanent, mystical mother god for her allegiance. In O'Neill's next play another neurotic protagonist, Reuben Light, repudiates the Puritanical father God of his parents and seeks forgiveness for his mother's subsequent death from the maternal god he discovers in electricity. *Dynamo* ends in a hydroelectric plant with Reuben's murder of his girl friend Ada, then sacrificial suicide to a generator, *"huge and black, with something of a massive female idol about it*" (II, 871). The play's titular symbol clearly alludes to "The Dynamo and the Virgin" chapter from *The Education of Henry Adams*, the famous American autobiography which introduced this powerful symbol for our modern technological god. But credibility of character falls victim to the play's schematic presentation of the "big subject" (as O'Neill described it after finishing *Dynamo* in August, 1928): the "sickness of today" and the "death of the old God and the failure of Science and Materialism to give any satisfying new One for the surviving primitive religious instinct to find a meaning for life in."[12] Another letter written while he wrote the play betrays the tired imagination of a playwright who consciously borrowed *Dynamo*'s interior/ exterior domestic settings from *Desire Under the Elms*, its industrial sounds from *The Hairy Ape*, and its thought asides from *Interlude*.[13] The characters also seem borrowed from earlier O'Neill plays (especially *Desire*), resulting in unintended self-parody. The Oedipal Reuben is a modern Eben Cabot without the dignity, his minister father a cowardly, watered-down Ephraim; Ada's mother, subject to spells of moody dreaminess around the dynamo she worships, recalls *Brown*'s Earth Mother, Cybel; Ada's father mocks like Dion Anthony, is a scientist like Ned Darrell.

   Dynamo failed on Broadway in 1929, as did O'Neill's final religious play, *Days Without End*, in 1934. Again, he reworks old material. Resembling Dion Anthony, protagonist John Loving is split between two selves, one attracted tentatively to his abandoned Christian faith (John, an unmasked character), the other toward Mephistophelean nihilism (Loving, who wears "*the death mask of a John who has died with a sneer of scornful mockery on his lips*").[14] Their word duel forms the central conflict of a play about John's progress on an autobiographical novel, whose plot reveals his recent adultery and current desire (fueled by Loving) for his ailing wife Elsa to die. But with the aid of a Catholic priest, John finally slays his masked alterego by recovering his lost faith in church at the foot of a crucifix, and Elsa miraculously recovers. The play does not. While *Days* offers in John's past a mildly intriguing resume of O'Neill's own spiritual journey, its underdeveloped characters, overloaded exposition, and blunt (and highly atypical) Christian conclusion render it O'Neill's dullest mature drama.[15] Perhaps sensing this, O'Neill cancelled plans for the third of the "Myth Plays for the God-Forsaken" trilogy begun by *Dynamo* and *Days*, and never ventured onto religious terrain again.

   In fact, a previous trilogy of myth plays had already given O'Neill's spiritual sensibility its most powerful expression. T. S. Eliot once observed that good poets borrow, while great poets steal; the plot for *Mourning Becomes Electra*, produced in 1932, was stolen from Euripides, Sophocles and (especially) the *Oresteia* of Aeschylus. But *Electra*'s title indicates O'Neill's interest in the daughter, Lavinia Mannon, who avenges the murder of her father Ezra (Agamemnon) by his wife Christine (Clytemnestra) and her lover, Ezra's cousin Adam Brant (Aegisthus). Part 2 of the trilogy, *Homecoming*, describes Ezra's poisoning upon his return to New England in 1865 from serving as a Union general in the American Civil War; part 2, *The Hunted*, depicts the outraged Lavinia manipulating her neurotic, Oedipal brother Orin (Orestes) into killing Brant and goading Christine into taking her life. The final play, *The Haunted*, finds Lavinia worried that Orin, driven half-insane by guilt and incestuous desire, will confess and tarnish the Mannon name. She drives her brother to suicide, then entombs herself within the family Greek revival mansion for the remainder of her life. She is helped by Seth, the family's old gardener, who also hosts the various choruses of townspeople whose gossip about the aristocratic Mannons opens each part of the trilogy.

Doris Alexander notes that *Electra* places O'Neill "in direct rivalry" with the ancient Greek playwrights.[16] Indeed, that competition of modern playwright with revered forefathers enacts the rebellion of child against parent at the heart of the play. O'Neill also challenged another father figure, Kenneth Macgowan, in his abdication of the theatrical expressionism his colleague had encouraged. "Hereafter I write plays primarily as literature to be read," he wrote Macgowan in June 1929; "my trend will be to regard anything depending on director or scenic designer for collaboration to bring out its full values as suspect."[17] *Electra* nonetheless betrays a lingering trace of the Art Theatre in the "*strange life-like mask*" expression of all the Mannons in repose (II, 897), a visual sign of their shared destiny as members of a cursed family. Moreover, the play's major relationships pattern themselves according to the Freudian family romance that Macgowan had helped popularize in a 1929 book he co-authored, *What is Wrong with Marriage*. Each Mannon child is enamored of the opposite-sex parent in a drama which features frequent fleeting glimpses of unconscious suppressed desires (as in Vinny's attraction to Brant, who resembles her father), and which exposes the repetition compulsion of characters whose later words and gestures reenact moments from earlier scenes, from the recent past.

The stranglehold of past on present is the play's central theme. *Electra* itself takes place in the past, participating in the broad alternation between historical and modern settings that marks O'Neill's middle period. Starting in 1934, however, the playwright set all his plays in prior periods, concurring with Mary Tyrone of *Long Day's Journey* that "the past is the present. It's the future, too" (III, 765). The line could summarize *Electra*. The past is governed by one's ancestors, the ancestral Mannon family portraits whose "*intense, bitter life, with their frozen stare*" (II, 1034) so dominates the sitting room that Lavinia addresses them like characters. Scenes occur there that underscore

Lavinia's growing resemblance to Christine, Orin's to Ezra, and Ezra's to the zealots, generals and judges who preceded him. O'Neill's determinism was in large part itself determined by the Greek tragedians, Freud, and early twentieth-century American culture, all of which figured the family as a form of fate.[18] Hence, "fate springing out of the family" became O'Neill's conscious intention as he revised the first draft;[19] and as Travis Bogard concludes, fate deliberately shapes the plot, the character descriptions, and even the Mannon speech rhythms.[20] The grim protagonist Lavinia, who ceaselessly prods others into action but herself moves *"like some tragic mechanical doll"* (II, 974), is fate's fool until her resignation to the Mannon destiny—and possible ironic triumph over it—in her final gesture of self-imprisonment.

The male family portraits also suggest another prominent theme: the sins of the fathers. The earliest colonial Mannon burned witches, but the family is not doomed until Ezra's father (recalling Cain) expels his brother, Brant's father, from the family when both lust after the same woman. If the theme of primal sin recalls Nathaniel Hawthorne's fiction, other Gothic features point toward Poe. *Electra* describes the fall of the house of Mannon, a powerful and respectable New England family; ghosts haunt the house; incestuous love and death commingle in the plot. Ultimately, death conquers all. At the play's heart, thematically and structurally, lies the corpse of Ezra Mannon, who himself killed Christine's love by his Puritanical Mannon belief (perceived and forsworn too late) that "life was a dying. Being born was starting to die. Death was being born" (II, 937–38). Though the carefree pagan life of the Blessed Isles in the South Pacific entices Adam and Christine, and briefly seduces Orin and Lavinia, "death becomes the Mannons," as Orin tells Ezra's corpse (II, 975). Mourning becomes Electra.

The play is quintessential O'Neill in its length (over five hours in performance), its repetitions, its power, its enactment of ancient tragic actions on native grounds. Also typically, tragedy shares the stage with melodrama in the play's strong narrative elements (blackmail, murder and revenge), the emotional intensity of its stage directions, and the manipulativeness of Lavinia and Christine—misogynistic nightmares who descend directly from Nina Leeds. But the family focus on this heaviest of the middle plays also points toward the lightest, *Ah, Wilderness!*, produced in 1933 on Broadway where it ran for a year. Several factors account for its popularity. It is set in a small Connecticut seaport—the New London of O'Neill's childhood—on 4 July 1906, in an era that offers not tragic entrapment but fond memories of simpler times. (The play thus aligns itself with numerous later nostalgic narratives of the 1930s, particularly Wilder's *Our Town*.) It also displays the familiar stereotypes of comedy (a clumsy servant, a funny drunk, an old maid, a Puritanical elder, even a traveling salesman) in familiar, hence reassuring patterns. Boy (the teenaged Richard Miller) briefly loses girl (the chaste, pretty Muriel Macomber), then fails to lose his virginity to a "tart" before he reunites with girl. The equilibrium of a social unit, the Miller family, is briefly upset by Richard's mild rebellion and his uncle Sid's alcoholic episode (upsetting the maiden Aunt Lily, whom he courts), then is restored upon their repentance. Finally, the play sentimentally affirms the respectable bourgeois family—headed by Richard's mother Essie and father Nat—as a source of love, support and wisdom. Recognizing that Richard is "just as innocent and as big a kid as Muriel" (III, 20), Nat tempers discipline with understanding when he lectures his son the day after Richard's drunken return from a bar. In the previous scene, a sober Richard and Muriel had reunited in innocent love on a moonlit beach; but the last moments extol the seasoned love of Essie and Nat, the latter wooing his wife with lines from a romantic text admired by both father and son, "The Rubaiyat of Omar Khayyam."

The source of the play's title, "The Rubaiyat" also provides several of the play's numerous allusions to *fin de siècle* texts. For Richard's adolescent rebellion is mediated by Swinburne's poetry, Wilde's fiction, and Ibsen's *Hedda Gabler*. Though never quoted, O'Neill's true Penelope is the Shaw of *Arms and the Man*: another initiation story about the partial disillusion of an appealing young protagonist whose temperamental romantic idealism expresses itself in a theatrical manner learned from art. The most literary of O'Neill's middle plays, *Wilderness* (anticipating the late work) foregrounds, questions, and sometimes parodies its sources. Richard's melodramatic poses and language are similarly recognized and more thoroughly mocked. "He ought to be on stage," his mother chuckles after one histrionic exit (III, 33), suggesting O'Neill's acknowledgment of the theatrical form (parodied again in *A Touch of the Poet*, the first Cycle play) that had both enriched and weakened his own work. Intriguingly, Richard's alternation between a *"plain simple boy and a posey actor solemnly playing a role"* (III, 12) finds O'Neill employing the favorite device of the middle period—the mask—in a strictly behavioral manner that deepens in the psychologically realistic portraiture of *Poet, Long Day's Journey* and *A Moon for the Misbegotten*.

Those final masterworks, rich in allusions, continue the project initiated in *Electra* to write for a literary audience. But O'Neill's earlier, expressionistic plays from 1925 to 1930 also advanced his own literary development, for they expanded his dramatic actions and deepened his characterizations while they indulged—and finally tempered—the obsession with "big subjects" that often threatened to turn his dialogue into rhetoric. Along with *Electra* and *Wilderness*, those middle plays contributed crucially to the artistic growth of the modern American theatre as well. O'Neill's earnestness during this phase about theatre's religious mission, for instance, has immeasurably influenced countless more secular successors, elevating their aims for their dramatic medium (with Arthur Miller's concern about tragedy and the common man only the most obvious example). Moreover, O'Neill's bold and restless imagination, whether playing with masks or incorporating novelistic techniques into commercially successful drama, has inspired subsequent generations of American playwrights to experiment without foregoing the hope of earning a living through their art. Perhaps most important, these plays exposed the large audiences of mainstream American theatre to the concerns and techniques of European dramatists. O'Neill thus paved the way for the Ibsenesque moral realism of Miller, the Strindbergian sexual battles of Tennessee Williams, the expressionistic allegories of early Edward Albee, even the Absurdist—and mythic—families of later Sam Shepard. Whatever their flaws, then, the plays of this phase by themselves merit our attention, for they represent what most playwrights would consider a lifetime's worth of achievement; but the full flowering of O'Neill's genius lay in the future, when he was borne back ceaselessly into the past.

Notes

1. *Provincetown Playbill* for Strindberg's *The Spook Sonata*, January 3, 1924; rpt. in Ulrich Halfmann, ed., *Eugene O'Neill: Comments on the Drama and the Theater* (Tübingen: Gunter Narr Verlag, 1987), p. 32.

2. Travis Bogard, ed., *Eugene O'Neill: Complete Plays* (New York: The Library of America, 1988), ii, p. 420. Hereafter documented in the text.

3. Rpt. in Halfmann, *Eugene O'Neill*, pp. 66–67.

4. Halfmann, *Eugene O'Neill*, p. 66.

5. Halfmann, *Eugene O'Neill*, p. 67.

6. For a New Historicist deconstruction of O'Neill's drama as both expression and critique of depth psychology, see Joel Pfister's *Staging Depth: Eugene O'Neill and the Politics of Psychological Discourse* (Chapel Hill: University of North Carolina Press, 1995), which claims that Brown's quick destruction by Dion's mask implies a parody of the "anxious quest for pseudo-spiritual depth" in which O'Neill's bourgeois audience was itself engaged (p. 83).

7. June 1927 Letter to Benjamin de Casseres, *Selected Letters of Eugene O'Neill*, eds. Travis Bogard and Jackson R. Bryer (New Haven: Yale University Press, 1988), p. 246.

8. *Modern Drama and the Rhetoric of Theatre* (Berkeley: University of California Press, 1992), pp. 64–67.

9. The play was staged in April 1928 at the Pasadena Playhouse by an amateur company directed by Gilmore Brown. For a scholarly analysis of the productions of this and other O'Neill plays from this period, see Ronald H. Wainscott, *Staging O'Neill: The Experimental Years, 1920–1934* (New Haven: Yale University Press, 1988).

10. "A Dramatist's Notebook," *The American Spectator*, 1, 3 (1933) 2. The last segment of a piece O'Neill wrote for George Jean Nathan's new journal also presents his final opinion on the theatrical potential of masks in general and for his work in particular. Rpt. in Halfmann, *Eugene O'Neill*, pp. 107–12.

11. *The Inner Strength of Opposites: O'Neill's Novelistic Drama and the Melodramatic Imagination* (Athens: University of Georgia Press, 1994), pp. 28, 106ff.

12. *Letters*, p. 311.

13. June 1928 letter to Theresa Helburn, *Letters*, pp. 300–01.

14. Bogard, ed., *Eugene O'Neill: Complete Plays* (New York: Random House, 1988), in, p. 113. Hereafter documented in the text.

15. See Bogard, *Contour in Time: The Plays of Eugene O'Neill*, rev. edn. (New York: Oxford University Press, 1988), p. 327.

16. *Eugene O'Neill's Creative Struggle: The Decisive Decade, 1924–1933* (University Park: Pennsylvania State University Press, 1992), p. 149. Though it persistently overinterprets the play as evidence of psychobiography, this is a valuable source study.

17. Quoted in Bogard, *Contour*, p. 340.

18. See Pfister, pp. 20–30, on the cultural construction of family as determinant.

19. Work Diary, 27 March 1930; rpt. in Halfmann, *Eugene O'Neill*, p. 90.

20. Bogard, *Contour*, 336–39.

Other sources relevant to this chapter include:

Floyd, Virginia, ed., *Eugene O'Neill at Work: Newly Released Ideas for Plays* (New York: Frederick Ungar, 1981).
Robinson, James A., *Eugene O'Neill and Oriental Thought: A Divided Vision* (Carbondale: Southern Illinois University Press, 1982).
Manheim, Michael, *Eugene O'Neill's New Language of Kinship* (Syracuse, New York: Syracuse University Press, 1982).

BARBARA VOGLINO

Feminism versus Fatalism:
Uncertainty as Closure in "Anna Christie"

"*Anna Christie*" (1920), O'Neill's second full-length play to win a Pulitzer Prize, gained him more popular fame than *Beyond the Horizon* (1918). The sentimentalized depiction of the regeneration of a prostitute, with its—as it was generally interpreted—"happy" ending, appealed to contemporary middle-class audiences as Robert Mayo's death from tuberculosis had not. But although the play opened (New York, November 1921) to predominantly favorable reviews, nearly all the critics found fault with what they considered the bogus "happy ending."[1] The consensus of opinion was that the closure had been "tampered with"[2] as a compromise to current tastes.[3] Far from being pleased with the theater audiences' acclaim for what some have considered one of the rare comedies in the O'Neill canon, the playwright was devastated by the ironic realization that the commercial success of the play depended upon the audience "believing just what [he] did not want them to [i.e., the happy ending]."[4] O'Neill insisted that he had intended a much more uncertain closure: "And the sea outside—life—waits. The happy ending is merely the comma at the end of a gaudy introductory clause, with the body of the sentence still unwritten."[5]

It is not surprising that audiences failed to grasp O'Neill's intention in "*Anna Christie*," since he had considerable difficulty formulating his goal even for himself while writing the play. He shifted his focus several times,

From "*Perverse Mind*": *Eugen O'Neill's Struggle with Closure*, pp. 35–45. © 1999 by Fairleigh Dickinson University Press.

which necessitated at least four different title changes (*Chris Christophersen,
The Ole Davil, Tides,* and "*Anna Christie*"). He also altered the stoker's name,
Anna's occupation, and details of the plot. The ending appears to have been
particularly problematic. The first draft (*Chris Christophersen*) concludes
with Chris accepting the steamship captain's offer to serve as his bo'sun, an
ending that Leslie Eric Comens interprets as a comic resolution—Chris
returning to end thereby making his peace with the sea.[6] A somewhat later
attempt, *The Ole Davil,* which concludes with the characters laughing at
Chris's superstitious fear of the sea, also suggests comedy. "*Anna Christie,*"
O'Neill's final version of the play, ends (contrary to early audiences' apparent
interpretation of the conclusion as "happy") with uncertainty. Despite his
repeated efforts, however, O'Neill apparently never devised a denouement
for this play that completely satisfied him.[7] Always considering "*Anna*" one
of his greatest failures, O'Neill refused to allow it to be published with his
collected plays by Joseph Wood Krutch (1932).

It seems a reasonable conjecture that O'Neill's inability to finish "*Anna
Christie*" satisfactorily derived at least partly from his tendency—acknowledged
even by himself in the previously cited letter to Beatrice Ashe[8]—to project not
one ending, but at least two for each play. In *Beyond the Horizon,* for example,
O'Neill's "perverse mind" prepares the audience for Robert's destruction
and then suggests the redemptive ending (which perhaps "delight[ed his]
soul"), only to immediately undercut the idea of redemption in the final bleak
sequence between Andrew and Ruth. In "*Anna Christie*" O'Neill's "double
vision" operates somewhat differently: he prepares the viewer for two very
different closures throughout.

He begins by setting up audience expectations for the traditional
"happy ending." The play opens in a New York waterfront saloon with
Anna, destitute and ill, having left her life of prostitution to join the father
she has not seen for fifteen years and begin a new existence. Overjoyed to
learn of his daughter's coming, Chris Christophersen, the Swedish-American
captain of a coal barge, explains to the bartender that the reason he left Anna
with her cousins on a Minnesota farm for all those years was to protect her
from "dat ole davil, sea," which had claimed many of his ancestors' lives and
widowed their spouses. The bartender, winking, suggests, "This girl, now, 'll
be marryin' a sailor herself, likely. It's in the blood" (1.964). Chris's irrational
fury at the very idea of Anna marrying a sailor suggests the direction the play
will take. The wary viewer instantly anticipates that closure will involve just
such a union as part of Anna's new life.

The comedic plot suggested early in the play proceeds on schedule
toward the expected conclusion. After ten days on Chris's coal barge, Anna,
appearing healthy and transformed, expresses her love for the sea and the fog,

which she feels has cleansed her. Filled with foreboding by Anna's apparently hereditary attraction to the sea, Chris's unnatural fear is further fueled when his barge rescues some survivors of a wrecked steamship immediately following his protestation to Anna, "No! Dat ole davil sea, she ain't God! (2.982). Among the battered men Chris ushers aboard is Mat Burke, whom "God," in the form of the sea, appears to have brought to the barge explicitly to meet Anna. Alarmed by his daughter's obvious attraction to the rescued stoker, Chris orders her to her cabin, but Anna refuses to obey. Instead, she guides the weakened Burke to her own bed to sleep off his ordeal. As Burke is being led off, he prattles about "marrying [Anna] soon" (2.992), leaving Chris stunned and furious about the trick perpetrated on him by "dat ole davil, sea."

In act 3, a week later in Boston, the triangular wrangling comes to a head. Mat attempts to persuade the old Swede to accept him as a son-in-law, but Chris is violently opposed. The arrival of Anna puts an end to their fighting. Claiming that she loves Mat but cannot marry him, she bids him a sobbing "Good-by" (3.1003). The two men, however, paying her scant heed, continue to battle over possession of her. Infuriated, Anna insists upon her independence from male domination by revealing her sordid past. Devastated, Chris and Mat go ashore to get drunk.

Act 4 opens two nights later with a heavy fog that seems an objective correlative for the condition of the three characters, who, overwhelmed as a result of Anna's confession, are unsure what to do. Anna has gone ashore and purchased a train ticket. However, still hoping that Mat will come back for her, she has found herself unable to use the ticket and has returned to the barge. Chris returns after signing on a ship bound for South Africa the next day, having first arranged that Anna will receive all his pay. Mat straggles in last, violently drunk and bruised from fighting; he begs Anna to assure him her confession was a lie. Refusing to retract what she has told him, Anna once again insists that she has changed and swears she has never actually "loved" any other man. This last oath helps to assuage Mat's ego, and he agrees to marry her. Their "honeymoon" will be brief, however, since by a strange quirk of fate Burke has signed on the same ship as her father and will sail the next day.

The projected comedic closure, Anna's successful attainment of a new life, which involves her marriage to a sailor despite her father's opposition, has been fulfilled. Anna, who arrived at the saloon feeling dirty and hating men, has undergone a significant change. Believing that she has been purged of her past by the sea, she acquires a new sense of identity. She also falls in love and struggles to retain her seafaring suitor despite numerous obstacles (her father's objections, her own past, and Mat's irritating possessiveness). A strong-willed young woman who knows what she wants, Anna appears capable of accomplishing what she sets out to do. The play being a comedy, with Anna as its titular heroine, generic expectations have induced the spectator to expect her to succeed.[9]

Anna, in fact, surpasses the audience's expectations. In affirming her own capacity to structure her life, she makes a surprisingly militant assertion of feminism:

> But nobody owns me, see?—'cepting myself. I'll do what I please and no man, I don't give a hoot who he is, can tell me what to do! I ain't asking either of you for a living I can make it myself—one way or other. I'm my own boss. So put that in your pipe and smoke it! You and your orders! (3.1007)

She refuses to allow either her father or lover to "own" or direct her, and she boldly defends her past conduct by equating it with the men's. She tells Mat, "You been doing the same thing ... in every port. How're you any better than I was?" (4.1022). Having asserted her independence from male domination, and having persuaded Chris and Mat to accept her as the ex-prostitute that she is, Anna has won particularly by the standards of 1920 audiences—a huge victory for her sex. When Mat returns to the barge still wanting her, closure—according to David F. Hult's definition of the process as an "inner movement in the direction of unity or completeness"[10]—appears imminent and the play is virtually over. Anna's proposition that the three live happily ever after in the "little house" she will prepare for them while they are away seems the inevitable—if overworked—comedic conclusion. Early audiences appear to have accepted the "happy ending" proposed by Anna because they unconsciously perceived the structure of the play to be complete at this point. The "satisfying ending," according to Murray Krieger, "fulfills internally aroused expectations."[11]

The simple comedic ending, however, was not the closure which "delight[ed the] soul" of Eugene O'Neill, admirer of Gerhart Hauptmann ("True drama is basically endless").[12] Thus, having allowed his heroine to achieve an identity and life for herself through her determination and courage, O'Neill's "perverse mind" proceeds to undermine her prospect of happiness in the final sequence. Mat's qualms upon learning that Anna's family was Lutheran, after she has sworn on his crucifix, rivals Chris's distrust of the sea in its fatalism: "Luthers, is it? ... Well, I'm damned then surely. Yerra, what's the difference? 'Tis the will of God, anyway" (4.1026). Immediately following, Chris voices his anxiety over the coincidence of them sailing on the same ship together ("dat funny vay ole davil do her vorst dirty tricks"

[4.1026]); and Mat, in his final speech of the play, starts to agree with him: "I'm fearing maybe you have the right of it for once, divil take you." Although Anna tries to "cut out the gloom" by proposing a toast, the play closes with Chris's fatalistic pronouncement: "Fog, fog, fog, all bloody time. You can't see vhere you vas going, no. Only dat ole davil, sea—she knows!" (4.1027). As the final speech of the play, Chris's words have a powerful impact. The fog suggests the dangers of the voyage to come, and also their futures, which are ultimately unknowable. The audience is left with the impression that the sea, which has already devoured generations of Christophersens, may be waiting for Chris and Mat to ship out so she can swallow them up.

If it seems remarkable that early audiences appear to have overlooked the final sequence in their interpretation of the ending, it seems doubly so in consideration of O'Neill's evident preparation for the subversion of his "happy ending" throughout this play. Numerous fatalistic allusions challenge the very possibility of purposeful self-determination such as that demonstrated by Anna. The many references to fog, for example, illustrate man's actual helpless or "befogged" condition of being cast adrift in the expansive universe mirrored by the sea, which may at times be malevolent. In this desperate, somewhat ignoble state, the personae of "*Anna Christie*" grasp at face-saving illusions that make existence more tolerable. O'Neill, himself, referred to these "pitifully humorous gesture[s] in the direction of happiness" as "symbol[s] of what most of us have to do—at any rate, *do* do—every now and then ... in order to keep on living."[13]

Chris, for example, cannot bear confronting any situations that might require him to accept responsibility for his actions. He cannot even speak frankly to his mistress, Marthy, about leaving the barge in preparation for Anna, but he has to ask the bartender to think up a lie. Fortunately, the good-natured prostitute volunteers to leave. When Anna tries to convince him of his responsibility for her downfall in act 3, he cannot bear to listen but puts his fingers in his ears, which she must physically remove in order to make him hear. Chris's attempt to stop up his ears is consistent with his deliberate avoidance of truth all his life. He refuses to acknowledge personal responsibility for anything—even his desertion of his wife for the life of a sailor—but uses the sea as a scapegoat for all his shortcomings and misdeeds. Regarding Anna, whom he left with his wife's cousins, Chris excuses his neglect of her by asserting his conviction that she would grow up healthier inland than if exposed to the sea. Preferring his illusion to factual verification, Chris never personally checked on Anna's condition. When Anna surprises him by descending upon him in act 1, Chris, finding unexpected solace for his increasing loneliness, cannot bear to lose her so quickly to Mat. Although he has allowed Anna to grow up bereft of his guidance, he (somewhat deludedly, at this late date) undertakes to play the role of concerned father by discouraging her relationship with the rescued stoker. "Don't you want no one to be nice to me except yourself?" (3.995), she asks perceptively.

Chris is not a bad man, only a weak one. His tenderness toward Anna, whom he never blames for her past, is moving. Furthermore, he does finally acknowledge the error of his ways in act 4: "Ay've been tanking, and Ay guess it vas all my fault—all bad tangs dat happen to you" (4.1014–15). When she responds that no one is to blame ("There ain't nothing to forgive, anyway. It ain't your fault, and it ain't mine, and it ain't [Mat's] neither. We're all poor nuts, and things happen, and we yust get mixed in wrong, that's all" [4.1015]), he eagerly reverts to his favorite illusion: "You say right tank, Anna, py golly! It ain't nobody's fault! (*shaking his fist*) It's dat ole davil, sea!" (4.1015).

Mat Burke is quick to condemn Chris's reliance upon the sea as his personal scapegoat. The stoker tells the old Swede he has "swallowed the anchor" (3.999), which the stoker in the earlier *Chris Christophersen* defines as "whin[ing] and blam[ing] something outside of yourself for your misfortunes ..." (3.2.881). Nevertheless, Mat relies on a number of comforting illusions himself. From his first meeting with Anna, Mat insists upon fabricating fictions about her. In just a few minutes she proceeds in his fancy from a mermaid rising from the sea, to the captain's mistress, to his sainted daughter with a golden crown upon her head (2.987). After Anna shatters her "halo" by revealing the truth about her past, Mat tries to escape from dealing with the truth by going ashore and becoming drunk. The liquor fails to have the desired effect, however, as does the liquor in the much later play *The Iceman Cometh* (1940) after its imbibers are forced to confront the truth. Unable to accept the destruction of his fantasy even while intoxicated, Mat returns to the barge begging Anna for a lie. He is desperate enough to accept any crumb of comfort she can bestow upon him, even the assurance that she has never actually "loved" any man before him. To give his renewed fantasy more substance, she must swear on the crucifix given him by his dying mother, which he firmly believes has always protected him from harm. The effectiveness of the icon, however, is soon called into question by the fact that Anna is not Catholic. Nevertheless, Mat is eventually able to accept Anna's "naked word" (4.1025), because he has replaced the vision shattered by her revelation with a new illusion about her—not only that it was his powerful influence that changed her, but that he will continue to transform her further and further into the wife of his dreams: "For I've a power of strength in me to lead men the way I want, and women, too, maybe, and I'm thinking *I'd change you to a new woman entirely*, so I'd never know, or you either, what kind of woman you'd been in the past at all" (4.1023, emphasis added). Mat has still not accepted Anna as she is.

Anna, as O'Neill presents her, is also difficult for the audience to accept at times. Perhaps in transforming his heroine from typist in the earlier *Chris Christophersen* to trollop in this play, O'Neill neglected to work out all aspects of her character. Anna's explanation of the reason she started working in a brothel—because she felt "freer" and less confined with her body beneath paying customers than as a "nurse" supervising other people's children—is incomprehensible. To those viewers who are able to construe her intense need for the freedom of self-determination as rendering her descent into prostitution credible, however, Anna appears franker and less given to self-delusion than her father and lover. Nevertheless, she deliberately encourages Chris and Mat in their illusions. She leads the newly rescued and still groggy Mat to believe her a lady: "... I must say I don't care for your language. The men I know don't pull that rough stuff when ladies are around" (2.985). Similarly, she encourages her father to trust in her innocence. When Chris makes insinuations about her dates with Mat, she replies with inappropriate outrage:

> Say, listen here, you ain't trying to insinuate that there's something wrong between us, are you? ... Well, don't you never think it neither if you want me ever to speak to you again.... If I ever dreamt you thought that, I'd get the hell out of this barge so quick you couldn't see me for dust. (3.994)

Even her admirable enlightenment of the men regarding her past is performed less to disillusion them than to discourage them from dominating her.[14] No paragon of virtue even after her confession, Anna continues to prevaricate. When Mat returns to the barge two nights later, she shows him the train ticket she has bought and insinuates that she will return to her former occupation the next day if he leaves again (4.1021). She does not tell him that Chris has provided for her financially and she will not need to work, but uses every means at her disposal to provoke Mat into claiming her for his own. What is more, her equivocal tactics succeed.

In her joy at regaining both men's affection, Anna attempts to varnish over any of their lurking fears and gloom with a new illusion—the "big happy family." She proposes to "get a little house somewhere and ... make a regular place for you two to come back to—wait and see. And now you drink up and be friends" (4.1025–26). This final illusion of Anna creating a home to which her men may return and live "happily ever after" is the illusion apparently shared by many of the viewers of O'Neill's day, who chose to accept Anna's fabrication as fact.

Nevertheless, the ever-pervasive fog that begins and ends the play seems an overpowering objective correlative for man's frequently befuddled, deluded, and/or drunken condition—his helplessness in the face of destiny, as represented by the sea. Furthermore, the frequent use of the word "fix" by the characters, as they, for the most part, futilely attempt to oppose the fog or take control of their lives, supports Chris's fatalism. Chris tries to "fix" (3.994) Burke so that he cannot marry Anna, first by attacking him with a knife, and then by purchasing a gun (for which, reconsidering, he never buys bullets). Both weapons are, therefore, ineffectual against the stoker. Later in the play Chris refers to "fixing" (4.1014) his salary for his coming voyage upon Anna, so that she will have no need to return to her old trade. Although Chris's intentions are good, he is once again abandoning Anna, which was the reason she became a prostitute in the first place. Money may prove an ineffectual substitute for his love. Mat, without using the actual word "fix," attempts to repair his wounded ego by having Anna swear on the crucifix. However, her oath as a Lutheran only exacerbates his doubts. Even Anna refers to "fix[ing]" their predicament at the end, by accepting the men's voyage together and promising them a home. When Chris voices his premonitions of doom, and Mat starts to support him, Anna attempts to distract them from their anxieties with a gay toast: "Aw say, what's the matter? Cut out the gloom. We're all *fixed* now, ain't we, me and you? ... Come on! Here's to the sea, no matter what!" (4.1026, emphasis added).

As the play comes to a close, Anna is attempting to will her happy ending into being, as does Maggie Verver at the end of Henry James's novel *The Golden Bowl* (1904). Both women's futures are left "open" at the end of the works. In his preface to *The Portrait of a Lady* James defended his inconclusive endings as a literary necessity: "The whole of anything is never told; you can only take what groups together."[15] Also acknowledging the falseness inherent in the very concept of "closure," O'Neill justified the open ending of "*Anna Christie*" as an attempt to represent continuity: "A naturalistic play is life. Life doesn't end. One experience is but the birth of another...."[16] As O'Neill seems to have anticipated in this statement, however, the audience cannot help speculating on the two women's futures. Endings, as June Schlueter points out, have a natural "afterlife" that prompts sequels.[17] The prospect before Anna may be even less optimistic than that facing Maggie, who will at least have the physical presence of her prince. Anna will be alone again after the men ship out, a condition that disheartened her when she first arrived at the saloon, and that may be even harder to bear now that she has known love. Whether or not her struggle for self-determination and happiness is even worthwhile seems unclear from the text: she may be deluded and a mere pawn of fate. Even if the men return to live out her fantasy of domesticity in her "little house somewhere," there is already a crack in the "golden bowl" of her happiness with Mat's desperate search for a supernatural sanction, which, as Clifford Leech argues, is "indicative of a never fully quenchable suspicion."[18] Furthermore, Mat's intention of "chang[ing]" Anna "to a new woman entirely" (4.1023) conflicts with Anna's new sense of identity and suggests a problematic marriage at best. Finally, there is the very real possibility that the men will not return; as Chris points out, sailors, for one reason or another, often do not. What will become of Anna if Chris's money runs out?

Despite the characters' desperate attempts to "fix" their destinies, images of man's helplessness pervade the play. The bulletless gun that drops from Chris's pocket suggests his castrated or powerless condition. Similarly useless, Mat's crucifix brings him little comfort in the society of ex-Lutherans. Finally, Anna's unused train ticket seems another objectification of the ineffectuality of man's efforts at self-determination. Far from being able to control their respective destinies, Chris, Mat, and Anna must wait for the fog to clear so that they can see what life brings.

Throughout most of the play, however, and most emphatically at closure, Anna's projection of happiness appears to conflict with Chris's forebodings of doom. The audience feels torn between the possibilities of self determination and the implications of fatalism together in the same play. One idea seems to undermine the other. Anna's assertion of independence and attempt to achieve harmony for the trio seem delusional in the face of the impenetrable fog and vast sea upon which, as Chris reminds the viewer in the closing lines, all their fates will ultimately be determined. Furthermore, Chris's fatalistic pronouncements, which, to some extent, may be dismissed as the self-exonerating fantasies of a gloomy old man, appear nearly equally delusional in consideration of Anna's hard-won "victory" over the men. The sea, as Travis Bogard points out, is not nearly so malevolent as Chris insists. Despite its implication in the deaths of Chris's ancestors and Mat's shipmates, the sea is also responsible for cleansing Anna, bringing Mat to her, and giving her hope for a new life.[19] Thus, Bogard concludes, "It is by no means inevitable that the sea [upon which the trio's future will be determined] will betray trust or that the ending will be tragic."[20] The only certainty about the ending is its uncertainty: "You can't see vhere you vas going" ([Chris] 4.1027).[21]

The inconclusive or "open" ending of "*Anna Christie*" represents one of O'Neill's early efforts to deal with what David H. Richter has more recently described as the perpetual dilemma of the artist: "how ... to bring a work to a satisfying conclusion without being false to the boundless nature of human life."[22] That the closure of "*Anna Christie*" is not satisfying, however, has been most convincingly demonstrated by its apparently widespread misinterpretation by early audiences, who, despite the numerous indications to the contrary in the text, appear to have "reconstructed" the ending to be "happy." They seem to have been able to accomplish this feat primarily because the production of meaning, which June Schlueter asserts is essential for dramatic closure,[23] is not clear. Uncertain whether the play is about self-determination and the equality of women, about the malevolent powers of an uncaring fate, or even about the exasperating uncertainty of individual destinies, audiences seem to have indulged in the type of creativity described by Wolfgang Iser[24] and have completed the play in the manner of their choice. The reader/viewer, according to Terence Hawkes, can close up and "make coherent virtually anything."[25]

The unsatisfactoriness of the conclusion to "Anna Christie," as acknowledged by many critics and, to some extent, even by O'Neill,[26] in no way indicates that open endings are inadequate per se, however. According to Marianna Torgovnick, open-ended works can also attain effective closure: "The test is the honesty and the appropriateness of the ending's relationship to beginning and middle, not the degree of finality or resolution achieved by the ending."[27] It is in regard to "appropriateness" that the closure of "Anna Christie" appears to fail. Unlike The Golden Bowl, a serious study of complex characters, "Anna" is a comedy featuring, to a large extent, stock comedic characters like Mat Burke, and as such invokes the generic expectation that things will "turn out right" in the end. In strong contrast to the "happy" resolution generally associated with comedy, the "open ending," according to Robert M. Adams, is most suitably used in connection with the somber view that "man is essentially alone with his responsibilities in a complex and divided cosmos."[28] Although O'Neill was basically in accord with this view of man's aloneness, it seems a heavy weight to attach to the personae of this particular play, whom O'Neill himself professed to see as "a bit tragically humorous in their vacillating weakness."[29] The incongruous combination of comic characters and action with cosmic solemnity may well have been responsible for the unintentional laughter provoked in the audience during a recent New York performance of the play.[30] The comedic context of "Anna Christie" seems to require a more conclusive ending for the viewer to obtain closural satisfaction.

As the various versions of the play bear witness, however, O'Neill wrestled with finishing "Anna Christie" to little avail. Disturbed by audiences' misinterpretation of his final version, he wrote a detailed explanation of his intentions concerning the ending to the New York Times (18 December 1921), the very length of which suggests that he had, as he suspected, "failed."[31] What appears to have happened is that, having prepared the play for two different endings, each of which negates the other, O'Neill was unable to end the play without vastly rewriting a piece upon which he had already been working for more than two years. "The devil of it is, I don't see my way out," he confessed to George Jean Nathan.[32] The feeling that it was time to put "*Anna*" aside and move on may have been a major factor in his resorting to inconclusiveness as an ending.

A more personal conflict may also have affected his capacity to complete the play. According to Henry J. Schmidt, "Endings that seem incommensurable with the preceding action may signify a philosophical crisis...."[33] The defense of women's equality is a new theme for O'Neill in "*Anna*," and one not in keeping with the function of servitude generally assigned to the heroines of his plays (Mrs. Roylston in *Servitude* [1914], Nora Melody in *A Touch of the Poet* [1939], Sara Melody Harford in *More Stately Mansions* [1939], Josie Hogan in *A Moon for the Misbegotten* [1943]). The women who do not minister to their men's needs in O'Neill's plays are usually depicted as misguided and made to suffer for their failure (Maud Steele Brown in *Bread and Butter* [1914], Martha Jayson in *The First Man* [1921], Ella Downey Harris in *All God's Chillun Got Wings* [1923], and Mary Tyrone in *Long Day's Journey into Night* [1941]).

During the composition of "*Anna Christie*" O'Neill had married the independent novelist Agnes Boulton, who refused to subordinate her own writing career to his, and whose character may have contributed to his creation of Anna. Although O'Neill had probably admired her self-determining character at first, he may have begun to doubt their compatibility by this point: Agnes apparently failed to satisfy his needs as a wife. In 1926 he began seeing the actress Carlotta Monterey, who, while fully capable of asserting herself (as she did on occasion), was willing to efface herself, to a large degree, in order to serve him in such various functions as mistress, mother, domestic organizer, and secretary. In 1929 O'Neill was finally able to divorce Agnes and marry Carlotta. Although O'Neill respected and was attracted to more overtly self-assertive women like Beatrice Ashe (1914–16), Louise Bryant (1916–17), and Agnes/Anna, he appears to have been more comfortable with a woman like Carlotta (with whom he remained, for the most part, until his death), who could subordinate herself to his needs. Perhaps it was this underlying conflict in his feelings about women that compelled him to undermine his theme of feminine equality in "*Anna Christie*" with the concept of fatalism.

Notes

1. The ending of "*Anna Christie*," as I shall proceed to demonstrate in this chapter, is not generally interpreted as "happy" by modern viewers. Travis Bogard offers the following explanation for the discrepancy in audience reactions since the play's debut:

"There is perhaps some doubt which ending [that of The Ole Davil or of the script as printed] was used in the original production [of '*Anna Christie*'].... Reviewers speak of the action ending in laughter, which is the ending of *The Ole Davil*, not *Anna Christie*" (*Contour in Time*, 162). More specific corroboration would be helpful. The numerous excerpts from reviews of the first production cited by Jordan Miller (*Eugene O'Neill and the American Critic*, ed. J. Y. Miller, 240–46), while frequently referring to the play's "happy ending," make no mention of laughter. Louis V. De Foe, in fact, hails "*Anna*" as "another grim O'Neill drama" (ibid., 241).

2. Louis V. De Foe, as cited by Bogard, *Contour in Time*, 163.

3. Sheaffer, *Son and Artist*, 67; *Eugene O'Neill and the American Critic*, ed. J. Y. Miller, 240–46.

4. O'Neill, as cited by Sheaffer, *Son and Artist*, 68.

5. O'Neill, to George Jean Nathan, 1 February 1921, in *Selected Letters*, ed. Bogard and Bryer, 148.

6. Leslie Eric Comens, foreword to *Chris Christophersen*, by Eugene O'Neill (New York: Random House, 1982), viii.

7. Sheaffer, *Son and Playwright*, 462.

8. O'Neill, to Beatrice Ashe, 14 January 1915, in "Letters to Beatrice Ashe, 1914–1916."

9. Bernard Beckerman, "Shakespeare Closing," *Kenyon Review* 7, no. 3 (1985): 80.

10. David F. Hult, preface to *Concepts of Closure*, ed. David F. Hult, Yale French Studies 67 (New Haven: Yale University Press, 1984), iv–v.

11. Krieger, "An Apology for Poetics," 96–97.

12. Gerhart Hauptmann, as cited by Schmidt, How *Dramas End*, 9. For the more complete quotation see chapter 1, page 22.

13. O'Neill, to Jonathan Cape, 15 May 1923, in *Selected Letters*, ed. Bogard and Bryer, 176.

14. John V. Antush, "Eugene O'Neill: Modern and Postmodern," *Eugene O'Neill Review* 13, no. 1 (1989): 21.

15. Henry James, preface to *The Portrait of a Lady*, from *The Notebooks* (1947), in *Perspectives on James's The Portrait of a Lady: A Collection of Critical Essays*, ed. William T. Stafford (New York: New York University Press, 1967), 4.

16. O'Neill, to Malcolm Mollan, December 1921, in *Selected Letters*, ed. Bogard and Bryer, 159.

17. Schlueter, *Dramatic Closure*, 20.

18. Clifford Leech, *O'Neill* (New York: Barnes & Noble, 1963), 31.

19. Bogard, *Contour in Time*, 157–58.

20. Ibid., 163.

21. The staging of the 1993 New York production appears to have conveyed the uncertainty O'Neill intended with fog billowing out over the thrust stage and the characters gazing in different directions. John Lahr describes the final misty tableau: "... Chris turns away from the new couple to look out to sea, Burke takes hold of Anna's wrist, but Anna is turned away from him, gazing upstage into the gray horizon" ("Selling the Sizzle," review of "*Anna Christie*," by Eugene O'Neill, as performed at the Roundabout Theater, New York; reprinted in *New York Theatre Critics' Reviews: 1993*, ed. Norma Adler, Pat Willard, Joan Marlowe, and Betty Blake [New York: Critics' Theatre Reviews, 1993], 10–12).

22. Richter, "Closure and the Critics," 287.

23. Schlueter, *Dramatic Closure*, 23.

24. Iser, *Implied Reader*, 279.

25. Terence Hawkes, "Opening Closure," *Modern Drama* 24, no. 3 (1981): 355–56.

26. O'Neill, to George Jean Nathan, 1 February 1921, in *Selected Letters*, ed. Bogard and Bryer, 148.

27. Torgovnick, *Closure in the Novel*, 6.

28. Robert M. Adams, *Strains of Discord: Studies in Literary Openness* (Ithaca: Cornell University Press, 1958), 33.

29. O'Neill, to the *New York Times*, December 1921. As cited by Quinn, *History of the American Drama*, 177–78.

30. Ward Morehouse III attests to unexpected laughter during a performance of the 1993 New York production of *"Anna Christie"* ("*'Anna Christie'* Sends Off Sparks," review of *"Anna Christie,"* by Eugene O'Neill, as performed at the Roundabout Theater, New York; reprinted in *New York Theatre Critics' Reviews: 1993*, ed. Adler et al., 6–7)..

31. As cited by Gelb and Gelb, *O'Neill*, 481.

32. O'Neill, to George Jean Nathan, 1 February 1921, in *Selected Letters*, ed. Bogard and Bryer, 148.

33. Schmidt, *How Dramas End*, 10.

ZANDER BRIETZKE

Masks and Mirrors

"Oh, Father, why can't you ever be the thing you can seem to be?"
   —Sara Melody in *A Touch of the Poet*

Despite O'Neill's antitheatrical prejudice, the need for illusion, or the pipe dream or the hopeless hope, figures as his dominant theme in early plays such as *Beyond the Horizon* (1918) and *The Straw* (1919), as well as mature plays such as *A Touch of the Poet, Long Day's Journey Into Night*, and most emphatically of all, *The Iceman Cometh*. Virginia Floyd defines the message in that play as one applicable to all of the plays: "humanity's desperate need for a life-sustaining illusion to lessen the despair of soul-destroying reality" (*Plays of Eugene O'Neill* 512). Action in *Gold* (1920), an expanded and unsuccessful retooling of an earlier play, *Where the Cross Is Made* (1918), seems to articulate this need explicitly. Captain Bartlett commits murder to obtain a treasure which he subsequently never looks at again for fear that it is brass instead of gold. He justifies his barbarism by maintaining that the treasure is real and that the victims attempted to steal it from him. For years, he stubbornly awaits the return of his ship with his former accomplices and the rest of the booty. A doctor observes his behavior and diagnoses his condition to Bartlett's daughter: "No, your father won't let himself look the facts in the face. If he did, probably the shock of it would kill him. That darn dream of his has become his life" (CP1 941). Obsession with an illusion of great riches allows

From *The Aesthetics of Failure: Dynamic Structure in the Plays of Eugene O'Neill*, pp. 59–92. © 2001 Zander Brietzke.

him to live. Without a dream, an illusion, life is not worth living. Indeed, Bartlett dies after finally acknowledging the truth that his few tokens are worthless junk.

The captain's need for illusion is analogous to O'Neill's ambivalent need for the theatre: it may be worthless junk, but it's all that there is. Theatrical trappings give him material form for his illusion/reality theme. O'Neill, however, twists this rather hackneyed theme into an original shape which challenges a pat understanding of his plays. He doesn't oppose the two terms so much as claim them as identical. For O'Neill, everything is an inevitable illusion, and the theatre becomes the perfect medium for his expression. Seen in this light, the binary opposition breaks down and leaves only layers of illusion to explore. In a 1922 interview with Oliver Sayler, O'Neill claimed that "The theatre to me is life—the substance and interpretation of life" (Cargill 107). Theatre serves as metaphor and medium to embody life. In *Lazarus Laughed*, the title character mocks Caligula: "Tragic is the plight of the tragedian whose only audience is himself! Life is for each man a solitary cell whose walls are mirrors" (CP2 572). O'Neill's notebook for *Marco Millions*, researched and detailed by Virginia Floyd in *O'Neill at Work*, records further identification of theatre with life: "Our lives are theatre—in the worst sense—the history of Man the forced posturing of an actor to empty benches. The Gods laughed once—then grew ashamed and went away" (67). The *Lazarus* notebook highlights still another theatrical image that posits life as a theatrical performance: "He [Man] thinks of himself as a hero fighting the dragons of evil. Alas, this dragon is a grave worm born in himself and he is a feeble actor making brave faces into a mirror and saying 'I am a warrior!' If he could see what applause his audience would give to his last gesture how happily would he die, acting the hero!" (*O'Neill at Work* 103).

Recurring motifs in these theatrical images require further unpacking in order to see clearly how O'Neill views life as theatre. First, O'Neill portrays life as an unconvincing performance played by feeble actors posturing before an empty house. The physical theatre provides the means for O'Neill to project his vision of the world. Lee Simonson, O'Neill's frequent designer at the Theatre Guild, reverses Shakespeare's phrase to make an acute point about great dramatists, including O'Neill: "All the world's a stage. But to the playwright, as he writes, any stage is all the world" (41). Existential crisis deepens the theatrical metaphor by virtue of the fact that no one watches the performance. The actor performs the role of life in a "solitary cell" and to "empty benches." In a Nietzschean universe, gods have vanished. O'Neill suggests that if there were an audience to applaud, the actor could finish his performance. Instead, actors perform for themselves and watch their show in a mirror. Their solo efforts try to convince themselves that they are who they pretend to be. In the absence of anyone watching them, they must convince themselves of the authenticity of their performance by making "brave faces into a mirror." Too often, the second-rate ham actor fails to do so. O'Neill characters struggle to be that whom they seem to be by casting themselves as heroes "fighting the dragons of evil." This projected melodrama of external events shades an internal struggle where the real dragon, according to O'Neill, is "a grave worm" born within the individual.

How to see this "grave worm" remains O'Neill's dramatic problem to solve. How does he access the hidden recesses of character where the real drama lies? O'Neill published his only contribution to dramatic theory in a series of short essays for George Jean Nathan's and H. L. Mencken's *American Spectator* magazine in late 1932 and early 1933 called *Memoranda on Masks*. In it, he advocated extensive use of masks in theatre to convey the inner truths of existence: "... the use of masks will be discovered eventually to be the freest solution of the modern dramatist's problem as to how—with the greatest possible dramatic clarity and economy of means—he can express those profound hidden conflicts of the mind which the probings of psychology continue to disclose to us" (Cargill 116). While the mask forces a fixed representation upon the actor's face, it simultaneously shields what is underneath the mask. The introduction of masks always begs the question: who and what is behind the mask? The presence of a mask seems to perpetuate the illusion and reality theme. What I hope to show in the following pages is not the reality beneath the mask so much as the frightening possibility that yet another illusion, another version of the self lies under the exterior presentation. For O'Neill, character is not a question of appearance and essence, but a matter of compatibility between multiple versions of the self.

Reflective surfaces such as mirrors play a key role in mask maintenance. The mirror allows characters, first of all, to see themselves. Certainly, the mirror in *A Touch of the Poet* is a most striking example, in which Cornelius Melody repeatedly observes himself striking Byronic poses, and into which he recites *Childe Harold*. Melody essentially plays the part of Byronic hero for himself in order to convince himself of his own aristocratic nobility. Equally important as an actual mirror, however, is the reflection that characters see of themselves in the eyes of another character. To see themselves in the unflattering light of how others see them proves a devastating blow in *The Hairy Ape, Mourning Becomes Electra*, and *Hughie*. O'Neill frequently mirrors characters as well: Andrew and Robert Mayo in *Beyond the Horizon*; Dion Anthony and Billy Brown in *The Great God Brown*; Jamie and Edmund in *Long Day's Journey Into Night*; Oedipal and Electra complexes in *Mourning Becomes Electra*; two sets of parents and a split stage in *Dynamo*; a split protagonist in

Days Without End; Hickey and Parritt in *The Iceman Cometh*. Mirrors both distort and reveal character by showing one character in terms of another or in terms of an opposite. Pairing characters is a visual means to demonstrate fractured identity.

Use of masks in the plays varies from literary description to expressionistic economy to metaphorical pretense. Initially, masks appear only in stage directions in which O'Neill tries to indicate the surface and depth of emotion. Later, when actual masks appear on stage, they function variously as symbols of inhumanity, as representative types of people, or as protective skin. O'Neill dispenses with masks altogether in his final plays. Paradoxically, however, pretense in these plays functions as a kind of mask and the process of unmasking in each play comprises the dramatic action. The mask transforms in these plays from a static image or a visual sign to a dynamic process that unveils in time. Plays end at the point when characters expose themselves fully to the spectator's, including the audience's, view. This marks the point of desire beyond which nothing more can be seen. The mask, then, is a means of survival for the characters and for the life of the play as well. Unmasking produces emotional tumult which precipitates the ending. Dramatic tension breaks when the barrier between the outside and the inside comes down. It is not so much that the world cannot be faced as it is; facing it as it is exacts a level of human courage that is impossible to sustain. At its best, O'Neill's drama celebrates and dramatizes the cost of vulnerability.

One of the first references to masks comes in the stage directions of *Diff'rent* (1920) describing Caleb Williams in Act 2: "His face wears its set expression of an emotionless mask but his eyes cannot conceal an inward struggle ..." (CP2 41–42). The fact that the audience cannot actually see his "inward struggle" in his eyes highlights the literary aspect of the description. Indeed, Caleb's lack of visible emotion marks a severe deficiency in the play. The action takes place in a New England whaling town over a thirty year interval during which Caleb arrives at Emma Crosby's annually to ask her hand in marriage. Each year she refuses on account of one affair Caleb had before they were supposed to marry. Ideals prevent them from marrying, despite the fact that they suit each other perfectly. Emma wears an "expressionless mask" as well. Action fails to convey the depth of emotion and feeling that each character has for the other. The mask in *Diff'rent* never comes off because it is identical to the face.

Similarly, Eleanor's face in *Welded* (1923) twice becomes mask-like when she tries to seek revenge against her husband Michael Cape by throwing herself into the arms of another lover. The mask represents her determination to act according to her cognitive will. Nervous twitching reflects conflict between external presentation and internal turbulence.

O'Neill takes pains in stage directions to show the physical burden that the mask exerts (e.g., rage, twitching, mad expressions, rigidity). Urge to show everything enhances the playwright's ability to communicate a message, but it detracts from the possibility to create an artistic experience. The idea of the mask registers psychological conflict within characters unambiguously and denotatively. The mask also serves as a protective shield for Eleanor. When John, her suitor, kisses her, he notices that he's not really kissing her, but only her shell: "Under his kisses her face again becomes mask-like, her body rigid, her eyes closed. John suddenly grows aware of this" (CP2 254). He exclaims that her body feels like a corpse. Ultimately, Eleanor almost collapses under the strain of her stated desire to exact revenge and her emotional feeling for her husband. She constructs a new mask, one of pride instead of revenge, and rushes back home to her husband. The "exultant pride" (258) of the stage directions indicates a similar feeling shared by Mrs. Royleston in *Servitude* and later Nora in *A Touch of the Poet*. Pride, too, functions as a kind of mask, which both projects character and protects vulnerability.

The literary use of masks reaches its most pervasive expression in *Mourning Becomes Electra*. The mask as shield ensures privacy, but it's also associated with death in this play. Christine describes the Mannon house as a kind of tomb, a whited sepulcher: "pagan temple front stuck like a mask on Puritan gray ugliness!" (CP2 903–904). Character descriptions in the text portray all the Mannon characters, including Christine, Lavinia, and Adam Brant as wearing a life-like mask. This mask functions as a kind of death mask, as if the Mannons were not quite alive, as Eleanor is not alive sexually in *Welded*, but able to give the impression of being alive. One of the town chorus remarks to the onlookers: "That's the Mannon look. They all has it. They grow it on their wives. Seth's growed it on too, didn't you notice—from bein' with 'em all his life. They don't want folks to guess their secrets" (896). Portraits of the Mannon family, too, all possess the same mask-like quality that suggests death and lifelessness. It is the curse of inheritance: Christine, the only non-Mannon by birth, has "growed it on" and she, understandably, is the character who resents the burden most of all and most wants to shake it off. Her husband's homecoming incites the action. Returning from the Civil War as a hero, General Ezra Mannon speaks as one who has seen too much of death in his lifetime. He describes the meeting house of worship among the Mannons as a temple of death. Clean-scrubbed and whitewashed, it, too, is a whited sepulcher, like the Mannon facade. He describes the repetition and meaninglessness of death in the war: "But in this war I've seen too many white walls splattered with blood that counted no more than dirty water. I've seen dead men scattered about, no more important than rubbish to be got rid of. That made the white meeting-house seem meaningless—making so much solemn fuss over death!" (938). Ezra returns home determined to live, having survived the war. He tells his wife that there has always been a barrier between them, "a wall hiding us from each other!" (938). Ezra regrets that he has not been able to show his love before: "Something queer in me keeps me mum about the things I'd like most to say—keeps me hiding the things I'd like to show. Something keeps me sitting numb in my own heart—like a statue of a dead man in a town square" (939). Mannon tries to tear off the mask of death that separates him from his wife.

After Mannon's murder, Orin, the son, returns home and sees his father laid out in the study. His address to the corpse echoes Mannon's own words earlier regarding his death in life posture: "Death sits so naturally on you! Death becomes the Mannons! You were always like the statue of an eminent dead man—sitting on a chair in a park or straddling a horse in a town square—looking over the head of life without a sign of recognition—cutting it dead for the impropriety of living! [*He chuckles to himself with a queer affectionate amusement.*] You never cared to know me in life—but I really think we might be friends now you are dead!" (CP2 975). The death-like mask that the corpse wears becomes the character in the play. Passed down from generation to generation, this mask marks the Mannon inheritance. O'Neill punned with the title of his play on two counts. First, he uses "becomes" in the sense that mourning befits Lavinia. She looks good in black; it is her best color; in black, she is most herself. But he also chooses "becomes" in the sense that mourning is her fate. Lavinia, in time, becomes mourning. She buries her father, mother, and brother in the course of the trilogy. She is the last to grieve for the Mannon dead. The mask of mourning, of black, of a funeral and military posture, is one that she cannot ultimately avoid. All the Mannons try to tear off the mask but they inevitably fail. They clutch for life and that struggle defines the dramatic action. Certainly, Lavinia's struggle is the most compelling of all. Lavinia rebels against her fate but, in the end, she submits and dons, once again, the mask of the Mannons.

The first actual use of masks in an O'Neill play occurred in the production of *The Hairy Ape* (1921).[1] The Fifth Avenue crowd of men and women, exiting from churches, stroll past Yank and Long without even noticing them. Although the published version of the play did not call for using masks, descriptions of the crowd make masks a reasonable choice in performance, emphasizing the inhuman quality of the crowd, as opposed to the very human Yank: "The crowd from church enter from the right, sauntering slowly and affectedly, their heads held stiffly up, looking neither to right nor left, talking in toneless, simpering voices. The women are rouged, calcimined, dyed, overdressed to the nth degree. The men are in Prince Alberts, high hats, spats, canes, etc. A procession of gaudy marionettes, yet with something of the relentless horror of Frankensteins in their detached, mechanical unawareness" (CP2 147). Despite Yank's oral and later physical assault against them, they do not react to his presence. The masks differentiate the crowd from Yank along class lines. They exist in a much different world than the world of Yank. This expressionistic moment, visualizing the protagonist's subjectivity, demonstrates Yank's impotence in the world.

All God's Chillun Got Wings (1923) features the marriage between a black man, Jim Harris, and a white woman. Race, itself, functions as a kind of mask in this play. Civic authorities at the time seldom saw past the masks, viewing the play as a treatise about miscegenation which featured the audacious image of a white woman kissing a black man's hand.[2] In the second act, an authentic Congo mask appears in the couple's apartment, a wedding present from Jim's sister, a reminder of his cultural heritage. Stage directions preceding the scene describe the mask: "a grotesque face, inspiring obscure, dim connotations in one's mind, but beautifully done, conceived in a true religious spirit" (CP2 297). Ella's hostility toward the mask increases as the action proceeds. The first half of the play concerns Jim's pursuit of Ella and their marriage. The last half of the play details Jim's recurring efforts to pass the bar exam and enter the white world as a lawyer. While he needs to pass the bar exam in order to feel worthy of her, she needs him to fail in order to feel superior to him and to punish herself for marrying a black man. At the end, after learning that Jim has failed to pass the exam once again, Ella plunges a knife through the mask and pins it to the table. She justifies her actions to Jim by arguing that she saved his life: "It's all right, Jim! It's dead. The devil's dead. See! It couldn't live—unless you passed. If you'd passed it would have lived in you. Then I'd have had to kill you, Jim, don't you see?—or it would have killed me. But now I've killed it" (314). Passing the bar exam would signal cross-over into the white world, and if Jim did so he would be able to integrate his cultural past as well, symbolized by the Congo mask. Ella can only love and accept Jim if he fails. Stabbing the mask kills any chance of true union between the couple. After this climactic moment, Ella relies upon Jim to play the role of old kind Uncle Jim, or the boy who used to play marbles with Ella. O'Neill graphically presents his theme of fractured identity in this play by working schematically on an oppositional basis. Black and white are juxtaposed not so much as a study of race relations, but as a visual study of opposites. The wedding scene is visually spectacular as the couple emerges from a church, blacks lining one side of the stage, whites the other. The Congo mask clearly symbolizes Jim's cultural past and heritage. When Ella drives a knife through it the irreconcilability of the relationship is clear along with Jim's failure to integrate all aspects of himself. The binary pull in the play simplifies a reading and eliminates ambiguity. Later works show the same concerns, but

O'Neill's technique appears both more subtle and more emotionally powerful and convincing in the final plays.

Use of masks in the above plays remains incidental compared to their widespread use in *The Great God Brown* (1925). The action creates a love triangle between two friends, William Brown and Dion Anthony, and one woman, Margaret. Architect Billy Brown steals the identity of his artistic and romantic rival, Dion Anthony, but the weight of his friend's mask destroys him. In the prologue, only Dion and Margaret wear masks. Dion's is "a fixed forcing of his own face—dark, spiritual, poetic, passionately supersensitive, helplessly unprotected in its childlike, religious faith in life—into the expression of a mocking, reckless, defiant, gayly scoffing and sensual young Pan" (CP2 475). The description of the mask and the face underneath visually details the two aspects of Dion's character and name. He is a combination of ascetic St. Anthony and sensual Dionysus. The mask operates as a protective barrier between the character and the outside world. As the play unfolds, characters repeatedly put on and take off their masks. Early in the first act, Dion precedes his first major speech, a monologue, by removing his mask when he observes that no one is around:

> Why am I afraid to dance, I who love music and rhythm and grace and song and laughter? Why am I afraid to live, I who love life and the beauty of flesh and the living colors of earth and sky and sea? Why am I afraid of love, I who love love? Why am I afraid, I who am not afraid? Why must I pretend to scorn in order to pity? Why must I hide myself in self-contempt in order to understand? Why must I be so ashamed of my strength, so proud of my weakness? Why must I live in a cage like a criminal, defying and hating, I who love peace and friendship? [*clasping his hands above in supplication*] Why was I born without a skin, O God, that I must wear armor in order to touch or to be touched? [479–480].

The alternation between masked and unmasked face fashions the entire character of Dion. The action indicates that the masks are necessary for protection in a hostile world, a disguise, the cost of which becomes evident at the outset of Act 1, in which Dion's mask hangs from a strap around his neck, giving him the appearance of having two faces. His real face seems older, more ravaged and more selfless than before. His masked face has become Mephistophelian. During the course of the action, Margaret can only accept and love the masked face. She does not recognize him with his mask off. Only in the company of the prostitute, Cybel, can Dion reveal himself as he is and relax. In another excellent speech, Dion recalls his father, reminiscent of one by Orin about his father in *Mourning Becomes Electra*: "What aliens we were to each other! When he lay dead, his face looked so familiar that I wondered where I had met that man before. Only at the second of my conception. After that, we grew hostile with concealed shame" (495–6). The masks visually embody the problem of how much to reveal and how much to conceal from others. Removal and replacement of the masks create tension in the work as well as show character through contrast of the masked with the unmasked face. The fact that Margaret can only remove her mask when Dion is wearing his makes the issue of intimacy and identity clear. Dion's despair over the necessity of wearing the mask, revealed in both of the examples above, shows the tenderness of his character that is hidden beneath the exterior drunken cynic.

Over the length of the drama, however, the use of the masks assumes other functions that obscure meaning in the play. Dion is an artist whose innate talent provokes William Brown's jealousy. After Dion dies, Brown hides the body, steals Dion's mask, and poses as his friend in order to take Margaret and her children as his own. Brown wants more than Margaret, however; he wants to be an artist himself. A rift between the two halves of Dion's personality, ascetic and Dionysiac, causes his demise. His artistic spirit, the exterior mask, leads him to the debauched pursuit of women and booze which kills him. Brown, as his stolid name seems to indicate, has none of the artistic spirit about him. O'Neill makes it clear that this character is incapable of creating or even understanding another creative and artistic spirit. Once Brown assumes Dion's mask, he shoulders a tremendous strain similar to Dion's, as though the artistic mask cannot fit properly on his head. The mask, which initially seems to represent only the barrier that separates characters from each other and from themselves, assumes the mantle of artistic sensibility. Why Brown cannot wear it comfortably remains a mystery. The mask literally becomes a character in the end. When Brown announces that Dion is dead, several policemen carry out his mask as if it were a body. The literal representation of this action reaches ritualistic levels.

The changing functions of masks (e.g., shield, symbol, ritual) confused scheme as a ruthless grain speculator in foreign markets and removes himself from the life he formerly loved. Although patently mechanical in construction, *Beyond the Horizon*, as creaky as it is, aspires to the same heights as *The Great God Brown*. Without resorting to masks or explanations about the "dualism of man's immortal soul," this play, which precedes *Brown* by seven years, effectively shows the split nature of human identity which threatens to cancel the best ambitions.

Lazarus Laughed (1926) requires the most elaborate use of masks found in any play. Stage directions specify masks for all except the title character.[3] The subtitle reads: *A Play for an Imaginative Theatre.* Apparently no such theatre exists.[4] There has never been a professional production of this play, although it always remained one of O'Neill's favorites.[5] His stage directions ask for masks to represent seven age groups and seven personality types. Instead of showing the dualism within an individual as in *The Great God Brown*, or the symbolic death mask in *Mourning Becomes Electra*, the masks erase individuality in an attempt to represent all of humanity. Permutations of masks according to period and type, in addition to oversized and half-masks, contribute to the bombast of the entire production scheme which completely overwhelms the significance of the play. Without the masks, though, without the huge ensemble and immense spectacle, no production seems warranted. Excess as a principal virtue makes production plans scarce.

Days Without End (1933), the last O'Neill play to use masks, does so in a limited fashion. It portrays the dualism of John Loving by splitting the character into two personas played by two actors. Frederic Carpenter notes that John and Loving are divided along melodramatic lines: "The one is wholly kind and good, the other, wholly malicious and bad" (140). The former is unmasked, while the evil one wears a half mask that resembles John's face. Loving's face "is a mask whose features reproduce exactly the features of John's face—the death mask of a John who has died with a sneer of scornful mockery on his lips. And this mocking scorn is repeated in the expression of the eyes which stare bleakly from behind the mask" (CP3 113). This trick enables the two characters to conduct dialogue with each other throughout the play until the good one finally vanquishes his evil twin at the foot of the cross at play's end. Visual representation of the two characters simplifies the play despite adding a veneer of technical sophistication. Religious content certainly contributed to the play's failure in production, but the form of the play destroyed any sense of mystery and intrigue that could have complicated the message and outcome.

The mask, in the above examples, is the means to represent character, but the idea of the mask functions more importantly as a dynamic audiences very much in performance, but they flocked to the production anyway (Wainscott 194). O'Neill argued that the confusion lay in the execution of the masks, not in the way they were conceived. His letter to Benjamin De Casseres thanks him for reading the play, an opportunity that afforded an interpretation that production completely wiped out. About the actual masks in production, O'Neill concluded: "They suggested only the bromidic, hypocritical & defensive double-personality of people in their personal relationships—a thing I never would have needed masks to convey" (SL 246).

Protestations aside, the best parts of the play detail frustrations of integrating the mask with what lies beneath it. Dion's two monologues, parts of which are quoted above, represent the best language in the play. The masks are, as O'Neill admits, completely dispensable in these scenes to the extent that they are redundant. In fact, the idea of the mask worn by Dion would be a much more powerful image if it were not represented literally. O'Neill apologized, in a way, for his unsuccessful use of masks, in a letter to critic John Mason Brown in 1934: "Perhaps I have sometimes been off the track, possibly my use of masks and asides is artifice and bombast— ... But I fully believe that my long absorption in the dualism of man's mortal soul has been worth while" (SL 440). *The Great God Brown* attempts to show the dualism of Dionysus and St. Anthony within a character, as well as the dualism between characters, Dion Anthony and William Brown, the familiar collision between the artist and the man of business. Absorption with dualism ends up showing only that and nothing more. Brown sums up the tragic condition resting upon such dualism by uttering the following banal pronouncement in the final act: "Man is born broken. He lives by mending. The grace of God is glue!" (528). Final moments manage to surpass everything previous in terms of straining the obvious and the mundane. After Brown dies, Margaret kisses the mask of Dion as if it were him: "Good-by. Thank you for happiness! And you're not dead, sweetheart! You can never die till my heart dies! You will live forever! You will sleep under my heart! I will feel you stirring in your sleep, forever under my heart! (532–533). When asked the name of the body on the floor, the prostitute Cybel looks at the body of Brown and says simply, "Man!" (533). The strain for a symbolic ending results in a grossly simplified ending that makes the subject of dualism obvious and thoroughly uninteresting. If audiences were confused by this play, they were confused by the opaqueness of its construction and not any ideas emanating from it.

Stripped to its essentials, the use of masks in *The Great God Brown* does not add anything that is not evident in an earlier play such as *Beyond the Horizon*. In the early play, the love triangle pits two brothers, Robert and Andrew Mayo, against one another. The former has "a touch of the poet" about him, while the latter is a successful farmer. The woman who is the focus of their desires, Ruth Atkins, chooses to marry the artist because he's different. Robert gives up his dream of travel in order to settle down on the farm with Ruth. Andrew, who loves Ruth deeply, betrays his own nature, too, by taking Robert's place at sea. Domestic life on the farm literally kills Robert, just as the mundane requirements of making a living and rearing children seem to destroy Dion Anthony. William Brown, who loves Margaret and wishes to be a family man, destroys himself through his jealousy of Dion. Similarly, Andrew Mayo pursues a get-rich-quick process in the essential dramatic action of the drama. O'Neill asks in *Memoranda on Masks*: "For what, at bottom, is the new psychological insight into human cause and effect but a study in masks, an exercise in unmasking?" (Cargill 116). Critic Eugene Waith points out that the mask is a primary dramaturgical device even in the many plays in which no literal mask appears: "The mask was a way of getting at the inner reality of character. In fact, it may be said that for O'Neill it was *the* way, for even in the many plays where actual masks are not used, we find the same preoccupation with concealment and discovery" (30). Visually, the mask externalizes the unseen forces at work in the mind. It works as a tool to reveal the loneliness and sensitivity of existence as well as the dividedness and multiplicity of human identity. The plays exhibit a pattern of movement from protection (concealment) to vulnerability (discovery). Addressing the early plays in particular, Ralf Remshardt observes that "Conflict arises out of being rather than action, while a character's actions and his nature are either completely synchronous or diametrically opposed" (131).

The mask of bravado that Yank wears in *Bound East for Cardiff* shields fear of death that can't be completely hidden. The degree to which he and his friend Driscoll avoid the inevitability of Yank's death creates the drama. In *The Moon of the Caribbees*, Smitty assumes a superior role to that of his drunk and coarse shipmates. Yet in the context of the beautiful landscape and hedonistic pleasure, Smitty's aloofness produces signs of his insecurity and weakness. Writer Stephen Murray in *The Straw* treats his loyal confidante and typist Eileen Carmody with professional respect and distance. When she drops her mask and admits her love for him, he retreats, but he can no longer write. When he meets her again, when she is on her deathbed, he agrees to play the part of a lover in order to help her get well. When he commits to the role of lover, however, he discovers that the mask no longer comes off. He discovers by throwing himself into a part and trying to save a friend, that he does love her. And, at that point, he realizes that he loves someone who is fated to die soon, a discovery which leads to the adoption of the hopeless hope, in which the probability of impending death negates any dreams of future happiness. As long as Murray remains disinterested, he lives in no danger. The moment at which he professes his love for another, he risks the pain of suffering which death will bring. In this play, Murray's projection of a mask becomes the character; he undergoes a transformation. The play ends once that transformation occurs, and stops with a question: what is the nature of love? How does Murray's play-acting become real? What this early play tentatively suggests, I believe, is that the dualism implied by the masks is much more complicated than the illusion/reality scheme allows. There are masks under masks and there is no question about which one is real and which one is not. It becomes a question of accessing or promoting a given mask to the surface. It's about seeing more masks.

Even in O'Neill's best plays, however, a metaphoric unmasking action fosters the illusion of dualism. Con Melody swaggers as an aristocratic gentleman, but ends up as an Irish drunk keeping bar at a third-rate tavern; Larry Slade thinks of himself as a wise philosopher in the game of life, but stares straight ahead at the end, fully aware of the hollowness of the game he formerly played; Josie Hogan pretends to be the town whore, but she remains a virgin; the Tyrones appear to be a happy family in the morning, but late night discovers them drunk, silent, and stoned to the world; "Erie" Smith plays the role of Broadway sport, but that game is a ruse to keep him from trudging up to his room alone. These examples show characters whose actions, in Remshardt's vocabulary, diametrically oppose their natures. Action in the plays always moves toward an unmasking in which oppositions become synchronous. Such synchronicity precipitates the end of the drama. All of the characters in *The Iceman Cometh* pretend to be one thing, but are truly something else. The characters exist in contented drunkenness as long as they collude in each others' fantasies. The game the bums play determines that Harry Hope is a popular local politician even though he hasn't ventured outside the bar in twenty years; Jimmy Tomorrow is a journalist; Willie Oban a brilliant lawyer; Joe Mott, owner of his own gambling house; Rocky is a bartender, not a pimp; Larry Slade a wizened philosopher; Piet Wetjoen and Cecil Lewis are Boer War heroes; Ed Mosher is a circus man, and Pat McGloin is a police lieutenant. The dramatis personae carefully introduces characters in terms of what they once were. Hickey unmasks each of them and forces them to see themselves as they are and face the truth. All the inhabitants of Hope's saloon, save two, restore their illusions about themselves and their actions at play's end. Of the two who do not restore a mask, one commits suicide, and the other, Larry, after pining for death theatrically throughout the play, longs for it to come in earnest. The mask keeps the illusion of dualism alive.

The unmasking action in *The Iceman Cometh* transforms a comic structure into a tragic one. In classical comedies, protagonists often appear as something other than who they are. The comic response recognizes the gap between pretense and reality and such plays usually end with the elimination of that gap and a new proclamation of moral order. O'Neill does something similar in *The Iceman Cometh*, but for different purposes than moral instruction. According to him, the play begins as a comedy before the tragedy comes on. He wrote to Lawrence Langner in 1940 that "there are moments in it that suddenly strip the secret soul of a man stark naked, not in cruelty or moral superiority, but with an understanding compassion which sees him as a victim of the ironies of life and of himself" (SL 511). By contrast, *Ah, Wilderness!* (1933), O'Neill's lone comedy, features a protagonist whose mask remains in place from beginning to end. Both plays adhere to a comic structure insofar as characters project a mask that shows one image and hides another. In tragedy, however, the characters glimpse the underside of their own masks, while comic characters seldom have to confront an unmasked image of themselves.

O'Neill wrote *Ah, Wilderness!* very quickly while he was struggling to find the right conclusion for *Days Without End*.[6] While he could not bear to bill it as a comedy, it plays as one. Without a doubt, it stands apart from all of his other plays. It hails the transition from examining the big, conceptual themes of the world, as in *Lazarus Laughed*, *The Great God Brown*, *Days Without End*, *Dynamo*, and *Strange Interlude*, to domestic themes and settings. Set in 1906, it also signals a preoccupation with the past that unites all of the final plays. *Ah, Wilderness!* reflects the flip side or mirror image of the later tragedy, *Long Day's Journey Into Night*. Too often, the earlier play is viewed as a light foray into the deeper and more painful truths of the later and greater play. A typical view recognizes the Tyrones as the true representation of O'Neill's family life, while the Miller family represents a fantasy. O'Neill, himself, once said in an interview: "That's the way I would have *liked* my boyhood to have been. It was a sort of wishing out loud" (Basso 48).[7] Removing the former play from the latter's shadow, seeing it on its own terms, the comedy loses none of its luster when sober implications of its action come to light. The dark side of this lovely play does not reside in the depiction of Uncle Sid's alcoholism, sexual politics, prostitution, or even the patriarchal relationships that dominate the Miller home, but in the mask of Richard Miller, the comic young hero of the play.[8]

Comedy in the play centers around the characterization of Richard. From the beginning, he spouts quotations from all sorts of worldly literature: Ibsen, Swinburne, Fitzgerald's translation of *The Rubáiyát of Omar Khayyám*, Shaw's *Candida*, Oscar Wilde, Kipling. His mother worries that he's having an affair with Hedda Gabler. Richard swings the plot of the play, what there is of it, in motion by sending Swinburne's poetry to his girlfriend. The girl's father intercepts the verses and visits the Miller household to voice his disapproval. The offending lines read as follows:

> That I could drink thy veins as wine, and eat
> Thy breasts like honey, that from face to feet
> Thy body were abolished and consumed,
> And in my flesh thy very flesh entombed! [CP3 23].

The comedy flourishes with the acknowledgment that Richard quotes poetry that he's read and admired in books but that he does not fully understand.

He is not the person whom he pretends to be. If he really were like Eilert Lovborg in *Hedda Gabler*, a character whom he professes to admire, then the play would not be nearly as funny. Indeed, Richard visits a bar, flirts with a kind prostitute, and gets drunk for the first time. That's a far cry from Lovborg's nocturnal trip to Mademoiselle Diana's boudoir where he inadvertently shoots himself in the bowels. Richard stays a sweet kid who doesn't have the least intention of fulfilling his prophesies of literary licentiousness. When he does meet Muriel for a clandestine rendezvous at the beach, one chaste kiss quiets his beating passion. An integration of Richard's outside mask with his inner consciousness never occurs. While the audience perceives the difference between Richard's affectations and his essential nature, Richard never has to remove his mask and examine himself in the mirror. Nat Miller, his father, justifies his refusal to explain the facts of life to his son: "You feel, in spite of all his bold talk out of books, that he's so darned innocent inside" (79). Innocence remains intact at the end. The pain in comedy never hurts for long. Mr. Miller finally punishes Richard by insisting that he must attend college at Yale and graduate, too.

Glare, from this sunny view of family life hides the foreboding portent of the play. Richard's mother believes that her son is destined for some kind of greatness and mentions the possibility of Richard becoming a great writer. If that were to occur, Richard would have to embrace the sort of attitudes and values that would be unacceptable in the Miller household and in the town in which he lives. Swinburne and Ibsen would be no laughing matters. O'Neill parodies *Hedda Gabler* in *Now I Ask You* (1916), an early unproduced play. In that play, the regular businessman humors the artistic hypocrisies of his young wife and tames her in marriage. In so doing, O'Neill seems to betray his own values and sensibilities regarding the artist in society. *Ah, Wilderness!* presents a nostalgic and flattering view of small town America and delights with warm humor, rich characters, and all the satisfactions of bourgeois life. If Richard Miller were to become an artist, he could no longer pose as one and still retreat to the safety of benign and loving parents. *Ah, Wilderness!* portrays the rewards of not pursuing an artistic life. The dark side of the play travels in the shadows of the road not taken.

Ah, Wilderness! is a play without pain precisely because Richard Miller never has to confront his mask. Everyone within the play protects him and his mask stays in place. In most O'Neill plays, though, characters recognize another identity under the mask which seems to be the real face. How do characters see themselves when the mask comes off? These moments of recognition indicate something much more profound than the illusion/reality opposition can supply. For example, the contest between Ezra and Christine Mannon in *Mourning Becomes Electra* resolves in the darkness of their bedroom in early morning. Playing the part of dutiful wife, Christine allows Mannon to make love to her. Much like Eleanor when she endures John's kisses in *Welded*, Christine only gives Mannon her body and not her spirit. The barrier, the mask, remains up between them and Mannon accuses her of not being his wife: "You were only pretending love! You let me take you as if you were a nigger slave I'd bought at auction! You made me appear a lustful beast in my own eyes!—as you've always done since our first marriage night!" (CP2 944). Pushed to the brink of what she can tolerate, Christine responds finally: "I loved you when I married you! I wanted to give myself! But you made me so I couldn't give! You filled me with disgust!" (944). New England Puritanism that regards sexuality as sinful pollutes Ezra's relations with his wife and contributes to his deviant behavior. Christine confronts her husband, admits her affair with Adam Brant, and boasts that he is her lover and not Ezra. When Christine reflects her feelings for Ezra back to him, he does not see himself as he is, necessarily, but he does see himself as Christine sees him. The image of a "lustful beast" proves intolerable to him, but it reflects the legacy of the Mannon family. When the mask drops, Christine resolves as a mirror and shows Mannon someone whom he cannot accept. Struggling with his anger, Mannon suffers an apparent heart attack, brought on by Christine's disclosures.

The Emperor Jones works by peeling away slowly the mask of civilization and superiority from the hero, but *The Hairy Ape* rips Yank's mask away in a single moment. He subsequently tries to avenge his honor and find his rightful place in the world. The third scene of the play, in which the rich and ghost-like Mildred descends from the deck above ship to see how the other half lives, produces the inciting moment. Her invasion of the stokehole surprises Yank and when he turns to see her, he frightens her with his dirty, brawny, sweaty appearance. "Oh, the filthy beast!" she exclaims, fainting (CP2 137). Her words are similar to the accusations that Christine Mannon levels at her husband in *Mourning Becomes Electra*, but in this case, Yank endures public humiliation that changes his view of the world and his place in it forever. Prior to this moment, Yank considered himself as the prime mover in the world and the one who most belongs in it as king of the stokers. O'Neill's opening directions name Yank as the stokers' "most highly developed individual" (CP2 121). In the modern world of speed, power, and reliance upon the machine, Yank reigns in his glory. He refutes easily romantic tales of the past spun by his mate Paddy which threaten the primacy of the stokers feeding coal to the engines. At the end of the first scene, he rebuts Paddy in front of his shipmates: "Tinkin' and dreamin', what'll that get yuh? What's tinkin' got to do wit it? We move, don't we? Speed, ain't it? Fog, dat's all you stand for. But we drive trou dat, don't we? We split dat up and smash trou—twenty-five knots a hour!" (130). Before Yank encounters Mildred, he rests secure in his power and confident of his position of dominance in the world. After enduring her slight against him and the laughter from his comrades, Yank assumes the pose of "The Thinker" in each subsequent scene. The shock of his collision with his exact opposite forces him to re-evaluate his view of the world.

Reflection creates crisis in the play. Yank tries to avenge his honor, an attempt to reassert his will on the world. He ends up at the zoo, staring in the face of a gorilla. Looking at the ape, Yank acknowledges that "yuh're what she seen when she looked at me, de white-faced tart!" (161). Yank finally sees what Mildred saw, he sees himself from her perspective, an image that destroys him. The stokehole in which he formerly worked was nothing more than a kind of steel cage in which ape-like men slaved to shovel coal into the ship's furnaces. At the end of the play, the image of Yank in a steel cage at the zoo echoes the initial image of the ship's stokehole. O'Neill's literary postscript, "And, perhaps, the Hairy Ape at last belongs" is ironic in the sense that Yank's position has unchanged (163). He belongs to the monkey cage in exactly the same way that he belongs to the ship's stokehole. The dualism of his character (the best among men/a filthy beast) is really an illusion. Only the perspective changes from how he envisions himself, initially, and how his friends see him, to how others see him, particularly Mildred and her ilk. Yank's refusal to recognize himself in that light constitutes the action of the play. To the extent that he rebels against the image that others have of him, Yank wears a mask of himself. Action in the play rips off that mask and Yank struggles mightily to put it back on again to restore his own self-conception of his role in the world. He's unable to accept a non-flattering version of his character. The irony of the ending points out that Yank fails to recognize and integrate all aspects of his character.

An impressive military uniform, a full-length mirror, vast quantities of alcohol and cultured speech are all means Cornelius Melody employs to promote one version of identity in *A Touch of the Poet* (1935). Even his nickname, Con, suggests the character who pretends to be one thing, but is truly another. In this play, however, all the other characters know him to be exactly who he is. Accoutrements that adorn his character do not convince others or the audience that Melody is other than a shebeen keeper in Ireland. All Melody's efforts to disguise his nature are attempts to hide himself from himself. Even the no account drunks who hang on his coattails only to drink his liquor see through Melody's pretenses. One of them, O'Dowd, remarks: "Ain't he the lunatic, sittin' like a play-actor in his red coat, lyin' about his battles with the French!" (234). In the same scene, Melody responds in such a way to indicate that he is not unaware of what goes on around him: "So you may go on fooling yourselves that I am fooled in you" (235). Melody constructs his game of pretense in the face of present circumstance. Despite the poverty in which he lives, Melody self-fashions his identity as an aristocrat and gentleman. The uniform recalls former days of valor. Melody constantly looks at himself in the mirror in order to see the image that he wants to see. Repeatedly, O'Neill directs the character to sag at first sight of the reflection before asserting control over the figure. It is as though Melody sees himself all too clearly with all his imperfections, as though he is completely aware of the disparity between who he is and who he aspires to be. Only through an act of will does he assume a military bearing which strikes regal comportment. He exerts discipline to maintain a mask that no longer fits. In the most poignant moment of the play, his daughter, Sara, who embodies the same split between peasant and aristocrat as her father and who will be the legacy figure in the cycle plays, pleads with him: "Oh, Father, why can't you ever be the thing you can seem to be?" (228). Characters enter rooms on three occasions to interrupt Melody's view of himself in the mirror. In short succession, scenes reveal who Melody is, who he wants to be, and how he presents himself to other characters. The action resolves with Melody's failure to embody the role that he fashions for himself and his inability to live without that part as well. By consuming alcohol in enormous quantities, Melody attempts to make the mask fit, to live with the knowledge that it doesn't. Final recognition that others see him for who he is finishes his attempt to hold onto the mask. After riding off to the Harford mansion to avenge the family honor, Melody returns to his tavern beaten and bloody, his once sparkling uniform torn and frayed. Mrs. Harford, an attractive woman who had rebuked his flirtation earlier, punctuated Melody's humiliation by witnessing the drunken street brawl. In the midst of the fight, Melody looked up and saw her: "that pale Yankee bitch watching from a window, sneering with disgust!" (267). She effectively rips off Melody's mask. The action sustains as long as all characters allow Melody to play his part. But in one look, Melody realizes that the game is up. He can no longer flatter himself once he sees his reflection in Deborah Harford's condescending eyes.

The pretender, Con Melody, finally sees himself as he truly is and reverts to form. Stage directions at the end describe Melody as a "loutish, grinning clown" (277). When he speaks, the brogue which he demonstrably mastered with perfect diction, returns. All pretense of grandeur vanishes, and Melody adopts a new role to play. Strangely, Sara, who had argued throughout the play that her father should see himself as he is, reverses herself at the end and implores: "Won't you be yourself again?" (277). She tries to rouse the old Melody, but he protests vehemently: "For the love of God, stop—let me go—!" (279). He cannot live without the illusion that he created for himself. Sara watches her father exit and offers a benediction: "May the hero of Talavera rest in peace!" (280). After the street brawl, his friend Creegan comments on Melody's ravings: "It's the same crazy blather he's talked every once in a while since they brought him to—about the Harford woman—and speakin' av the pigs and his father one minute, and his pride and his honor and his mare the next" (267). Melody fails to integrate two dominant strains of his character. He can no longer reconcile who he is and what he's become with who he used to be and who he'd like to be. When Sara asks herself, "Why do I mourn for him?" she halts at the contradictions in Con's personality (281). Michael Manheim astutely observes: "She panics at the realization that Con is caught between two irreconcilable natures—both genuine yet at the same time both poses" ("O'Neill's Transcendence of Melodrama in *A Moon for the Misbegotten*" 152). Throughout the play, there has been an insistence that Melody pretends to be a gentleman but that he's really just a tavern keeper. This division between illusion and reality is, as it turns out, another illusion.

Melody's "performance" at the end is no more authentic than his performance as Major Melody of Wellington's dragoons. Sara begins to realize only at the end that her father is neither one nor the other but, at least, both. Her own dividedness and multiplicity forms the subject in O'Neill's next play, *More Stately Mansions*, in which she battles to balance her love for Simon Harford and her lust for money and power. For his part in that play, Simon tries to integrate his desire to write books with a competing desire to build more stately mansions as a captain of industry. The mask, then, does not shield the essence of character so much as other aspects of character. In the recognition scenes I've outlined in *Mourning Becomes Electra*, *The Hairy Ape*, and *A Touch of the Poet*, characters glimpse other parts of themselves which they would rather not see. Their inability to integrate these aspects leads to their downfall. The mask is a strategy that above all else, simplifies an approach to character. It allows characters to see themselves as they would like to be seen. Mannon is a sensitive lover; Yank is a powerful leader; Melody is a brave aristocrat. These readings of respective characters are true but incomplete. Characters in O'Neill can never be the thing that they can sometimes seem to be. They can never accept less than that either, even as they can never see more of themselves.

A Moon for the Misbegotten culminates O'Neill's conception of character as mask and acting as necessary pretense. O'Neill juxtaposes the sham of theatre with a painful unmasking of human vulnerability. Very little happens in this play. A dying man confesses his sins on the altar of a virgin's breast. That summarizes the dramatic action and emphasizes the unmasking that occurs between James Tyrone and Josie Hogan. Action strips away all pretense, an ironic pattern in a play that builds itself around acting and scheming.

Phil Hogan, Josie's father, operates as a playwright within the play who designs schemes within schemes to bring the two reluctant lovers together. Ultimately, such scheming results in heart-breaking failure, but it also forces a transvaluation of values as it confers a state of grace upon the three principal figures. Religious imagery, blasphemed early and often in the play, emerges in a fresh new context at the end of the play. Despite the fact that the two lovers do not end up together for a happy ending, love remains the positive value as it has in no previous O'Neill play. Hogan and Josie reach new levels of understanding and intimacy. Romantic love transforms into love as sacrifice, the same value championed first in O'Neill's unproduced *Servitude*. While the message remains the same, the medium in which O'Neill conveys his theme achieves tremendous emotional richness in his last play.

The three principal characters are all actors who mask interior thoughts and feelings with a very different exterior presentation. Josie is the greatest actor of all. She plays the part of the village wanton, who has been with so many men that none will marry her and make a decent woman of her. In truth, she is a virgin. She concocts her elaborate charade as a defense system against her own conception of herself as ugly and unworthy. Rather than feel the shame of being scorned by men, she invents a scheme in which she pretends to have slept with the entire town. When Hogan raises the possibility that she might catch Tyrone for a husband, a man whom she does love and admire, she responds: "Och, Father, don't play the jackass with me. You know, and I know, I'm an ugly overgrown lump of a woman, and the men that want me are no better than stupid bulls" (CP3 870). Josie pretends that her appearance prevents Tyrone from loving her: "If I was a dainty, pretty tart he'd be proud I'd raise a rumpus about him. But when it's a big, ugly hulk like me—[*She falters and forces herself to go on.*] If he ever was tempted to want me, he'd be ashamed of it" (903). Josie refuses to see herself as desirable although both Tyrone and her father love her deeply. Josie plays the part of the wanton precisely because she fears that men perceive her as sexually unattractive. She protects herself from ever having to realize her worst fears.

Her father, Phil Hogan, delights in his role as a combative Irish curmudgeon. He presents himself as cynical and hard-hearted, but he remains the most sentimental character in the play. His rough talk belies a loving father who tries to get what's best for his daughter. As an act of kindness, Hogan props up Josie's story of herself as promiscuous woman. Knowing that Josie will never accept a compliment directly from him, Hogan conveys affection in third person reference to Tyrone: "You're a pure virgin to him, but all the same there's things besides your beautiful soul he feels drawn to, like your beautiful hair and eyes, and—" (901). From the outset, Hogan sees his daughter clearly and knows why she plays the game of the wanton. He does not destroy her illusion out of great pity, understanding and love. To make her face the facts would be too harsh for her. Hogan proceeds with his elaborate schemes to marry his daughter to Tyrone on the basis of his knowing precisely who Josie is and the nature of the mask she wears. He plays the matchmaker in the play in order to give her a shot at happiness.

Even before James Tyrone enters at the end of Act 1, his character precedes him onstage by way of description. Hogan and Josie spy him down the road on his approach to their farm, and Josie announces him: "Look at him when he thinks no one is watching, with his eyes on the ground. Like a dead man walking slow behind his own coffin. [*then roughly*] Faith, he must have a hangover. He sees us now. Look at the bluff he puts up, straightening himself and grinning. [*resentfully*] I don't want to meet him. Let him make jokes with you and play the old game about a drink you both think is such fun. That's all he comes for, anyway" [*She starts of again.*] (874). Tyrone plays the part of the Broadway sport who revels in the gambling life of hotel bars and prostitutes. His demeanor and wardrobe suggest, according to O'Neill's stage directions, "that he follows a style set by well-groomed Broadway gamblers who would like to be mistaken for Wall Street brokers" (875). Yet the description of him as a "dead man walking" aptly characterizes his true nature beneath the jovial and joking exterior. Tyrone harbors a secret that the action of the play will reveal. When Josie surprises Jim with a friendly kiss later in the first act, she reacts: "Och, there's no spirit in you! It's like kissing a corpse" (882). Like Eleanor Cape in *Welded*, Tyrone is dead on the inside. At the very end of the play, Josie laments the fact that her would—be lover has gone: "I didn't know he'd died already—that it was a damned soul coming to me in the moonlight, to confess and be forgiven and find peace for a night—" (937). Tyrone is dead before he enters the action of the play. His mask, the opposite of the Mannon mask, provides the illusion that he's alive. He performs his role when he comes onstage and an audience watches him. Just as Josie reveals herself in the course of the action, Tyrone unburdens himself of his secrets and the mutual unmasking of the two concludes the play.

Characters play games to establish bonds of affection between them. Since they all wear masks, they agree upon certain games to play that have rules which allow them to act roles without fear of exposure. These games communicate affection without having to reveal intimate thoughts and secrets. The games spark rituals of good feeling. Invective and blarney are two means to hide inner feelings among the principals. Tyrone and Hogan good-naturedly trade insults about the condition of the farm, their relationship of landlord and tenant, and proceed to engage in a match of wits in which Tyrone begs for a hospitable drink and Hogan cheerfully refuses. Josie, listening to the entire charade, finally interrupts: "Ain't you the fools, playing that old game between you, and both of you pleased as punch!" (879). Father and daughter play similar games with each other. Hogan makes his entrance calling his only daughter a "great slut" and an "overgrown cow" (862). Josie counters these jibes by insulting her father as a "bad-tempered old hornet" and an "ugly little buck goat" (862), and then flattering him as a fighter: "Sure, you could give Jack Dempsey himself a run for his money" (863). The initial confrontation ends with Hogan threatening to beat his daughter, calmed only by the fact that she wields a club: "A fine curse God put on me when he gave me a daughter as big and strong as a bull, and as vicious and disrespectful. [*Suddenly his eyes twinkle and he grins admiringly.*] Be God, look at you standing therewith the club! If you ain't the damnedest daughter in Connecticut, who is?" (863–4). Banter, in the form of insult or compliment, establishes a bond between characters and communicates affection. Each character agrees to sustain the others' illusion. They engage the mask of each other, but politely leave the private face alone.

Tyrone and Josie, too, combine compliments and complaints to keep each other at a respectful distance. Tyrone, from the outset, knows that Josie is not whom she pretends to be, and welcomes her with an appropriate, yet satirical address: "and how's my Virgin Queen of Ireland?" (877). Josie, in turn, needles Tyrone by suggesting that he would feel more at home in the arms of some of his tarts on Broadway than on the Connecticut farm of his tenants. Tyrone forces her to blush with his new admission: "I like them tall and strong and voluptuous, now, with beautiful big breasts" (878). With her, Tyrone tries to drop his role as a Broadway sport and prove himself a gentleman. Josie reluctantly drops her guard, fearful that she will make herself vulnerable if she admits her love for Tyrone. She repeatedly, in the first two acts, tries to play the familiar part of the promiscuous woman, but Tyrone won't let her play the game. At the end of Act 2, he says: "Lay off that line, for tonight at least. [*He adds slowly*] I'd like tonight to be different" (910). Tyrone instinctively knows that the games interfere with what he wants to say. The irritation that Tyrone expresses when Josie attempts to resume the ritual of play indicates that something unusual will happen between them. Absence of play indicates a change in Tyrone's character. He appears differently than he has on previous occasions, a fact attributed to two things. Josie believes that his inability to play the usual games results from his decision to sell the farm to the rich neighbor, T. Stedman Harder. When Tyrone arrives late for his moonlight date with Josie in Act 2, Josie suggests that he has a bad conscience, implying that he feels guilty about what he has done to sell the farm which he had promised to the Hogans. Tyrone responds by staring at her guiltily and asking: "What put that in your head? Conscience about what?" (909). Tyrone is guilty, but not about selling the farm. Both characters misunderstand each other at this point and only in the final act does Tyrone unveil his secret. His guilt stems from the death of his mother and his behavior surrounding it. The issue around the sale of his farm supplies only the overt melodrama that provides suspense. "Some viewers of the play," according to Michael Manheim, "never do get the point that melodramatic intrigue is not finally the central interest of this play" ("O'Neill's Transcendence of Melodrama in *A Moon for the Misbegotten*" 154). The real drama, however, takes place before the action of the play begins. The plot, in this case, is an excuse for something revelatory to happen. That event discloses Tyrone's haunted past and his desperate plea for forgiveness (Manheim 153–157).

Scheming within the play makes up the plot. Hogan, of course, invents the scheme that Josie falls for in which Tyrone sells the farm for quick cash in order to return to his high rolling life of New York. But even before Hogan appears, the importance of scheming manifests itself in the opening scene between Josie and her brother, Mike. The scene is a leave-taking, in which Mike follows the pattern of his other brothers, Thomas and John, and leaves the farm for the city. Josie helps Mike escape from Hogan by preparing his bags, distracting Hogan, and even stealing a little of the old man's money to support Mike's trip. When Hogan discovers that Mike has left, he feigns outrage and blusters against his daughter. The initial scene of Mike's departure establishes Josie's tenderness and goodness toward her brother, whom she does not like, and feigned hostility toward her father, whom she does like. Scheming binds father and daughter together in fun and affection. Hogan and Josie revel in the memory of tricking their neighbors, the Crowleys, on the sale of a lame horse, and Josie's flirtations as a young girl with Tyrone's father in order to stave off paying the rent. Hogan tells Josie, admiringly, "You should have gone on the stage" (869). Josie's analysis of her father hints at the structure of the entire play: "You old divil, you've always a trick hidden behind your tricks, so no one can tell at times what you're after" (869). The play works as artifice packed within artifice, scheme within scheme, in order to unpack human truths at the center. What the play's after and what Hogan is after is withheld until the end of the action.

The arrival of T. Stedman Harder, the Standard Oil millionaire whose fence borders the Hogan's land, provides the opportunity to put acting and trickery on full display. Apparently, Hogan repeatedly breaks down the fence in order for his pigs to wallow on the banks of Harder's ice pond. Harder arrives in Act 1 to make his complaint in person and to demand restitution. O'Neill's long description of Harder puts him at a decided disadvantage against the likes of Hogan. The initial description begins: "Harder is in his late thirties but looks younger because his face is unmarked by worry, ambition, or any of the common hazards of life. No matter how long he lives, his four undergraduate years will always be for him the most significant in his life, and the moment of his highest achievement the time he was tapped for an exclusive Senior Society at the Ivy university to which his father had given millions" (884). The college boy, for O'Neill, always represents an individual who cannot master a situation. Bounded by institutional thinking and an easy life, the college educated character lacks the ability to act, to perform a role, and he cannot fool others. Despite all Harder's money, he proves no match for Hogan and Josie in a battle of wits. Hogan seizes the offensive quickly by accusing Harder of breaking down the fence and encouraging the pigs to risk pneumonia in the winter at the ice pond!

The duplicitous nature of the Hogans on display against Harder amplifies the main scheme of the action. While the audience watches the confrontation between Hogans and Harder, Tyrone listens and laughs behind the wall of the Hogan farmhouse. The Hogans act for the benefit of Tyrone. His presence as an auditor heightens enjoyment of the performance and creates a play within a play. This scene also stimulates an impetus for Hogan's grand improvisation that follows. The squabble provides a motive for Tyrone to sell his farm to Harder. After Harder rides away in defeat, Tyrone refers to the farm as a gold mine on three separate occasions. He confides that Harder wants to buy the farm in order to throw Hogan off the property. Jim predicts that Harder's humiliation at the hands of Hogan will triple the value of the farm and that he will make a lot of money on the sale. Of course, he's kidding, he would never actually sell the farm to Harder. He loves the Hogans. But Hogan, ever scheming, uses Tyrone's words to hatch his matchmaking plot upon his unsuspecting daughter.

Hogan improvises and modulates his scheme as the action progresses. It begins as a question of how to get a rich man to marry Josie. Honest son Mike, no match for Hogan either, actually first breathes life into the scheme for Josie to catch Tyrone for a husband. Reasoning that she cannot marry a decent man, Mike figures Tyrone for a possible mark: "I know it's crazy, but maybe you're hoping if you got hold of him alone when he's mad drunk—Anyway, talk all you please to put me off, I'll bet my last penny you've cooked up some scheme to hook him, and the Old Man put you up to it. Maybe he thinks if he caught you with Jim and had witnesses to prove it, and his shotgun to scare him—" (860). When Josie discloses Mike's plot to Hogan, the father allows that it might just work. To calm Josie's outrage, Hogan intimates that the future of the farm would be settled if Josie were to marry Tyrone, the landlord of the property. Hogan's scheme, hiding a good hearted desire inside a pecuniary motive, elaborates in Act 2. He feigns heavy drunkenness in order to proclaim his profound sadness that Tyrone has, in fact, promised to sell the farm to Harder. He manipulates Josie into accepting a revenge plot for an act of betrayal. She agrees to lure Tyrone into bed in order for Hogan to bring witnesses to catch them there in the morning. They employ the time honored bed trick to ensure that she marries him and that they save the farm. Hogan stages his departure from the farm in front of the approaching Tyrone, assuring Josie and Tyrone that he will not return again until morning.

Prior to leaving, however, Hogan reveals his true motivation. After Hogan goads Josie into collusion with him, she exits to her bedroom, ostensibly to freshen up and re-apply her makeup. Alone on stage, Hogan's demeanor changes. O'Neill's directions read: "Abruptly he ceases to look like a drunk who, by an effort, is keeping himself half-sober. He is a man who has been drinking a lot but is still clear-headed and has complete control of himself" (906). He observes that Josie's room remains dark. She cannot even look at herself in the mirror and face the task for which she has set herself. Hogan speaks: "God forgive me, it's bitter medicine. But it's the only way I can see that has a chance now" (906). In an instant, the mask drops to show the scheme within the scheme. Such a moment reveals the loving father beneath the feisty curmudgeon. Later, after having been found out, Hogan vents his full motivation for his devious conniving: "All you said about my lying and scheming, and what I hoped would happen, is true. But it wasn't his money, Josie. I did see it was the last chance—the only one left to bring the two of you to stop your damned pretending, and face the truth that you loved each other. I wanted you to find happiness—by hook or crook, one way or another, what did I care how? I wanted to save him, and I hoped he'd see that only your love could—It was his talk of the beauty he saw in you that made me hope—And I knew he'd never go to bed with you even if you'd let him unless he married you" (944).

Tyrone's own counter scheme makes marriage impossible and thwarts Hogan's plot. He arrives at the farmhouse late for his moonlight date with Josie and not noticeably drunk, a significant sign for the occasion. In the following act, Act 3, Josie brings him her father's liquor and he accepts it gratefully, acknowledging that "The booze at the Inn didn't work tonight" (910). Alcohol does not provide refuge for him on this night from haunting memories of the past. Typically, the alcoholic mask shields a character from bitter self-knowledge. O'Neill's description of Tyrone's entrance for his date with Josie reads in part: "... his eyes have a peculiar fixed, glazed look, and there is a certain vague quality in his manner and speech, as if he were a bit hazy and absent-minded" (907). That the alcohol doesn't work leads to Tyrone's desperation. When the bums in *The Iceman Cometh* return from the streets to Hope's saloon, fresh from realizing the vacuity of their pipe dreams, they complain in unison that the booze doesn't work. They can get drunk only when they restore their life illusions. Tyrone, unlike the characters in *Iceman*, possesses no illusions, but the booze helps him to numb the pain of his guilty past deeds. Before his first entrance, Hogan and Josie discuss the mask-like function of alcohol on Jim's character:

> JOSIE: He only acts like he's hard and shameless to get back at life when it's tormenting him—and who doesn't?
>
> HOGAN: Or take the other kind of queer drunk he gets on sometimes when, without any reason you can see, he'll suddenly turn strange, and look sad, and stare at nothing as if he was mourning over some ghost inside him, and—
>
> JOSIE: I think I know what comes over him when he's like that. It's the memory of his mother comes back and his grief for her death [872–873].

The action of *A Moon for the Misbegotten* picks up at the precise moment at which Jim can no longer erase memory of his performance surrounding his mother's death. The inability of alcohol to do its work motivates him to visit Josie, although the real reason remains a mystery at this point: "Had to get out of the damned Inn. I was going batty alone there. The old heebie-jeebies. So I came to you. [*He pauses—then adds with strange, wondering sincerity*] I've really begun to love you a lot, Josie" (908–909). Debauched to the core, Tyrone sees through the hollow pretenses of Josie. Her purity and simple goodness attract him. While Josie masks her innocence, Tyrone fears that his fine dress, good manners, and college education cover up a rotten soul and dirty secrets. Aware of the polarity between them, Tyrone fears that he will ruin Josie. Alone at the end of Act 2, after Josie goes in search of another bottle, Tyrone reviles himself for his need to see Josie. "You rotten bastard!" he says, failing miserably to light a match with a trembling hand as the curtain falls (911).

Physical desire for Josie leads to self-loathing and the threat of violence in the first part of the third act. Josie continues to assume her role as a wanton, but Tyrone threatens her: "If you don't look out, I'll call you on that bluff, Josie. [*He stares at her with a deliberate sensualist's look that undresses her.*] I'd like to. You know that, don't you?" (913). Jim assures her that he's over his case of heebie-jeebies, and adds: "Let the dead past bury its dead" (914). But as the scene unwinds, Tyrone, filled with memories and booze, begins to confuse Josie with the blonde woman whom he met on the train while taking his mother's body back East for burial. And as they converse, he also begins to force an intimate conversation with Josie in order for them both to drop their masks and see each other: "You can take the truth, Josie—from me. Because you and I belong to the same club. We can kid the world but we can't fool ourselves, like most people, no matter what we do—nor escape ourselves no matter where we run away. Whether it's the bottom of a bottle, or a South Sea Island, we'd find our own ghosts there waiting to greet us—'sleepless with pale commemorative eyes,' as Rossetti wrote" (923).

The allusion to the South Sea Islands usually refers to a libidinous zone of health and sexual freedom, a counterpoint to the Puritanism of New England, in plays such as *Beyond the Horizon*, *Diff'rent*, and *Mourning Becomes Electra*. Here, Tyrone argues that sexuality only excites ghosts of the past. Josie misreads Tyrone's intentions when she finally admits that she is a virgin. She follows this painful admission with a plea for love and a longing to take Tyrone to her bed. He, however, can only accept sexual relations in terms of sordid transactions. His demeanor changes and his language reflects the fact that he sees Josie now as the blonde woman on the train: "Sure thing, Kiddo. What the hell else do you suppose I came for? I've been kidding myself. [*He steps up beside her and puts his arm around her and presses his body to hers.*] You're the goods, Kid. I've wanted you all along. Love, nuts! I'll show you what love is. I know what you want, Bright Eyes" (925). Tyrone's transformation into a hustling john kills any possibility of romance between the two. Sex, for Tyrone, satisfies his self-hatred and the conviction that he destroys everyone whom he touches. "... when I poison them, they stay poisoned!" (926). His performance for Josie allows her to view him as he sees himself. She responds as he wishes and reacts with fear and disgust.

About to walk away, Tyrone adds a final plea: "I came here asking for love—just for this one night, because I thought you loved me" (926). The love Tyrone needs is not sexual. His desire for this night to be different than all the others is now clear. He doesn't want to defile or poison Josie like all the other whores he's bedded. Tyrone wants this night to be different in order for him to tell, finally, the story about the blonde woman on the train. He wants to confess his sins that make him hateful to himself. Josie welcomes him back to her arms and allows him to lie down with his head back against her breast. He tells about how his mother's death angered him by leaving him all alone. Unable to cry at her funeral, he remembers feeling obliged to act the part of the bereaved: "So I put on an act. I flopped on my knees and hid my face in my hands and faked some sobs and cried, 'Mama! Mama! My dear mother!' But all the time I kept saying to myself, 'You lousy ham! You God-damned lousy ham!'" (931). He goes on to describe how he slept with the "blonde pig" on the train for fifty bucks a night while his mother lay in a coffin in the baggage car. He remembers lines from a tear-jerker song, voiced out of context at the start of the act, but which now, given the situation, reveal the depth of Tyrone's pursuit of self-defilement:

> "And baby's cries can't waken her
> In the baggage coach ahead" [932].

The connotations of the above dramatic situation strike a grotesque image. Tyrone constructs the entire story theatrically as though he were a performer. He describes his revenge against his mother as an actor in a play: "It was like some plot I had to carry out. The blonde—she didn't matter. She was only something that belonged in the plot" (931–932). Tyrone sleeps with the prostitute on the train in order to express his anger against his mother for leaving him all alone. He asks Josie, for one night, to play the part of his mother in order to hear his confession. That she agrees attests to the power and strength of her love for him. After confessing all, Josie hugs Tyrone to her. She wanted to take Tyrone as a lover, but she ends up in the role of his mother. The act ends with Tyrone sobbing against Josie's breast, later falling asleep, and Josie staring into the moonlight: "You're a fine one, wanting to leave me when the night I promised I'd give you has just begun, our night that'll be different from all the others, with a dawn that won't creep over dirty windowpanes but will wake in the sky like a promise of God's peace in the soul's dark sadness" (933). What began with the prospects of romance, ends with a scene of wish fulfillment enacting the past: a son asking for and receiving forgiveness from his mother.

When Hogan reappears to find Josie still clutching a sleeping Tyrone to her breast in the pre-dawn hours of Act 4, Josie speaks of a miracle: "A virgin who bears a dead child in the night, and the dawn finds her still a virgin. If that isn't a miracle, what is?" (936). The wanton woman transforms into the Madonna. Josie sacrifices her own physical desire for Tyrone as a supreme gift of love. Whereas themes of sacrifice receive rhetoric in early plays such as *Servitude*, *The Personal Equation*, *Welded*, and a mature play such as *Days Without End*, *A Moon for the Misbegotten* dramatically represents sacrifice through Josie's enduring pose of cradling Tyrone. As she accepts him into her arms at the end of the preceding act she recognizes the trade she makes for Tyrone's love: "It's easy enough, too, for I have all kinds of love for you—and maybe this is the greatest of all—because it costs so much" (927). Josie sacrifices her one chance for romantic love in exchange for giving Tyrone one night of peace. The dawn which rises is beautiful, not another gray dawn creeping over dirty windowpanes, but Tyrone first tries to cover up his response to the scene with customary cynicism: "God seems to be putting on quite a display. I like Belasco better. Rise of curtain,

Act-Four stuff" (942). Tyrone distances himself from the immediate experience by casting the sunrise in theatrical terms. He seems unaware of what transpired during the night. After imbibing an eye-opener, the flood of the night's memories rush back to him and he tries to leave quickly. Josie stops him, though, and he finally confesses that he does remember what happened and what Josie did for him: "I'm glad I remember! I'll never forget your love! [*He kisses her on the lips.*] Never! [*kissing her again*] Never, do you hear! I'll always love you, Josie. [*He kisses her again.*] Good-bye—and God bless you!" (944). Tyrone exits for the last time immediately after this farewell, certain never to return. Josie offers the final benediction of grace: "May you have your wish and die in your sleep soon, Jim, darling. May you rest forever in forgiveness and peace" (946).

The tragedy of *A Moon for the Misbegotten*, a love story, is that the two lovers cannot come together. As Josie says to her father, she didn't know that Tyrone was dead already when he came to see her. The moon provides the perfect atmosphere for romance. Josie dresses up in anticipation of the event. When Tyrone reveals, too, that he has no intention to sell the farm to anyone except the Hogans, no obstacles seem to stand between the two lovers. Sexuality, itself, becomes the final hurdle. Tyrone didn't come to meet a lover, he came to ask forgiveness from the one person who could best represent his mother's memory. The action of the play strips Josie naked and sets up an expectation, at least a hope that she will get Tyrone as a reward. The painful realization comes when Tyrone doesn't accept what Josie first offers and she has to transform herself completely from a wanting and willing lover to a forgiving mother. Josie first masquerades as a promiscuous woman, but Tyrone sees through her performance. But when she tries to give herself to him as a woman, he rebuffs her. His encounter with her in which he pretends that she's a whore is disgusting. But Josie is not a willing virgin, either. It is a part she's forced to play. The tragedy lies in the fact that she is forced to play first one role and then the other. Only at the end do the two lovers embrace in a way that reveals the depth of their sexual passion for each other. Only after eliminating the possibility for romance do they come together. The two would-be lovers finally see each other completely and honestly but the moment is fleeting. Once they face each other without masks, there is nothing left in the drama.

At the end of the play, Hogan begins a curse, but apologizes quickly to Josie in deference to her love for Tyrone: "I didn't mean it. I know whatever happened he meant no harm to you. It was life I was cursing—[*with a trace of his natural manner*] And, be God, that's a waste of breath, if it does deserve it" (945). The curse faintly echoes the curse of old Chris looking out to sea, in the wake of his daughter's marriage proposal from Burke, at the end of

"*Anna Christie.*" Hogan, the observer in the play and the matchmaker, fails to write the happy ending that he intended. Surprisingly, though, absence of a lifetime romance makes the love story more moving. The brief final contact between the two lovers conveys an enduring intensity of feeling. Josie forgives her father for all his scheming and the end of the play marks a return to the beginning. After all the masks of the characters have been removed in the course of the action, daughter and father agree to put them back on and resume their old games of friendly antagonisms. They fit comfortably back into their old roles and restore bonds between them. The performative mode in which they lead daily life once again girds the underpinnings of love, familiarity and respect which sustain their relationship. Everything is the same, but unspeakably different.

The action in *A Moon for the Misbegotten* seems to unmask character in a fairly straightforward way. The town whore is revealed as a virgin. The virgin/whore dualism that governs Tyrone's behavior prevents him from accepting all the love that Josie wants to give him. As she says to Tyrone, "I have all kinds of love for you...." The painful realization in the play is that she can only give one aspect of her love to Tyrone. Just at the point when Josie stands unmasked, naked before him, and is ready to take him as a lover, Tyrone demands that she limit her love to only one role. He can only accept her innocence and purity and love as a substitute mother, but he cannot tolerate her sexuality. The dualism of *this* or *that* simplifies an approach to character as well as a response to the world. Josie is not this or that, necessarily, but this *and* that, a crucial distinction. Unmasking is ultimately an illusion in O'Neill. It promises through time to reveal the essence of character and provide an easy answer. But in fact, the process of unmasking doesn't reveal an essence so much as show more masks, the unknown sum of which make up the range and depth of human feeling and experience. Failure to embrace the totality of identity, in oneself and in others, accounts for a tragic response to this play. In Tyrone's and Josie's final embrace, it is finally clear that he loves her passionately and wants her as a lover. Their final kisses at last simultaneously fulfill and frustrate audience expectations. But to paraphrase from *The Great God Brown*, the characters remain broken and unable to mend each other. Nevertheless, the effort that they put forth to try and heal each other, given their limitations, inspires awe and compassion and confers a state of grace upon them.

NOTES

1. Wainscott 110. Masks were not O'Neill's idea, but costumer Blanche Hays', for the Fifth Avenue chorus in scene 5 (117). Wainscott emphasizes the collaborative nature of this successful and influential production: "The work of director, designers, and actors

melded most perfectly here [scene 5] in capturing an unforgettable style which was not only emblematic but also established a stylistic staging model for American expressionism of the 1920s" (118).

2. See Wainscott 147–156. The mayor prevented children from acting in the first scene of the play, ostensibly because they were "too young"; consequently, director James Light read the scene to the audience. Most of the critical commentary focused on the racial issue.

3. The number of masks reached 300 for the initial production in Pasadena (Wainscott 221).

4. See Miller 363–364. The first production of this play was staged on April 9, 1928, by the Pasadena Community Playhouse in California, directed by Gilmor Brown. Fordham University produced the play in 1948, but both play and production received poor reviews in the New York premiere.

5. See O'Neill's letter of 1926 to Kenneth Macgowan explaining the novelty of the play (SL 204). One of the biggest obstacles in staging the play was that O'Neill could think of no actor who could play the title role (SL 207). In a letter to Benjamin De Casseres, O'Neill suggested the Russian actor Chaliapin for the role, but he didn't speak English (SL 246). In a letter to critic Barrett Clark in 1930, he thought Paul Robeson would be a good Lazarus, though he thought his race might be disconcerting (SL 365). In a letter to Lawrence Langner in 1943, O'Neill puts forward the unlikely candidacy of Spencer Tracy for the part (SL 548).

6. In a letter to Eugene O'Neill, Jr., dated November 11, 1932, O'Neill tells his son that he wrote the first draft of *Ah, Wilderness!* in one month.

7. This interview in 1948, the second in a three part series in *The New Yorker*, was the last one ever granted by O'Neill.

8. See Thomas F. Van Laan, "Singing in the Wilderness: The Dark Vision of O'Neill's Only Mature Comedy," in Bloom 99–108 for analysis of the unresolved social ills depicted in the play.

ROMULUS LINNEY

O'Neill

When I was an undergraduate at Oberlin College, from 1949 until 1953, the reputation of Eugene O'Neill, in spite of his general recognition as America's most successful playwright and his great fame abroad, was under attack. The English faculty of that distinguished college was persuaded that O'Neill's sun had finally and deservedly set. He was considered, as I remember it, an overrated practitioner of a collapsing Broadway art form, finally getting what he deserved critically. The scorn engendered by his (to them) awkward language, tough-guy posturings, lamentable tastes in almost Robert Service-type poetry, his depressing nostalgia for filthy steamers at sea and his self-destructive lifestyle, his failure to lift melodrama into higher conflict, and his constant crude preference for the elementary instead of the complex, was scorching.

As an eager student, I read the plays, took notes, and could not quite agree with my instructors ... but, alas, I pretended to. I remember this faculty with affection and admiration, but I was not so young or naive that I did not guess the source of their disdain: They were embarrassed by O'Neill. They considered him adolescent, a rube New England-style. A glib poseur whose sarcastic dramatic structure rested on bogs of sickening sentimentality. I actually remember that phrase from someone. The only professor who had a good word to say about him was the man who quietly and skillfully directed

From *The Southern Review* 38, 4 (Autumn 2002), pp. 842–848. © 2002 by *The Southern Review*.

the student plays, but the only O'Neill he did while I was there was *The Long Voyage Home*, hardly a daring foray into O'Neill waters. I played Olson the Swede in that production, felt its impact on audiences, and wondered what was sentimental about it.

I am grateful to those teachers for an otherwise first-rate education in literature, but I have since wondered why we all came down on O'Neill quite so hard, and why, as time proved, we were all so wrong. We were of course in the grip of New Criticism, that era's reverse mirror-image of postmodernism, but it was not a shrill or preposterous dogma. My mentors were good teachers, trying to be dedicated and fair as scholars, and as readers sensitive and understanding. I was an intelligent enough youngster. What was it that bothered us so much?

The flaws, as in any daring writer's work, were wildly obvious. He was not only melodramatic but sometimes downright corny. His characters did sometimes have a preference for bad poetry you can't quite believe he didn't like too, with the right whiskey. And on and on. He was often taken to task outside academia as well, by esteemed professional critics like Mary McCarthy, who wrote of *The Iceman Cometh* that its iceman-and-the-wife joke was simply vulgar, that the author was a victim of the same self-pity exhibited in his characters. Even recently, a *Times Literary Supplement* review of Elizabeth Hardwick's new biography of Herman Melville noted by the way Hardwick's comment that she could not understand why O'Neill's plays, so crudely written, could still affect her deeply. At least she could admit to being touched. We couldn't. And so on and on with the trendy trashing of O'Neill. But the plain truth was that no one else in the American theater, before or since, has matched the magnitude of his achievement, and few American writers in any genre can match his life's work. It seems to me only Henry James and William Faulkner did so very much so very well.

There were superficial reasons for the decline in his reputation. He had been commercially successful, after all, during his lifetime, as playwrights' careers go. George Jean Nathan has it he made half a million dollars from *Strange Interlude*, and maybe so; anyway, with films and worldwide productions, he did better than anyone else, eliciting no doubt further hostility, since playwrights in this country, once they make a living, never mind a killing, seem to the literary world more racetrack gamblers than writers. He was not always or even often a very pleasant man, though that smile in some photographs is winning, youthful and charming. He didn't have time to do people many favors, or make much attempt to attract the influential to his work; nor did he need to. His dramatic subjects could be grandiose to say the least: a modern Greek tragedy in Civil War dress; Marco Polo with the soul of Babbitt; Apollo and Dionysus in small-town America; Lazarus, if you please, laughing. My goodness. How adolescent, indeed.

This all changed when the José Quintero–Jason Robards *Iceman* and *Long Day's Journey into Night* appeared on our stage. At the time of *Long Day's Journey*, I was a graduate student in drama at Yale, and in New Haven we all went to see Fredric March and his wife, with the young actor named Robards, in the at-the-time "last" play of O'Neill. And here it was that my life was not just touched but scalded by Eugene O'Neill.

I had been an actor, but became a director. I was directing as my student thesis *Marco Millions*, a play the school forbade me to do because it was too complicated and royalties had to be paid. I wrote Carlotta Monterey O'Neill, then living in New York, described my admiration of her husband, my army time in Asia, and some mask and scenic devices I thought would be worthy of the play. She wrote me a charming letter saying she thought I did understand the play, would do it well, and could perform it sans royalties. She also took the trouble to write the same thing to the dean of the drama school, and that quickly settled that. While rehearsing *Marco Millions*, I was told that Alfred Lunt, who first played Marco Polo in the Theatre Guild production, was in town with Friedrich Dürrenmatt's *The Visit*; why not invite him to a rehearsal? Well, all right. At the Taft Hotel I left a Hallmark sort of card addressed to Mr. Lunt and Ms. Fontaine, and one afternoon, to my amazement, Alfred Lunt walked quietly into one of my drama-school rehearsals. He just wanted to sit there, and watch us work, so we did that for a while; then I called a break, and we got him designs and told him what we were trying to do. With that major generosity I have since often seen in major artists, he approved our young efforts and spent some memorable time with us, describing the play as the Guild did it—how the costumes Lee Simonson designed for Kublai Khan's guards were so heavy that if anyone knelt or fell he couldn't get up again, and how despite all that you must play Eugene O'Neill for what he is and let the chips fall where they may. Our production, with its many Oriental inventions by me, went well for a student work, and that was fine, but when it was over I knew something was very wrong, just didn't know what. I had by that time of course gone to see *The Visit*, and my friend Alfred. I came out stunned not only by his performance and by that of his wife, but by a work of the kind of power I had so treasured in O'Neill. *Play O'Neill for what he is*, said Lunt, *and let the chips fall where they may*. Coming out of *The Visit*, I knew what was wrong with my *Marco Millions*. I meant well, but I had not been honest. With my many inventions, I was trying to make the play look like I wrote it. As much as I loved *Marco Millions*, it was not mine. It belonged to O'Neill. He wrote it, and I didn't. I had that daunting experience of being made to face my young self, forced to it by that other look O'Neill has in photographs, the ones in which he isn't smiling.

If a live Alfred Lunt could speak to me, so could a ghostly Eugene O'Neill. I heard it all very clearly. Lunt said, "Let the chips fall where they may." O'Neill said, "Kid, stop messing with my stuff and write your own." And so I became, for better or for worse, a writer myself, and I have never been sorry how those chips have fallen. In the secrecy of my imagination, I am affectionately grateful to both.

Fredric March was wonderful in *Long Day's Journey* as the father, but when I saw him, the play was in its second week on pre–New York tryout, and he had not yet mastered his lines in the last act and had to pound the table a lot to remember them. Florence Eldridge seemed a little muted to some of us as the mother, and so did Bradford Dillman as Edmund, the personification of the young O'Neill. But Jason Robards was perfection, living proof that O'Neill's sardonic, arrested development drunks, so clumsy in their thrashing about, were, given an actor who understood them, people of measureless depth and sensitivity, ravaged and loving and raging and descended in a direct line from that tortured young man he portrayed as himself in the early sea plays.

I know O'Neill had trouble finding actors he really liked. I think Charles Gilpin in *The Emperor Jones* was one and Walter Huston in *Desire under the Elms* another. It is my loss never to have seen Gilpin, but Walter Huston had exactly that knife-edged intelligence, mature humor, and savage irony that so many miss just reading the plays. I would guess that the British actor Edward Petherbridge, playing Charlie in *Strange Interlude*, a part found impossible by most actors, would be a third. Petherbridge made Charlie not just an earnest bumbler, as it can read, but a man of Henry James depth and sensibility, with boundless love for his Nina and a great personal misery—all of which is there in the bones of the part.

In any case, no one had any doubt that Jason Robards brought to the stage, both as Hickey in *Iceman* and Jamie in *Long Day's Journey*, that combination of sarcasm and suffering of which O'Neill was the absolute master, a combination that many otherwise intelligent people could not grasp for so long, but could never forget after that performance. If plays at their greatest are love and death fused and incarnate before us, there they were, love and death in one person, in a theatrical performance I have never seen surpassed.

But there wasn't much analysis when the curtain came down in New Haven in 1958. Even the young and self-centered graduate students we were, with our ambitions and illusions, and dreams and defenses, felt the transcending power of the event. We were very quiet, and sat down to our beer with reverence.

Because the play we saw was about the man's own family. Plainly. Openly. Not disguised in any way. This was something we had never before seen attempted so baldly. He had put his father on the stage and called him a miser. He had put his mother on the stage and called her a dope fiend. He had put his brother on the stage and called him murderous. And as if this weren't enough, he had put himself on the stage as a loving, innocent, unmarried, non-alcoholic victim of the other three. Adolescent? Yes.

But he created, out of an unfair and incomplete scenario, a tragedy of the first magnitude, so filled with truth and power that there seemed nothing in our memories or our books to compare it with. Gone now the awkward language, replaced by utterances tempered, razor-sharp, and soaring. Gone the maudlin reproaches and the vague pessimism, replaced by the devastating and the inevitable. Gone melodrama and facile characterization, replaced by terrible human complications, those realities that theater at its best can, despite their tragedy, glory in, even celebrate—with that seemingly impossible combination affecting human beings unlike any other creation we possess.

I have never stopped marveling at this play, the greatest work of autobiographical art I know. I have never stopped thinking about how the playwright my good teachers disliked so much could write it.

I am not very good at suggesting categories, nor do I wish to be, since I distrust them in artistic matters. But if I can say, and feel reasonably content about it, that the great writers of the past—Homer, Sophocles, Dante, Shakespeare, Molière, Tolstoy, Chekhov, and company—generally went about their work in an objective manner, that is, by describing the world around them first, and injecting their personal experiences into it second, in disguise; and if I can say that many modern writers—Franz Kafka, Samuel Beckett, Philip Roth—found an alternative, that is, to place themselves at the center of their work, and make no bones about it; then I can also say that O'Neill in this play did both. He constructed a drama like writers of the past, giving it strength and dignity, then plunged into it like a writer of the present, giving it its raw anguish.

Someone will no doubt know better, but I can't think of any other writer who labored in fields so traditional and then crowned his life's work with a masterpiece so utterly radical. That O'Neill was aware of this I am sure, since aside from its emotional dedication, he also said of *Long Day's Journey* that it did the most with the least. Only August Strindberg, a playwright O'Neill learned from and profoundly admired, attempted anything like it, but Strindberg's autobiographical plays, novels, and memoirs are marred by mental obsessions that disappear only in realistic works like *Miss Julie* or the fantastical *Ghost Sonata*, where he can't be constantly seen as himself.

This kept him from O'Neill's achievement: the transformation of his most personal experiences into one single great work.

Who else did this so well, after writing so long in so different a manner? Chekhov? Ibsen? Shaw? The autobiographical element is there with them, as with all writers, but classically hidden within the story told. Arthur Miller? Tennessee Williams? Edward Albee? Harold Pinter? Caryl Churchill? Peter Handke? Franz Kroetz? Who, in other words, can transform a life into a work entirely of our time, a task that would seem to demand honesty at the expense of form, and yet manage to keep candor and form in a perfect harmony worthy of Shakespeare and Sophocles?

Now perhaps my curiosity about my teachers and our wrong verdicts can be reasoned out, to my satisfaction at least. What bothered us most were those early spurts of awkward, peering-out puerility in the plays, those willful and seemingly childish details O'Neill relished and would not give up. His straightforward critic and good friend George Jean Nathan said, I think rightly, that aside from their other virtues, O'Neill's plays carried you away simply because no other writer ever cared about his work with such desperation.

Nathan also wrote this: "O'Neill and Sinclair Lewis are alike in one respect. Both have naturally a boyish quality, an innocent artlessness in a number of directions, that will doubtless remain with them to their last days." These are prophetic words about O'Neill. My trusty *Webster's Second* begins its definition of *adolescence* this way: "The state or process of growing up from childhood to manhood or womanhood." Good definition, since it encompasses both state and process, suggesting that what has changed can in memory remain.

The same dictionary defines *genius* as "Extraordinary mental superiority," following this with a quote from James Russell Lowell: "Talent is that which is in a man's power; genius is that in whose power a man is."

It was evidently impossible at Oberlin College to believe a genius also adolescent. But I really did like *The Long Voyage Home* With everyone else deep in Jean-Paul Sartre and Albert Camus, it may have seemed clumsy and primitive. But I liked it. I respected it. I knew the hush it drew from its audiences, because I had stood on a stage and both heard that hush and felt the understanding that was behind it.

In those days of the frozen '50s, of the objective correlative, *explication de texte*, and the banishment of the author's life from the purity of his work, O'Neill challenged us with the stubborn remainders of adolescence in the plays, residues he perfectly well knew and treasured. He insisted on exercising a self-indulgence that we all thought a mature artist would know enough to shun.

And what is fascinating to me even now is that those embarrassing moments O'Neill insisted on preserving, the stuffing in of poems and asides and slangy remarks, the stilted quotations and half-digested pseudo-philosophy—it is at those points that I now consider him most wise, and most mature. He was keeping, in his life and work, a part of himself adolescent. Think Mozart, Mark Twain, *Ah, Wilderness*. No less an authority than Goethe pronounced the single most important element in the makeup of an artist the preservation of childhood inside maturity. O'Neill was learning his lessons, as adolescents must, but in that unique and idiosyncratic way every great artist finds, seeking the contradictory truth, looking past the technical innovations and tours de force to something else. But what?

Instead of the dour, sour creature he no doubt often was, instead of the futile parent and fierce, dangerous husband, instead of that sad man he was burdened with, he sought to find in hard work, as his father had taught him, the man he could respect and want to be. That was indeed a man still awkward, crude, posing, yes, all those youthful things, for in them lay powers I think even at the end he knew he had not yet attained and that he still ardently sought.

Just read the final scene between the two brothers, Edmund and Jamie, in *Long Day's Journey*. Just read it, aloud.

Slowly, over the long career, working out one sophisticated stage conception after another, he prepared himself to do something else. Finally, he did. He moved suddenly toward devastating autobiography. The sublimation in earlier plays of the one woman surrounded by several men, the taste of the exotic, the grandiose, and the theatrical—all resolved themselves into the harrowing reality of his own childhood and adolescence. As he wrote *The Iceman Cometh*, *Long Day's Journey into Night*, and *A Moon for the Misbegotten*, he penetrated the core of his hard life and wrote about it, briefly and intermittently at first, but finally as the great master and the great adolescent I believe he always knew he was, and wanted always to remain. In this way, unlike any other great artist I know, in his best work he found himself.

ANDREW GRAHAM-YOOLL

Eugene O'Neill in Buenos Aires

"O'Neill's time of dereliction in Buenos Aires was important to an understanding of the genius down and out on the beach, and the creative seeds that were planted in him at the time for his writing to come."
—Arthur Gelb, letter to editor of *Buenos Aires Herald*

Arthur Gelb's remark sparked my renewed interest in the life and writings of Eugene O'Neill, the man who revolutionized theater in the United States and the only U.S. playwright to win the Nobel Prize. Gelb, formerly a theater critic for the *New York Times*, and his wife co-authored the most substantial recent biography of the playwright, *O'Neill: Life with Monte Cristo* (Applause Books, 2000). This biography makes clear that Buenos Aires, capital of Argentina, played a role in the life, creative quality, and development of O'Neill as strong as the complicated relationship with his dominating actor father, James.

This story of O'Neill starts on a sidewalk in Montevideo, close to the main port of Uruguay which was built by the French in 1901, outside an old-fashioned office window that bore the name J. R. Williams. In a high display window was a sailing ship, a tall ship with ragged, sand-yellow sails, looking as if it had been hit by a southern wind. J. R. Williams, shipping agents in the River Plate countries since the nineteenth century, still have offices in

From *The Antioch Review* 60, 1 (Winter 2002), pp. 94–99. © 2002 by *The Antioch Review*.

Buenos Aires and Montevideo. It was aboard one of the ships they handled that Eugene O'Neill left Argentina in 1911.

As I stood outside the current J. R. Williams office, imagining O'Neill admiring the ship model in the old-fashioned display window of the company's earlier building, a voice asked, "What are you looking for?" The voice belonged to Andrew Cooper, a manager at the shipping agency. He listened to the story about O'Neill, then said, "My grandfather went aboard in those days. Perhaps they met."

So, with the help of the biography by Arthur and Barbara Gelb, and some recent discoveries, this is the story of Eugene O'Neill in Buenos Aires.

The sailing ship *Charles Racine* anchored in the Buenos Aires roads, which is the entrance to the channel dredged in the shallow River Plate to allow ships to sail into the port, on August 4, 1910, according to the log of Captain Gustav Waage. The arrival was confirmed in the *Buenos Aires Herald* shipping section, on Saturday, August 6: "Norwegian Barque, *Charles Racine*, 1,526 tons, from Boston, with timber. Christophersen Bros. (agents)." On the following Wednesday, the paper reported that the ship had moored in the Riachuelo, a filthy river, heavily polluted since it became the drain for the cattle slaughter companies on its banks in the late eighteenth century. The Riachuelo is the southern boundary of Buenos Aires, the federal capital of Argentina.

Eugene Gladstone O'Neill (1888–1953), a supernumerary on that sailing ship, came ashore in La Boca, on the Riachuelo, then a district shared by Italian immigrants and local cutthroats. It was O'Neill's first voyage at sea and it would remain in his memory, and in his plays, for the rest of his life. The Irish community in Buenos Aires, who are not reliable for their stories but tell them beautifully, say that the young O'Neill looked pale, stupid, and beaten.

The *Charles Racine* would inspire O'Neill to collect maritime gadgets, models, statistics, and stories. In 1946 he told an interviewer that the most beautiful thing ever built in the United States were the clipper ships.

August 10, 2001, marked ninety-one years since Eugene O'Neill arrived in Buenos Aires, where he spent an awful, drunken, derelict nine months. The journey to Buenos Aires was O'Neill's second departure from the United States in ten months. The first had been to Honduras, on a gold mining expedition. Both were attempted escapes from Kathleen Jenkins, a woman who had become pregnant in a summer courtship. As middle-class young ladies could not bear children unmarried, Kathleen and O'Neill had secretly married in New Jersey on October 2, 1909. This was shortly before O'Neill's twenty-first birthday on October 16, although he registered his age as twenty-two. O'Neill had admitted the pregnancy to his father, James, an established actor born in Kilkenny, Ireland, but had not confessed the secret marriage, which he assumed would incense his father. Eugene O'Neill, Junior, was born on May 4, 1910, when the estranged father was presumed to be in Honduras, although he was back in New York.

Confused by his marriage and paternity, O'Neill fled again. He sailed out of Boston on June 6, one month after the birth of his son. Confusion beset him in other ways: from his alcoholic mother, and from his stern and at the same time protective father, who had put sixty dollars in Eugene's pocket for his going to sea. The father, James, had become well known in the theater, ever since February 1882, when he had stepped into the role of Edmond Dantes in the play *The Count of Monte Cristo*. Acting had kept O'Neill in work and money for nearly thirty years.

Eugene O'Neill planned to find work in Buenos Aires with one of the several U.S. companies then starting up business in Argentina. A literary career was distant; his only occasional work in the United States had been acting parts imposed by his father.

Arthur and Barbara Gelb suggest that O'Neill's early interest in a seafaring life was inspired by the writings of John Masefield (largely remembered for just one poem of the sea, which has crossed the decades: "I must go down to the sea again, / The lonely sea and the sky, / And all I need is a tall ship, / And a star to guide her by ..."), and the novels of Joseph Conrad. The sea would stay with O'Neill and in his writings. For example, Edmund Tyrone, an autobiographical character in *Long Day's Journey into Night* (1941), was inspired in part by a summer holiday with his family in 1912—and also by his first job at sea and residence in Buenos Aires. Scenes and scraps in *The Iceman Cometh* (1939) also originated from his season in Buenos Aires.

O'Neill checked into the Continental Hotel (not the one that still exists by that name on the city center's Diagonal Norte, but another near the terminal of the British-owned Southern railway, Plaza Constitución), and then sought the camaraderie of the bars used by sailors on Paseo Colón, a wide avenue that combined business and brothels on the way south out of town. A bar known as the Sailor's Opera, which some older residents place near the corner of Juan de Garay street (named after the founder of the city) and Paseo Colón, was his preferred watering hole.

O'Neill wanted a short-term job to accumulate some savings, then to go to sea again, but he was qualified for no employment. An acquaintance made at the Continental, a Californian engineer, Frederick Hettman, introduced him to potential employers. Hettman was impressed by his meeting with the son of actor James O'Neill and took him to the newly opened offices of the Westinghouse Electric Company. O'Neill described himself as a draughtsman, but it was soon obvious that he had never drawn a straight line and he was put to work tracing plans. He resigned after six weeks.

Hettman was to come back into O'Neill's life later in his stay, but in the early days they lost touch when the Californian left Buenos Aires to work in one of Argentina's provinces. Hettman was recently used as the narrator of the story of O'Neill in Buenos Aires in a novel, *El largo viaje del Conde de Montecristo* (Ediciones de la Flor), by Miguel Sottolano, who won the Leopoldo Marechal book prize in 2000. O'Neill's life in Buenos Aires has also been used in fiction by Juan José Delaney, a young Irish-Argentine author and contributor to the Irish community's monthly newspaper, *The Southern Cross*.

O'Neill checked out of the Continental Hotel because he could not pay the rates, and checked into a sailors' "digs," a *pensión* off Paseo Colón. He got a job in the wool shed in the South Dock of Buenos Aires at the Chicago-based Swift Meat Packing Company, established in La Plata, thirty miles south of Buenos Aires. The shed burned down soon afterward, which saved him from having to resign. He blew what was left of his wages in bars along Paseo Colón, and especially at the Sailor's Opera. But even that series of outings came to an end as O'Neill ran out of cash.

O'Neill later described the rough side of New York as a vicar's tea party compared with the underbelly of Buenos Aires and Barracas, an industrial port-side suburb where he would go to see pornographic movies. In the Sailor's Opera he made a friend who would become the character Smitty in three of his future plays, *Bound East for Cardiff* (1914), *The Moon of the Caribbees* (1917), and *In the Zone* (1917). The morose personality in the plays was in fact the young son of an English aristocrat who was down on his luck and, at twenty-five, rapidly following the road to severe alcoholism. With what they had left of their money, they shared still cheaper rooms next to the port.

O'Neill would later recall that there was no park bench in Buenos Aires he had not slept on, but that jocular remark was mixed with the thought that his months in the city were a descent into Hell. He and his sailor friends who were ashore and out of work had the additional distress of being accosted by police, who were eager to extract bribes from or to blackmail the penniless gringos whom they threatened with arrest as vagrants. According to the Gelb biography, O'Neill begged for food and lived under lean-to shelters in the port, one of which he shared with a half-starved waif. With one acquaintance he considered staging a holdup at an exchange office, but backed out; later he admitted that he lacked the courage.

Hettman, the Californian, on his return to Buenos Aires went to one pensión on Paseo Colón and paid in advance for lodgings for O'Neill for several months. Hettman immediately went to work again up country; when he returned to the city from a visit to Córdoba, he found O'Neill had vanished. The future playwright had gone to sea again, on a cattle ship bound for Durban, South Africa. However, he was not allowed ashore there because he did not have the one hundred dollars required for landing in the British colony.

O'Neill came ashore again in Buenos Aires after at least two cattle ship tours to South Africa. A reporter and part-time poet working for the *Buenos Aires Herald*, Charles Ashleigh, found him quite broken and drunk most of the time. O'Neill was just twenty-two. However, Ashleigh enjoyed O'Neill's enthusiasm when discussing the writings of Conrad or the poetry of Keats.

O'Neill decided it was time to go home. He had contracted tuberculosis, was a hard drinker, was quite young, and had no future in Buenos Aires. On March 21, 1911, nine months after his departure from Boston, O'Neill boarded the Glasgow-registered tramp steamer *Ikala*, which had a crew of thirty British and Scandinavian seamen. The ship, represented locally by J.R. Williams and which had been looking for cargo for nearly a month moored in the port, sailed that same day. The *Ikala* was later used in another of O'Neill's plays, according to Gelb.

The *Ikala* reached New York on April 15. To avoid meeting his parents, O'Neill went straight to a "hotel" and bar known as Jimmy the Priest, demolished in 1966 to make way for the World Trade Center. That was not the end of O'Neill's seafaring. He made one last journey to Ireland, on the *New York*, to see his father's birthplace. On his return to New York, on August 26, 1911, he collected $14.84, after bar discounts. A seaman's pay was about twenty-seven dollars a month.

In 1913, Eugene O'Neill published three one-act plays (*A Wife for a Life*, *The Web*, *Thirst*). The playwright's career had begun, and it would go on to revolutionize American theater. In 1937 he was awarded the Nobel prize. Scenes from the *Charles Racine*, from life in Buenos Aires, and from the return home on the *Ikala*, would recur repeatedly in his plays—for example, in *The Long Voyage Home* (1917), *Strange Interlude* (1927), *Mourning becomes Electra* (1931), and others.

Perhaps appropriately, and in line with O'Neill's inebriation, his months in Buenos Aires are a blur. People in this city talk of the playwright who became famous, but his condition is conveniently ignored. In doing so, however, it is easy to forget just how important the sea and Buenos Aires were to the man's creative genius.

PATRICK J. CHURA

"Vital Contact":
Eugene O'Neill and the Working Class

> O'Neill entered upon the scene as one darkly handsome sailor with burning eyes and burning ambition, with undiscovered talent and unproduced plays.
>
> —Leona Rust Egan (153)

A famous photograph of Eugene O'Neill shows the playwright at the threshold of his career, gazing calmly seaward from the shore in Provincetown.[1] He is wearing the navy-blue sailor's uniform jersey that he had been given upon his promotion from ordinary seaman to able-bodied seaman on board the American Line cruise ship *Philadelphia* in 1911. O'Neill's attitude is contemplative and tranquil, his posture reposed and dignified, but his clothing suggests physical labor. He is inwardly a poet-playwright and outwardly a sailor. Well-groomed, relaxed, and pensive between sea and land, he advertises affiliation with the working class while engaged in a type of leisure that excludes him from it.

As an icon of the playwright's life and work, O'Neill's sailor's jersey has been variously interpreted, but it was certainly more than just a souvenir of his last voyage as a seaman. In nearly every interview he gave during the first decade of his career, O'Neill was careful to mention his apprenticeship as a common sailor, often adding other working-class credentials, including a stint doing "manual work for the Swift Packing people" (qtd. in Mindil

From *Twentieth Century Literature* 49, 4 (Winter 2003), pp. 520–546. © 2003 by *Twentieth Century Literature*.

4), but rarely failing to draw attention to what the jersey certified—that he "became an able seaman on the American Line ships" and spent almost all of two years at sea. More than 20 years after he had left his seafaring life, his third wife Carlotta had the moth-eaten sweater mended and presented it to him; the gift left him speechless with pleasure (Sheaffer 197). All his life, O'Neill kept the jersey.

A recent biographer interprets the significance of the jersey in somewhat conventional terms, speculating that it expressed "the first outward indication ... that Eugene might ever have the least success in the world or be self-supporting" (Black 115). On another level, however, the uniform sweater with bold white letters spelling out American Line bespoke not conventionality but its denial, symbolizing a determined if conflicted rejection of middle-class canons.

In 1916, O'Neill seems to have attempted to use his sailor's uniform to facilitate his first entry into the theater. At the age of 28, five years after his sea voyages, he donned his old American Line jersey for his arrival in Provincetown and his audition with the Provincetown Players, costuming himself as a seasoned seaman and carrying a sailor's knapsack full of plays. "Dressed slackly like a sailor who had just jumped ship" O'Neill "had come to town trampishly" (Kemp 95), apparently drawing on a somewhat remote seagoing experience to lend credibility to his current dramatic efforts. The decision to present himself as a worker to the Provincetowners was shrewd; the Players themselves wore flannel shirts to identify with the working class.

Partly because some of the original Players saw through O'Neill's staged working-class identity[2] and partly because the play he initially offered to the Provincetowners was "a very slight piece" (Ranald 506),[3] O'Neill's first tryout did not go well. At the second meeting between O'Neill and the Players, however, "something decidedly clicked" (Kemp 96). When "Bound East for Cardiff," a one-act play about the death of a common seaman in a ship's forecastle, was read for the Provincetown group, approval was unanimous. It was "the breakthrough they had hoped for" (Egan 11). Susan Glaspell's Provincetown memoir recalls that after this O'Neill reading, "Then we knew what we were for" (254). As Harry Kemp explained, "This time no one doubted that here was a genuine playwright" (96). If the fledgling theatrical company had found its dramatist, the dramatist had also discovered, apparently through trial and error, a social theme and artistic formula that would sustain his rise to prominence.

Though "Bound East" may legitimately be called an innovative play, its attempt to provide the middle class with intimate access to working-class reality was not an unusual social phenomenon or artistic theme in the 1910s. Numerous nonfictional downclassing experiments suggest a high level of historical concern with both experimentally motivated and reform-driven affiliation with the lower classes by genteel interlopers beginning around the 1880s and peaking—along with the furthermost inroads of socialism into American politics—in the decade and a half preceding World War I.[4] Mark Pittenger's study of nonfiction narratives produced by middle-class writers who "passed" as poor workers in order to investigate the underclass or experience poverty identifies 49 such texts in the Progressive era alone (55). By the 1910s, a new phrase—"vital contact"[5]—had become current among rebellious Harvard undergraduates and New York political liberals, giving a name to the frequent experimental interaction between genteel radicals and workers. Christine Stansell's recent work, *American Moderns*, observes that "vital contact" a term in general use in the pre–World War I decade, "distilled an ethos of cross-class exchange" (64). The theory was that "privileged youth ... were enervated by overeducation and overrefinement and that they could revivify themselves through contact with supposedly simpler, hardier, more spirited people" (61).

For male seekers of "vital contact" class descent ideally resulted in a restored masculine identity through the exchange of the softening conditions of privileged life for the rugged hardships of a labor environment.[6] Intertwining masculine self-renewal with themes of pastoral escape, downclassing mirrored aspects of Theodore Roosevelt's ideal of the "strenuous life" as a method of physically rebuilding overly domesticated male selfhood in the late Victorian age. William James made explicit the link between Roosevelt's masculine ideal and the downclassing of the Progressive era in *The Varieties of Religious Experience* (1902). Searching for a vibrant, creative middle ground between what he termed "military" and "saintly" asceticism, James concluded that socioeconomic self-denial was the logical answer: "May not voluntarily accepted poverty be 'the strenuous life,' without the need of crushing weaker peoples?" (367). Alluding directly to Roosevelt's behavioral standard and terminology, James argued that "poverty indeed is the strenuous life" while implicitly admonishing snobbery, cautioning against material measures of social worth, and condemning the obscene acquisition of wealth that characterized turn-of-the-century finance capitalism.

Not surprisingly, female "vital contact" differed from the male model, producing for its devotees a different kind of sociological authority. When Jane Addams founded Hull House in 1889 in one of Chicago's most impoverished wards, her example inspired educated upper-class young women in Chicago and several other northern cities to relinquish material comforts to live and work among the poor. The female paradigm of the proletarian journey in the Progressive era involved ameliorative social work, not simply passing through and embodying the lower class but reforming it—actively inculcating bourgeois moral, spiritual, and aesthetic standards among working-class subjects. Through their desire to nurture and make over the lower classes in their own image, the "old maids at Hull House" embodied a surrogate maternal function that attenuated their declarations of sexual independence and bespoke only a partial liberation from the conventions of gender.

In addition to these models of class interaction, the Paterson silk workers' strike of 1913 produced an influential theatrical display of cross-class interaction during the formative period of O'Neill's dramatic career. The Paterson strike brought Bohemian intellectuals and the working class together before 20,000 spectators on the stage of Madison Square Garden to create the spectacular Paterson Strike Pageant, an unprecedented display of possibilities for cross-class unity that is now understood by art historians as "an important incident in the history of radical self-consciousness and in the history of public art" (Nochlin 64). The Paterson Pageant—which reenacted events from the Paterson strike as a way of publicizing the violent reality of the class war and raising money for the strike fund—forged an innovative coalition between striking workers and leisure-class intellectuals, exemplified a fascinating ideal of societal revitalization, and produced an expressive, revolutionary dramatic text that is still actively being interpreted.[7] As the principal force behind the pageant, Harvard graduate and Greenwich Village radical John Reed exerted enormous influence on public perceptions of the strike in particular and the class war in general.[8]

A number of the founding members of the Provincetown Players had been involved in or present at the Paterson Pageant, ensuring that what awaited O'Neill at Provincetown in 1916 was a highly class-conscious group of politically engaged artists who were particularly receptive to the notion of dramatizing working-class experience.[9] Reed himself was probably the most dynamic member of the Players in 1916; he was the group's co-leader and author of the Players' constitution. Reed's play *Freedom* was performed in Provincetown in the same summer as O'Neill's authorial debut in "Bound East for Cardiff," which Reed acted in. In terms of personality, "O'Neill shared with Reed that drive to rub elbows with the tough lower-class elements of society" (Rosenstone 250), a drive that is as visible an influence in Reed's Paterson experience as it is in O'Neill's early life and early plays. Years later O'Neill acknowledged that it was Reed's influence that first brought him to Provincetown.[10]

While Reed was "particularly instrumental in developing the Players" (Rosenstone 248), he did so in coalition with George Cram "Jig" Cook, the Players' artistic director, who had organized the group's first season in the summer of 1915. Two years before founding the Players, Cook had sat enthralled at the Paterson Pageant, which he said had given him insight into "what the theater might be" (Glaspell 250). Reed and Cook were "the first to believe" in the Provincetown Players' idea of an experimental theater that would provide "vital drama" by portraying "the passion of the primitive group." That such language curiously resembles eye-witness descriptions of the Paterson Pageant is perhaps not coincidental. Cook had referred to the pageant as "the first labor play" and profusely praised the "feeling of oneness" with the strikers that Reed had conveyed (qtd. in Glaspell 250). Thus the artistic stances of both of O'Neill's major collaborators at Provincetown were in some way derivative of Paterson. As at least one historian of American theater has noted, "The Paterson Strike Pageant prepared the way for the Provincetown plays" (Egan 106).[11]

The pageant's artistic success was undeniable, but the assumptions upon which Reed's Paterson intervention had been predicated were infinitely more complicated. In financial terms, for example, the pageant was a fiasco that actually lost money for the strike fund; in terms of striker solidarity, the effort may have been even more harmful. Whether or not organizers like Reed fully realized it at the time, their exertions caused enormous disharmony and a loss of morale among the workers they had meant to help.[12] Though Reed himself came to embody an example of class cooperation that is still legendary in the annals of the American Left, it is likely that his personal actions were ultimately deleterious to the cause of the strikers.[13] Foremost among the problematic lessons adumbrated at Paterson was the crucial indication—clear in hindsight but apparently not to the Paterson activists— of the impracticability of political union between the laboring class and sympathetic bourgeois intellectuals. Could a middle-class radical/dramatist first seamlessly cross classes and "be" a worker, then interpret workers' lives in ways that ultimately aided them in the class struggle? What are the real effects—for both downclasser and working-class subject—of class barrier transgression?

Judging by his early career, Eugene O'Neill seems to have been extremely intrigued by these questions. In his early plays, O'Neill repeatedly explored situations that would have both troubled the pageant and complicated the thinking of the settlement movement—situations that suggested that the harsh lessons from Paterson, along with the practical limitations of the Hull House paradigm of "vital contact" were ultimately not lost on the self-proclaimed sailor-playwright. The result is that while O'Neill's actions, public persona, and public discourse explicitly accept the viability of "vital contact" as a method of both self-realization and social progress, his plays betray other, less sanguine conclusions.[14] Moreover, the relation between O'Neill's personal "vital contact" and the deeper theorization of identically situated class issues in his early drama is defined by disillusionment—disillusionment engendered by a willingness to confront the contradictions and potentially negative effects of cross-class interaction.

Joel Pfister has referred to O'Neill's role as author of the early *Glencairn* plays as that of a "tour guide" for a middle and upper class that was "fascinated by exhibits of 'exotic' workers" (109). This formula seems applicable not only to O'Neill's audition in Provincetown but also to the premier evening of "Bound East for Cardiff"—the first O'Neill work ever produced—on 28 July 1916. The atmosphere in the wharf theater, notes Susan Glaspell, recreated the feeling of a ship at sea: "There was a fog, just as the script demanded, and a fog bell in the harbor. The tide was in, and it washed under us and around, spraying through the holes in the floor, giving us the rhythm and the flavor of the sea" (254). As Glaspell indicates, "the people who had seen the plays, and the people who gave them, were adventurers together. The spectators were part of the Players." What the spectators saw was "a kind of realism and naturalism unexplored on the American stage" (Pfister 109), a new type of drama with a focus on the working-class subject as its crucial element. In the play, Kemp recalls, "we heard the actual speech of men who go to sea; we shared the reality of their lives; we felt the motion and windy, wave beaten urge of a ship" (96).

For the Provincetown group, the play confirmed that O'Neill's assumption of the outward markers of the laboring class—a class identification previously judged dubious—was not shallow or exterior but deep, visceral, and genuine enough to move middle-class audiences. While the playwright's adopted sailor's clothing was certainly part of the equation, what impressed the group about O'Neill had more to do with the illusion that this play fostered—the creation of a form of shared experience between the classes.

Several critics have viewed the play as a turning point in theater history, and the long-term collaboration between O'Neill and the Provincetown Players that began with this play as a milestone in the development of American drama.[15] The artistic merits of the work stem from its plausible treatment of tragic emotions under lower-class conditions and its accurate rendering of working-class dialect. As Pfister has noted, O'Neill's depiction of the lonely last hours of a sailor's life in the stifling forecastle "brought the lower class life and idiom to the American stage" (109). The play's setting, considered along with O'Neill's self-identification as a common seaman, suggests the correspondence between what Reed and "Jig" Cook termed "native art" (qtd. in Glaspell 252) and radical social theory.

Considering the reception of O'Neill's early subject matter among not only the Provincetown players but also the wharf theater audience, the playgoing experience as described by Glaspell indicates the ways in which O'Neill's drama satisfied the needs of a middle class seeking self-validation in the laboring class. Eric Schocket describes this process as "middle class angst cured by proletarian pain" (121), a form of which was inherent also in the Paterson Pageant. Glaspell's recollections of O'Neill's premier are curiously similar in vocabulary to famous accounts of the emotional effect of the pageant: "It is not merely figurative language to say the old wharf shook with applause.... I have never sat before a more moving production" (254). Like the Paterson Pageant, the play's catharsis would have been a joint function of its aesthetic power and its role in allowing the audience to experience a substitute form of "vital contact."

Thus O'Neill's propitious merging of sailor's garb with sailors' lives is problematic. It may indicate that, in gaining his first professional foothold in Provincetown, O'Neill presaged and intentionally accommodated his audience's desire to form lower-class affiliations. It may suggest that at this stage of his career, O'Neill genuinely accepted certain premises of "vital contact" as an ideal form of class interaction. It may mean that he did both. In any case, Glaspell's observation that "The sea has been good to Eugene O'Neill. It was there for his opening" (254) asserts the central importance of the sailor's world—the locus of the author's personal encounter with the lower classes—among O'Neill's distinguishing artistic innovations.

An equally important but rarely considered document from O'Neill's early career is the unpublished and unperformed play "The Personal Equation," one of O'Neill's first dramatic efforts, completed about the same time he wrote "Bound East," or about one year before his arrival in Provincetown. This play suggests the degree to which O'Neill, from the inception of his career, had been interested in the political meaning and psychological effects of cross-class interaction. The central character is Tom Perkins, a middle-class college dropout who has become a radical labor activist as a member of the International Workers of the Earth (IWE). Described by O'Neill as "a broken-down college boy" (9), the protagonist is in several ways a self-portrait of the young O'Neill (Floyd 90). Tom's experience in the play is similar to O'Neill's: he is the same age as O'Neill would have been in the play's 1911 setting, and he ships as a stoker on an ocean liner and witnesses preparations for a general strike in Liverpool, as O'Neill did in his first sea voyage. Like the middle-class radicals at Paterson, Tom has trouble finding a tenable position on either side of the class war. The labor activist Enwright notes that he "isn't our type" (8) and attributes Tom's motives to either his love for the beautiful fellow radical Olga or a puerile combination of "curiosity" and "craving for adventure."

When the play opens, Tom is the picture of vacillating radical commitment. Among the radicals of the IWE, as O'Neill's stage directions indicate, "His manner is one of boyishly naive enthusiasm with a certain note of defiance creeping in as if he were fighting an inward embarrassment and was determined to live it down" (8). Tom's love for Olga has led him into the inner circle of the IWE, where he is informed that the organization plans to use him in a project that will involve a risk of imprisonment or death. He nevertheless accepts the assignment as a way of proving the depth of his labor-class commitment to himself and to Olga. When he learns that the scheme involves the dynamiting of the engine room of the SS *San Francisco*, the very ship on which his father is second engineer, he still does not hesitate. The climactic moment of the play pits Tom against his father in a confrontation over control of the engine room.[16] Here Tom's father holds at bay a crowd of strikers led by his son, who is intent on smashing the ship's engines, to which the elder Perkins feels a strong attachment.[17] Perkins is thus forced to choose between his love for the engines and his love for his son. When he wounds his son in defense of the engines, he demonstrates his allegiance to capitalist industrial purposes and capitalist-defined aspirations.

The play's final scene is in a hospital weeks after the incident. A doctor explains to Perkins and Olga that the maimed Tom will probably be "like a child for the rest of his life" (69). Ironically, Perkins has received a promotion to chief engineer for the stand he took against the strikers, though he explains to Olga that he never intended to harm Tom. Meanwhile, war has broken out in Europe, and the "great radical leaders" (74) have decided to forgo the revolution in order to "crush German militarism." Though Olga calls them "blind fools" (75) and expresses her lasting faith in social revolution, she personally withdraws from the radical movement in order to become Tom's caretaker, nurse, and the mother of Tom's child, with which she is pregnant. At the play's close, the principal characters are reconciled—Tom and Olga as conventional husband and wife, and Tom and Perkins as father and son. They will all live together in the comfortable middle-class home that was to be Perkins's wedding present to Tom and Olga—the home that, as O'Neill indicates, had been "meant" (70) for them all along.

In "The Personal Equation," the final reconciliation of the three principals belies the social and political conflicts that had alienated them from each other, suggesting that the downward affiliations of radicals are only as deep as a need for personal fulfillment that is, after all, available within the parameters of a bourgeois society. Olga, for example, realizes that she loves Tom more than she does the class war and embraces the traditional social roles of mother and caretaker. Tom disguises himself as a worker and rejects the bourgeois moral code, but because of deeper commitments within his own class milieu, he is less than completely viable as a revolutionary.

A similar development and class trajectory are apparent in the history of the Paterson Pageant and John Reed, who claimed that he belonged among the workers but ultimately returned to the comforts of the leisure class. Tom's politics and the actions of Reed were motivated, at least in part, by "curiosity," "craving for adventure," and a desire to impress a woman who took the side of social revolution. Referring to Tom's radicalism, Olga remarks, "he was doing it only for me" (71). After his complex impulses have played themselves out, Tom's revolutionary activity becomes recognizable as only an approximation of his real desires and permanent commitments.

It is interesting to note that Perkins's 30-year love for his ship's capitalist-produced engines is validated by the play's denouement, while Tom's affiliation with radicals is belittled. At the end of the play, when Olga sees what the class war has done to Tom, she profusely apologizes both to him and to his father for leading him into the conflict. Considering that the crux of the division between Tom and Perkins had been one of class affiliation—as Tom argues, "you're in one world and I'm in another"—O'Neill's play ultimately affirms the superiority not only of familial ties but of innate, intrinsic class loyalties over those formed in response to the extrinsic ideological promptings of radicalism. The downclasser is physically maimed, and the ideals of labor activism are, though not fully dismissed, subordinated to what are positioned as deeper psychic promptings—romantic love and familial affiliation. This dialectic essentially describes radicalism and class-transgressing ideology as temporary and ineffectual substitutes for the genuine psychological needs of the middle class.

Not until 1922, with *The Hairy Ape*, would O'Neill develop an interpretation of cross-class relations that fully reveals the split between the personae of seaman and playwright, between the sailor-poet who both assumed and acted upon the ability to translate perception across class boundaries and the more deeply questioning artist who perceived the disabling paradoxes of downclassing expeditions. In *The Hairy Ape*, the contact between classes intended to result in mutual understanding is presented as a violent confrontation that produces only heightened suffering and alienation on both sides of the class divide. The unmistakable apex of the play's dramatic action is a harrowing cross-class encounter—the face-to-face meeting between Mildred Douglas, a self-absorbed social worker on a slumming expedition, and Yank, a powerful, hairy-chested, coal-blackened engine room stoker. The meaning of the play derives from the confusion that occurs in Yank's sense of self as a result of Mildred's intrusion into the stokehole[18]—an intrusion that epitomizes a potentially harmful social transaction basic to both reform-driven and adventure-driven "vital contact."

The play's opening scene presents life in the cramped stokehole, where "the ceiling crushes down on the men's heads" (121) and the attitudes of the stooping, proto-simian workers suggest beasts in a cage, "imprisoned by white steel." As the action begins, Yank has achieved a modus vivendi within the capitalist system, a position more fulfilling than Mildred's empty posing as a sincere social reformer. As the "most highly developed individual" in the fireman's forecastle, Yank represents to the stokehole workers "a self-expression, the very last word in what they are. "Yank is the authority among the stokers and refers to the stokehole as "home" (124). He is self-aggrandizing, arrogant, given to outbursts of rage, and he exults in his ability to cause the ship to move, giving him a form of control over his environment. As he sees it, he is a servant of the ship's engine, but the engine also responds to him: "I start somepin and the woild moves" (128). Yank has achieved what Maria Miliora refers to as "self-cohesiveness" (415), a sustaining sense of self that enables him to function within a milieu to which he has adapted both physically and emotionally. The central enabling construct of Yank's sense of well-being is a belief that he is superior to the upper classes. "We're better men dan dey are" (125), Yank asserts: "One of us guys could clean up de whole mob wit one mit.... Dem boids don't amount to nothin." While Yank's relation to his labor and to the world may exemplify what Miliora terms a "blissful grandiose fantasy" (419), he nevertheless "feels relatively cohesive ... because his self-object needs are met by his social milieu" (418).

The first assault on Yank's cohesiveness comes from Long, the socialist activist who attempts to induce Yank to embrace class consciousness by blanketing his experience in the vocabulary of the class war. Calling the stokers "Comrades" (125) who have been made "wage slaves" by "the damned Capitalist clarss," Long offers socialist terminology as a way of superficially reordering Yank's relation to his environment. But Yank rejects Long's theorization of labor as "Salvation Army–Socialist bull" that he has heard before. His response emphasizes two points. First, Long's view involves a loss of masculinity because it responds verbally rather than physically to material conditions: "Talk is cheap," Long is told, and "the job" that "takes a man" is what "belongs." Under Yank's direction, Long is called cowardly and reminded that "we don't need no one cryin' over us.... Makin' speeches" (128). Second, Long's socialism involves an unwelcome recognition of the inherent powerlessness of the laboring class—a cancellation of Yank's fantasy of cohesiveness: "Slaves, hell! We run de whole woiks" (129). Yank's contempt for Long's outlook therefore stems from its implicit denial of his superior relation to the higher-ups on the social scale. Revealingly, Long fails to influence Yank because his "talk" is insufficient to induce Yank to contemplate an interconnected relation between the upper and lower classes: "What's dem slobs in the foist cabin got to do wit us?" (125).

Later in scene 1, the Irishman Paddy attempts to awaken Yank to another essential feature of modern working-class life—alienation from contact with a natural environment as a result of technological progress. Paddy nostalgically describes the now-numbered days of sailing vessels, when "men belonged to ships ... a ship was part of the sea, and a man was part of the ship, and the sea joined all together and made it one" (126). Yank's response is to claim an identity that he admits is "new stuff" but apparently no less spiritually satisfying because he feels himself a part of the engines. Not needing the wind and the sun to which Paddy refers, Yank resolves to "eat up the coal dust" and dismisses Paddy as he does Long: "I belong and he don't" (128). Thus Yank's state of being in scene 1 allows him both to function in a manufactured security and to be a "man" to himself—an insular position, but one tenable enough to withstand assaults from within his own class.

Scene 2 introduces and describes Mildred Douglas, a "bored" do-gooder who has been playing at social work, experiencing the "morbid thrills of social service" (131) on New York's Lower East Side, and who is attempting to use her influence as the daughter of a steel magnate to arrange a tour of the ship's stokehole in order to "see how the other half lives." Mildred is now on her way to England on a journey her aunt refers to as a "slumming international." Like Yank, she is outwardly arrogant about the position—a credentialed worker for social reform—that she has achieved within her own milieu, but her "superiority" (130) is "discontented" and "disdainful" even toward her formidable aunt.

The conversation between the two women on the promenade deck suggests a strongly cynical view of Mildred and indirectly of the motives of the female settlement workers who were conspicuous in the play's early-twentieth-century setting. Effectively foreshadowing the transaction between Mildred and Yank, the aunt states, "How they must have hated you, by the way, the poor that you made so much poorer in their eyes" (131). Conflict thus derives from the aunt's perception that the type of social work practiced by Mildred is actually a form of predation on the lower classes. Despite Mildred's claims of sincerity, her aunt scornfully refers to her as "artificial" (130) in her social concern and a "poser" in her expressed desire to find a "new thrill" and "touch life" by visiting the stokehole. Described by O'Neill in relation to the natural environment of the sea, Mildred is "incongruous ... inert and disharmonious." As the stage directions indicate, Mildred's possibilities for sincerity and empathy have been "bred out of her" by an effete class with neither vitality nor integrity—a class whose ostensibly ameliorative efforts only further degrade the poor.

The crucial moment of the play is the brief but intense scene 3 confrontation in the stokehole between Mildred and Yank. During this encounter, O'Neill's stage directions indicate that Yank "feels himself insulted in some unknown fashion in the very heart of his pride" (137). In general terms, the effect on Yank is twofold: it "makes him painfully aware of his social inferiority and suddenly conscious of his inadequacies as a human being" (Floyd 241). In attempting to fathom particulars about the manner in which Yank is victimized by Mildred, we ascertain essentials about the class relationship as O'Neill pictured it at the peak of his creative association with the Provincetown Players.

As the numerous disdainful allusions to Mildred as a "skoit" (for example 142) confirm, issues of both class and gender are at the core of the encounter. The ship's engine that gives Yank his identity, and which Yank is in the process of servicing as Mildred intrudes, is not only figured as unequivocally feminine, but "she" is also the focus of tumultuous activity that bears strong connotations of a frenzied sexual act—a fact insistently indicated by Yank's repeated exhortations to "pile some grub in her ... open her up! ... trow it into her belly! ... let her have it! ... sling it into her!" (135). For her part, Mildred seeks contact with the lower classes not simply in order to enhance her social service credentials but as a response to psychological deficiencies including sublimated sexual desires. She enters the stokehole because she "would like to be sincere, to touch life somewhere" (131). When the anemic, pale, "slender, delicate" (130) Mildred appears dressed in white, she seems an attenuated feminine entity, one whose vitality has been "sapped before she was conceived." She lacks sexual energy of the kind that flows naturally from Yank and permeates his every movement. In the stokehole, Yank's "naked and shameless" (137) masculinity is appalling to Mildred. Having been interrupted in his furious and sexually charged stoking of the engine, Yank turns a gaze upon Mildred that is physically menacing and suggestive of sexual penetration. At the moment of their interaction, "he glares into her eyes, turned to stone ... his eyes bore into her." As O'Neill indicates, her "whole personality" is "crushed" in the stokehole. That the symbolic rape Yank enacts destroys both him and her— that their victimization is mutual—is a figurative indication of the depth of effect and potential trauma that, as O'Neill undoubtedly realized, could be comprehended by the cross-class transaction, an exchange that could not but reproduce several types of psychic and social power disparities—for which rape is an apt metaphor.

This relation is further emphasized by the surrounding group of workers, who witness the Yank–Mildred encounter and sense a deep emotional parley between them. Paddy taunts Yank with having "fallen in love" with Mildred. Yank retorts, "Love, Hell! Hate, dat's what. I've fallen in hate, get me?" Paddy's remark that "Twould take a wise man to tell one from the other" elucidates the potentially destructive, ambivalent relationship at the center of cross-class contact.

Concerning this bipolar class relation, Robert J. Andreach theorizes that Yank feels love for Mildred because she has "descended into his world to awaken him. As he awakens his love changes to hatred because she rejects him" (53). By her very presence, Mildred awakens Yank to the purposelessness of labor-class life without offering the real chance of anything higher. After the encounter, as Andreach points out, Yank's fury "changes from that of a spurned lover to that of a betrayed questor." His quest is a search for identity prompted by the complex awakening or awareness aroused by Mildred. Yank is bewildered since he cannot understand what motivates Mildred, what she seeks in the stokehole, and why she would awaken him to a reality higher than himself: "I don't get her. She's new to me. What does a skoit like her mean, huh?" (142). Yank cannot know that in seeking "reality," Mildred is driven by the same need for cohesiveness that compels him. The "reality" she seeks through a downclassing foray eludes her, and she is instead deeply harmed by her awareness of Yank. That relations between laborer and downclasser are inevitably destructive underscores the ways that downclassing forays are not exempt from the identical power relations that create class disparity in the first place.

While Mildred's intrusion into the stokehole stages the disabling paradox of "vital contact" it is not the only example of psychologically disruptive cross-class contact in the drama. The play may be viewed as a series of calculated trespassings of class boundaries, punctuated with dramatic situations that are recognizable as paradigms of social conflict in the era in which O'Neill wrote. Scene 5 finds Yank and Long on New York's Fifth Avenue, where "the adornments of extreme wealth are tantalizingly displayed" (144) and Yank and Long are "trespassers." In contrast to his surroundings, which he describes as "too clean and quiet and dolled up" (145), Yank is covered in coal dust, unshaven, dressed as a stoker in "dirty dungarees" (144) and a fireman's cap. Yank admits that he seeks another encounter with Mildred's "kind" (145) in order to "get even with her." Throughout the scene, Long again tries to indoctrinate Yank to socialist political ideals and vocabulary, which are summarily rejected by Yank: "Votes for women ... Force, dat's me!" (147). Though there is cross-class juxtaposition here as in scene 2, there is no interaction between Yank and the rich because the barrier transgression is not downward but upward. The change in setting—out of the stokehole and onto Fifth Avenue—enables the upper-class "gaudy marionettes" (147) to remain oblivious to Yank's presence. Even direct physical contact between Yank and a "fat gentleman" (149) is "as if nothing has happened."

Scene 7 is located at a chapter of the Industrial Workers of the World near the city's waterfront. Yank seeks membership, asking "Can't youse see I belong?" Yank's interaction here is not with another worker but with a radical intellectual whose politics come from the IWW manifesto. For the real worker this is another upward class encounter, and the contrast in spoken dialect and social philosophy between Yank and the secretary is nearly as pronounced as that encountered on Fifth Avenue. In an exchange that underscores a basic lack of understanding of the worker among the intellectual class, Yank's desire to "fix tings" (158) through violence and sabotage is viewed as a "wrong slant" by the IWW secretary. Yank is, however, only taking literally the espoused IWW determination "to change the unequal conditions of society by legitimate direct action" and seeking a concrete solution in order to "square tings" with Mildred. The IWW official reacts bureaucratically and intellectually to Yank's subjective anarchism and to his expectation of anti-industrial action, wrongly concluding that Yank is an "agent provocator" (159). If the Fifth Avenue capitalists fail to see Yank at all, the IWW secretary fails to see Yank for what he is.

The play's final scene portrays an encounter between Yank and a caged gorilla in "the monkey house of the Zoo" (160). Whereas Mildred's downward intrusion into Yank's realm had destroyed Yank's self-concept and "crushed" the "personality" of the slumming reformer, "Yank's intrusion into the world in which the gorilla is king also brings about his physical destruction" (Ranald 281). The affinity between the two scenes is explicit: looking at the gorilla, Yank remarks, "I was you to her" (161). Significantly, it is only in the play's downclassing interactions and class barrier transgressions that real psychological action and interaction are precipitated. Yank's entrance into the gorilla's cage, like Mildred's descent into Yank's stokehole, underscores the intruder's failure to countenance the true condition of the "primitive" and alleges the production of injurious rage and confusion within the intrusion's subject. Arguably, this is the central problem of the play, and it is the problem of all class-crossing efforts as O'Neill has come to understand them throughout his early drama and up to The Hairy Ape, the play that marks his last productive association with the Provincetown group under Jig Cook's leadership and the culmination of O'Neill's early career.

Placed within its historical context, The Hairy Ape may be understood as O'Neill's drastic reevaluation of both his adventurous personal downclassing ethos and of the reform-driven "vital contact" endemic to the play's 1910s setting. Throughout the play, Yank experiences "the disorienting affects of the rapidly shifting social environment of early twentieth century America" (Miliora 416), among which both "progressive" social ideology and "drastic distinctions in social class" are crucial. This ideology is exemplified by Mildred Douglas, the settlement worker with "social service credentials." Mildred stands for an army of middle- and upper-class women who worked in settlement houses and strived for social progress through philanthropic contact with lower-class life. In *The Hairy Ape*, the socialist Long refers to this multitude when he warns, "There's a 'ole mob of 'em like her, Gawd blind 'em."

In interviews throughout his early career, O'Neill had often relied on "progressive" suppositions to express the purpose of his art, and in doing so he had voiced a social theory quite similar to that which motivates Mildred Douglas to visit the stokehole (see for example Bird). But as O'Neill meticulously explores the class paradoxes of the early twentieth century in *The Hairy Ape*, he seriously questions the basic precepts of "social progress" that underlie the historical setting of the drama. In *The Hairy Ape*, ostensibly progressive social forces become agents of a harmful assault on lower-class selfhood. Primarily through Yank and Mildred's interaction in scene 3, *The Hairy Ape* thus gives us an "ironic disfiguration" of the concept of progress, "dramatizing not a pattern of progression but of regression" (Zapf 36). Yank the worker becomes "a mere object of the historical process, being imprisoned in the very structures which were originally intended to serve him" and, we must add, being alienated and destroyed by the process of cross-class "understanding" personified by Mildred in the stokehole.

In ways that illuminate *The Hairy Ape*, cultural historian T.J. Jackson Lears has analyzed the central goals of the settlement movement, and of the downwardly focused social service efforts of which Mildred is a representative. Lears describes the ways in which the movement founded by Jane Addams, with its attempts to create a "fuller life" for factory workers, "paralleled the longings of her own class for more intense experience and was in a way a projection of those longings" (80). As Lears notes, "The recoil from overcivilized gentility pervaded the ethos of reform at the turn of the century. Determined to revitalize their own lives, reformers became convinced they could revitalize working-class lives as well." As this happened, the focus of efforts to share experience with lower classes "began to shift from social justice to personal fulfillment."

Lears identifies this shift as "a key moment in the re-formation of capitalist cultural hegemony" (80), and it is a shift that O'Neill dissects in *The Hairy Ape* with painstaking precision. If, as Lears asserts, Addams and her followers "began unwittingly to accommodate themselves to the corporate system of organized capitalism" resulting in an attitude of "unctuous paternalism" an exaggerated version of such an attitude is reflected in Mildred. Her manipulation of capitalist power relations by drawing on her status as a millionaire in order to acquire access to the stokehole epitomizes what Lears refers to as a "compromise with modern industrial capitalism at … key points" (81). For this analysis, the most relevant of these compromises is that of treating voluntary forays into lower-class conditions as "a source of therapeutic revitalization," as Mildred does in pursuing her desire to "touch life somewhere." Under O'Neill's control, such therapeutic interaction is transformed into a crushing defeat for Mildred's ethic of social progress.

In *The Hairy Ape*, O'Neill suggests the stark alienation of lower-class existence and views this alienation not as mitigated but as exacerbated by upper-class intrusions. At the Hull House Labor Museum, as Lears notes, workers learned the historical and industrial significance of their jobs—a process that may ultimately have played a role in legitimizing their exploitation. From Mildred, who creates an awareness in Yank of what he actually does in the ship and who he actually is, Yank gains a similarly ambivalent self-knowledge. The identical ambivalence of effect, which seems persistently to attend both real and fictional representations of class-crossing in the period, including that of the Paterson Pageant—which "exhibited" starving and destitute workers on the stage of an opulent capitalist pleasure palace while causing irreparable harm to the strike itself—is by O'Neill both concretized and corrected in *The Hairy Ape*. What is striking and innovative about O'Neill's method of interaction between classes is not simply that it portrays an impossibility of synthesis between workers and downclassers but that "vital contact" becomes a pernicious and malignant force, incompatible with the workers' subjective needs.

By the time O'Neill began writing *Long Day's Journey into Night* in 1939, he seems to have understood not only the ineluctable harm of cross-class interventions like Mildred's but also a potentially injurious oversimplification underlying his own youthful and adventure-driven "vital contact." In acts 3 and 4 of this play, Edmund Tyrone clearly espouses the social theories of the young Eugene O'Neill, while Edmund's father James Tyrone just as persuasively expresses the social conclusions reached by the mature playwright.[19] Reading Edmund this way suggests that the Eugene O'Neill of the early 1910s had imbibed a spirit of class antagonism that colored his perceptions of class interaction in idealistic shades. Like O'Neill in 1912, Edmund has recently returned from a slumming adventure at sea where he has damaged his health while apparently forming a rudimentary socialist class consciousness. In act 4 of *Long Day's Journey*, Edmund extols the socially productive effects of his "vital contact," claiming that it has enabled him to relate more sympathetically to his father:

> God, Papa, ever since I went to sea and was on my own, and found out what hard work and little pay was, and what it felt like to be broke, and starve, and camp on park benches because I had no place to sleep, I've tried to be fair to you because I knew what you'd been up against as a kid. (109)

Tyrone realizes, however, that his own childhood had been essentially different from Edmund's adventures—"There was no damned romance in our poverty"—and asserts there is no way Edmund can understand its actual consequences:

> You said you realized what I'd been up against as a boy. The hell you do! ... You've had food, clothing. Oh, I know you had a fling of hard work with your back and hands, a bit of being homeless and penniless in a foreign land.... But it was a game.... It was play. (110)

Although Edmund expresses nostalgia for his self-imposed ordeal and pride in its effects, Tyrone views Edmund's temporary downclassing as "a game of romance and adventure" (146–47). Tyrone's childhood in authentic poverty enables him to discern the pretense of his son's voluntary privation. Edmund's brother Jamie also offers a perceptive appraisal when he remarks that although Edmund has "had the guts to go off on his own" (35), he "always came home broke finally," presumably to live off his father. Edmund's crude theorization of "vital contact"—reflective of a period when O'Neill's class views were at an embryonic stage—is thus framed with ironic rejoinders.

But Edmund's contempt for the values of his own class and his compulsion to share experience with the working class are as central to *Long Day's Journey* as they are to O'Neill's early art. The two key crises of the drama—Mary's relapse into morphine addiction and the diagnosis of Edmund's consumption—are the direct results of Edmund's downclassing adventure. The drama unfolds on the very day he and the other Tyrones learn the physical price of the young man's slumming excursion before the mast, the "stunt" of "working his way all over the maps as a sailor ... living in filthy dives, drinking rotgut" (35). Edmund's "ruined health" (33) is attributed by Tyrone to the "mad life" he has led "ever since he was fired from college"—a life centered around formative downclassing experiences. As in *The Hairy Ape*, the consequences of the downclassing excursion are utterly negative. That they are the result not of reform-oriented female "vital contact" but its adventure-driven male counterpart supports Alexander's assertion that with this play O'Neill "renounced the ideas of his years of revolt" (*Tempering* 61), a process that involved a severe questioning of his own and his generation's downclassing impulse.

O'Neill often claimed that his "real start as a dramatist" came when he "got out of an academy and among men, on the sea" (qtd. in Downes 10). This seems credible, for without his sailor's jersey and sailor's plays it is unlikely that he would have realized the important professional acceptance and encouragement of like-minded experimentalists in Provincetown. The Provincetowners "embraced O'Neill, encouraged him, and helped him to crystallize and articulate his philosophy" (Gelb 315). Temporally and ideologically, it is not far to Provincetown from the Paterson Pageant, and so another conjecture supported by this analysis involves the intriguing centrality of John Reed's Paterson Pageant as an artistic influence. Cosgrove has noted that the "association of worker and intellectual" (265) first formed at Paterson "became traditional and a crucial influence on Workers Theatre in America. "This influence has been underestimated, undeniably extending into the canonical drama of Eugene O'Neill and the beginnings of American theater at Provincetown, justifying the recognition of the pageant as a meaningful event in American literary history.

It is to O'Neill's credit that his drama bespeaks a growing internalization of the lessons of Paterson, and that after his acceptance at Provincetown he went on to question the very class philosophy that facilitated that acceptance. While it may be true, as Pfister has asserted, that O'Neill's representation of the working class "tells us less about the actual working class ... than about what O'Neill wanted this class to signify for him" (114), there is a qualitative difference between the act of escorting a middle-class audience into the forecastle to experience the pathos of a common seaman's death in "Bound East for Cardiff" and escorting an audience into the stokehole for the harrowing encounter between Mildred Douglas and the "hairy ape."

Looking at the development of O'Neill's early plays through *The Hairy Ape* makes it easier to understand why Edmund's father James Tyrone gets the condemnatory last word on his son's slumming adventures in *Long Day's Journey*. Tyrone's persuasiveness does not simply indicate a change in O'Neill's attitude toward "vital contact" or an acknowledgment of the impermeable nature of class barriers. It is also a ringing recognition that the "game of romance and adventure" involves consequences more harmful even than Edmund's tuberculosis, on both sides of the class divide.

Notes

1. Lendley Black has dated the photograph from 1911, before O'Neill arrived in Provincetown (n. pag.). Joel Pfister, however, locates the photo in Provincetown and offers the "late 1910s" as its date (9). The exact location of the photo is not crucial, but its emphatic indication of O'Neill's bifurcated class identification is central to my essay.

2. Harry Kemp recalls that the Players easily identified O'Neill as middle class. Though O'Neill "had been a sailor, it was said" (96), the Players were at first "dubious of their new member's ability and doubtful of his future worth to them" (95). When O'Neill showed the group a book of one-act plays but also acknowledged that he had paid for them himself, this "did not materially forward his case." Kemp claims that while O'Neill may have looked like a vagabond worker, the group was aware that he was actually still

supported by his father, who sent him a small allowance, "enough to keep him under shelter and alive" (97).

3. The first play O'Neill offered to the Provincetown group was called "The Movie Man," a one-act play about an American filmmaker who finances a Mexican revolution for the sake of filming its battles. Kemp remembers the play as "frightfully bad, trite and full of preposterous hokum" (96). See also Margaret Loftus Ranald 506.

4. From 1888 to 1894, Nellie Bly disguised herself as an unskilled worker and made well-publicized forays into sweatshops and factories, inspiring numerous imitators. In the mid-1890s, Stephen Crane made celebrated incognito excursions into the New York slums, producing numerous "city sketches" including "An Experiment in Misery," which detailed the temporary transformation of a middle-class youth into a "bum" or "hobo" of the Bowery. In 1899, Josiah Flynt published *Tramping with Tramps*, a collection of studies and sketches of "vagabond life" in Russia, Western Europe, and the United States. Hutchins Hapgood, a Harvard graduate and *Globe* reporter, made frequent forays into the lower and "criminal" classes, publishing *The Spirit of the Ghetto* in 1902 and *Autobiography of a Thief* in 1903. Also in 1903, Jack London contributed *The People of the Abyss* to the crowded field of "down-and-outer" chronicles.

5. Harvard student and radical socialist Lee Simonson is widely believed to have coined the term in 1908, but its repeated use in print by Princeton sociology professor Walter Wyckoff in an 1896 nonfiction narrative entitled *The Workers: An Experiment in Reality* contradicts this notion. Wyckoff explained the motivation for disguising himself as a laborer and voluntarily descending into lower class life: "Poverty, I had thought, would at once bring me into vital contact with the very poor" (1:16). Historian Robert A. Rosenstone attributes the coinage of the term to Simonson, as does Christine Stansell: "The phrase originated with the Harvard dissident Lee Simonson" (Stansell 355). Both scholars locate the term's origin in an article in the January 1908 Harvard *Advocate*, in which Simonson "excoriated both students and faculty for their indifference to the problems racking the modern world and the vital forces striving to change it" (Rosenstone 43). Actually Simonson used the term only once in the article, to refer to the need to introduce innovative plays into the university's dramatic repertory, thus bringing the school "into vital contact with all that is significant in modern drama. "John Reed gave the phrase a wider significance, if only by directly quoting Simonson, in his unpublished 1912 essay "Harvard Renaissance." Reed applied the term as part of a broad political discussion that called for a more relevant curriculum that would include courses in socialism and bring the school into "vital contact" with the class struggle.

6. While not referring to "vital contact" by name, James A. Robinson notes that when O'Neill "repudiated ... the values of the middle-class lifestyle his parents strove to maintain ... he unwittingly followed a late nineteenth-century paradigm of masculine behavior" (96).

7. IWW leader Elizabeth Gurley Flynn described the pageant as "the most beautiful and realistic example of art that has been put on stage in the last half century" (215). Nochlin calls the pageant "a major event in the history of radical theater ... stunningly effective as drama, spectacle and political propaganda" (67). More recently, Louis Sheaffer has suggested that the "mammoth pageant" was "perhaps the most stirring event ever staged in the Garden" (435). Stuart Cosgrove cites the 7 June 1913 date of the Paterson Pageant as "the first significant date in the history of twentieth century American Workers Theatre" (265). Christine Stansell observes that the pageant epitomized "an attraction to modern, 'revolutionary' and 'political' art" that "would henceforth run through American culture, leading enlightened audiences and artists to advertise their solidarities with 'the people'" (150).

8. Reed has been called the "Byronic hero" (Kazin 216) of pre–World War I radicalism. From his participation at Paterson in 1913 until his death in Moscow in 1920, Reed "sincerely desired an imaginative intimacy with workers and peasants ... a passionate identification with the oppressed" (Leach 33). As Walter Bates Rideout argues, Reed was "the prototype of the adventurous young American intellectual who refused to be simply a vagabond, who gave up all his middle-class advantages for solidarity with the working class, who even sacrificed his life to the Revolution" (127). Praising Reed's actions in labor conflicts at Paterson and Ludlow and in later political revolutions in Mexico and Moscow, leftist leader Michael Gold had reverently proclaimed that "there was no gap between Jack Reed and the workers any longer" (154). Among the Paterson images that Upton Sinclair vowed "would never pass from [his] memory" (263) was that of John Reed as pageant director, "with his shirt sleeves rolled up, shouting through a megaphone, drilling those who were to serve as captains of the mass."

9. Along with Reed and George Cram "Jig" Cook, this list includes Robert Edmund Jones, who designed the sets for the Paterson Pageant and several of O'Neill's Provincetown plays, including *The Hairy Ape*. Mary Heaton Vorse, Susan Glaspell, Mabel Dodge, Floyd Dell, Max Eastman, Ida Rauh, Hutchins Hapgood, and Harry Kemp were also present at Paterson and involved in Provincetown.

10. The most detailed account of the friendship between Reed and O'Neill, which began in Greenwich Village in 1914, is provided by Arthur and Barbara Gelb. The Gelbs speculate that O'Neill may actually have accompanied Reed to Mexico in 1914 while Reed was reporting about the Mexican Revolution for the Metropolitan, concluding, "Whether, in fact, O'Neill ever got to Mexico ... is a riddle" (263). In any case, Reed and O'Neill admired each other from their first meeting in 1914: "Reed was enchanted with [O'Neill's] stories of his wild youth, his adventures at sea, and his moody charm. O'Neill was equally taken with Reed" (262).

11. This is not to suggest that O'Neill had witnessed or shared directly in the Paterson Pageant. When the pageant took place on 7 June 1913, O'Neill had yet to write a play and had been discharged only four days earlier from the Gaylord Farm Sanatorium in Wallingford, Connecticut, where he had spent five months under treatment for tuberculosis.

12. As several historians have asserted, "the publicity gained from the pageant was purchased at the cost of the workers' unity" (Tripp 156). Elizabeth Gurley Flynn claimed that jealousies over roles in the pageant created "much discord ... in the ranks" (217) and that the pageant diverted attention from more important work of the strike: "The first scabs got into the Paterson mills while workers were training for the pageant."

13. As well-intentioned as his temporary intervention in the Paterson strike may have been, there were several ways that John Reed's actions may have hurt the cause of the Paterson strike. First, the disappointment that followed when it was revealed that the pageant had lost money, all historical accounts agree, was disastrous to striker solidarity. Second, almost immediately after the pageant, as the strike apparatus began to crumble, Reed and millionaire Fifth Avenue salon hostess Mabel Dodge left New York on a luxurious first-class passage for Europe, apparently without telling the strikers, who had come to appreciate Reed's uplifting cheerleading. Reed's departure at the moment when it became clear that the pageant had been a financial failure had an "immense psychological impact" (Rosenstone 124) in deepening the strikers' disillusionment.

14. Asked about the protracted working-class focus of his drama in a 1924 *Theatre Magazine* interview, O'Neill acknowledged that he wrote often about the lower classes, about what he referred to as "our brothers far down on the social scale" (Bird 53). In

explaining his rationale for doing so, however, the playwright expressed himself in starkly contradictory terms. In the first part of the interview, O'Neill stresses a "wish to arouse compassion" in his drama to create sympathy for "the unfortunate. The suffering." If after viewing the drama his audience is "inspired to help those unhappy brothers," O'Neill explains, the "tragic play is worthwhile."

Later in the same interview, O'Neill's description of the working class changes drastically, stressing not the suffering endured by exploited laborers but their guilelessness and freedom from social pretense: "They have not been steeped in the evasions and superficialities which come with social life and intercourse.... They are more direct. In action and utterance" (52). His characters lack a voice—"in many ways they are inarticulate ... they cannot write of their own problems," O'Neill explains—and so the playwright must be their spokesman: "I like to interpret for them."

A third perspective on the working class appears in the interview as O'Neill waxes nostalgic for his days as a seaman, the time when he was "one of" the workers: "Life on the sea is ideal. The ship for a home. Meals provided. A resting place" (53). Only for a class interloper like O'Neill, however, could the ship be so described—as a site of respite and disengagement, an escape from bourgeois artificiality, a place that comprised "no economic pressure." If O'Neill had discerned an inconsistency between his views of the working class as embodying this "ideal" and his first-hand experience of the "tragic" conditions of working class life—between a desire to "help" the working classes and a view of their lives as free of economic pressures—he does not so indicate in the interview. Yet nothing, it seems, could be more paralyzing to the impulse for social reform with which O'Neill begins his discussion of the laboring class than the attitude, expressed later in the interview, that there is a kind of freedom and manly virtue in enduring poor food and low pay. As I will argue, it was left to O'Neill's drama to confront these theoretical contradictions.

15. Maya Koreneva asserts that the performance of "Bound East for Cardiff" on 28 July 1916 "may be regarded literally as the birth of American drama" (148).

16. As Floyd notes (97), Olga's appearance with Tom among the stokers in "The Personal Equation" foreshadows scene 3 of *The Hairy Ape*—the stokehole visit of the female reformer Mildred Douglas.

17. The elder Perkins's commitment to his engines—"I love those engines—all engines" (27)—is described so as to resemble the central psychological device used by Yank in *The Hairy Ape* to justify his position in the stokehole. Asked if he sees himself as a "flesh and blood wheel of the engines" Yank replies, "Dat's me" (127). Yank's fully developed metaphor, "I'm steel" (129) suggests the origin of such "environmental" identifications in the primal psychic needs of the working class.

18. Mildred's intrusion causes a profound alteration in what clinical psychologist Maria Miliora, in a discussion of the play, refers to as the "self-object milieu" (415) of the working-class inhabitant.

19. Undertaking an analysis of the autobiographical sources of O'Neill's class views, Pfister also concludes that in *Long Day's Journey* "O'Neill can be read as both Edmund ... and as Tyrone" (106).

WORKS CITED

Alexander, Doris. "O'Neill as Social Critic." *O'Neill and His Plays*. Ed. Oscar Cargill, N. Bryllion Fagin, and William J. Fisher. New York: New York UP, 1961. 390–407.

———. *The Tempering of Eugene O'Neill*. New York: Harcourt, 1962.

Andreach, Robert J. "O'Neill's Use of Dante in *The Fountain* and *The Hairy Ape*." *Modern Drama* 10.1 (1968): 48–56.

Bird, Carol. "Eugene O'Neill—The Inner Man." Estrin 50–55.

Black, Lendley. *Eugene O'Neill: Beyond Mourning and Tragedy*. New Haven: Yale UP, 1999.

Cosgrove, Stuart. "From Shock Troupe to Group Theatre." *Theatres of the Left 1880–1935*. Ed. Raphael Samuel, Ewan MacColl, and Stuart Cosgrove. London: Routledge, 1985. 259–79.

Downes, Olin. "Playwright Finds His Inspiration on Lonely Sand Dunes by the Sea." Estrin 6–12.

Egan, Leona Rust. *Provincetown as a Stage*. Orleans, MA: Parnassus, 1994.

Estrin, Mark W., ed. *Conversations with Eugene O'Neill*. Jackson: U of Mississippi P, 1990.

Floyd, Virginia. *The Plays of Eugene O'Neill: A New Assessment*. New York: Ungar, 1985.

Flynn, Elizabeth Gurley. "The Truth about the Paterson Pageant." *I Speak My Own Peace*. New York: Masses and Mainstream, 1955.

Gelb, Barbara, and Arthur Gelb. *O'Neill*. New York: Harper, 1974.

Glaspell, Susan. *The Road to the Temple*. New York: Stokes, 1941.

Gold, Michael. "John Reed and the Real Thing." *Mike Gold: A Literary Anthology*. Ed. Michael Folsom. New York: International, 1972. 152–56.

James, William. *The Varieties of Religious Experience*. 1902. Cambridge: Harvard UP, 1985.

Kazin, Alfred. *On Native Grounds*. New York: Harcourt, 1942.

Kemp, Harry. "Out of Provincetown: A Memoir of Eugene O'Neill." Estrin. 95–102.

Koreneva, Maya. "One Hundred Percent American Tragedy: A Soviet View." *Eugene O'Neill: A World View*. Ed. Virginia Floyd. New York: Ungar, 1979. 145–71.

Leach, Eugene. "The Radicals of The Masses." *1915: The Cultural Moment*. Ed. Adele Heller and Lois Rudnick. New Brunswick: Rutgers UP, 1991. 27–47.

Lears, T.J. Jackson. *No Place of Grace: Antimodernism and the Transformation of American Culture 1880–1920*. New York: Pantheon, 1981.

London, Jack. *The People of the Abyss*. New York: Macmillan, 1903.

Miliora, Maria. "A Self Psychological Study of Dehumanization in Eugene O'Neill's *The Hairy Ape*." *Clinical Social Work Journal* 24.4 (1996): 415–27.

Mindil, Philip. "Behind the Scenes." Estrin 3–5.

Nochlin, Linda. "The Paterson Strike Pageant of 1913." *Art in America* 62 (May 1974): 64–68.

O'Neill, Eugene. "Bound East for Cardiff." *The Provincetown Plays*. 1st series. New York: Shay, 1916. 5–25.

———. *The Hairy Ape*. *The Complete Plays*. Vol. 2. New York: Library of America, 1988. 119–65.

———. *A Long Day's Journey into Night*. New Haven: Yale UP, 1956.

———. "The Personal Equation." *The Unknown O'Neill*. Ed. Travis Bogard. New Haven: Yale UP, 1988. 3–75.

Pfister, Joel. *Staging Depth: Eugene O'Neill and the Politics of Psychological Discourse*. Chapel Hill: U of North Carolina P, 1995.

Pittenger, Mark. "A World of Difference: Constructing the 'Underclass' in Progressive America." *American Quarterly* 49.1 (1997): 26–65.

Ranald, Margaret Loftus. *The Eugene O'Neill Companion*. Westport: Greenwood, 1984.

Reed, John. "Harvard Renaissance." 1912. Unpublished essay. John Reed Papers, Houghton Library, Harvard University.

Rideout, Walter Bates. *The Radical Novel in the United States, 1900–1954: Some Interrelations of Literature and Society*. Cambridge: Harvard UP, 1956.

Robinson, James A. "The Masculine Primitive and *The Hairy Ape*." *Eugene O'Neill Review* 19.1–2 (1995): 95–109.

Roosevelt, Theodore. "The Strenuous Life." *The Strenuous Life*. New York: Macmillan, 1902.

Rosenstone, Robert A. *Romantic Revolutionary: A Biography of John Reed*. New York: Random, 1981.

Schocket, Eric. "Undercover Explorations of the 'Other Half,' Or the Writer as Class Transvestite." *Representations* 64 (Fall 1998): 109–33.

Sheaffer, Louis. *O'Neill: Son and Artist*. Boston: Little, 1973.

Sinclair, Upton. *American Outpost*. Port Washington: Kennikat, 1932.

Stansell, Christine. *American Moderns: Bohemian New York and the Creation of a New Century*. New York: Holt, 2000.

Trilling, Lionel. "Eugene O'Neill." *Eugene O'Neill*. Ed. Harold Bloom. New York: Chelsea, 1987. 13–20.

Tripp, Anne Huber. *The I. W. W. and the Paterson Silk Strike of 1913*. Urbana: U of Illinois P, 1987.

Wyckoff, Walter. *The Workers: An Experiment in Reality*. 2 vols. New York: Scribner's, 1897, 1898.

Zapf, Hubert. "O'Neill's *Hairy Ape* and the Reversal of Hegelian Dialectics." *O'Neill and His Plays*. Ed. Oscar Cargill, N. Bryllion Fagin, and William J. Fisher. New York: New York UP, 1961. 35–39.

Bound East for Cardiff

O'Neill valued *Bound East for Cardiff* highly. In the chronological list of the plays he made at Skinner's request he remarked that the play was "very important from my point of view. In it can be seen, or felt, the germ of the spirit, life-attitude, etc., of all my more important future work" (Skinner viii).

The play is set in *"the seamen's forecastle of the British tramp steamer Glencairn on a foggy night midway on the voyage between New York and Cardiff."* Corresponding to the unity of setting is the extreme unity of time. The play is one of these fairly rare examples where playing time coincides with fictional time. Being a one-act play, the action revolves around a single situation (Schnetz 31). Characteristic of O'Neill is that this situation is described both in its interpersonal, intrapersonal, and superpersonal aspect. Superficially a realistic play about the rough life at sea, *Bound East for Cardiff* is actually a parabolic drama about the plight of humanity with a focal character who characteristically lacks a proper name. Nicknamed Yank, he is not only *homo Americanus* but, essentially, *homo universalis*.

The overall structure of the play, determined by Yank's situation, bears a striking similarity to Kipling's "The Rhyme of the Three Sealers," which O'Neill has Jim Tyrone (mis)quote from in *A Moon for the Misbegotten*. Kipling

From *Eugene O'Neill: A Playwright's Theatre*, pp. 167–175. © 2004 by Egil Törnqvist.

was one of young O'Neill's favorite writers (C 14, Bowen 18, 42–43). The relevant passage in Kipling's poem reads:

> Then Reuben Paine cried out again before his spirit passed:
>   "Have I followed the sea for thirty years to die in the dark at last?"
>   "Curse on her work that has nipped me here with a shifty trick unkind—
>   "I have gotten my death where I got my bread, but I dare not face it blind.
>
>   "Curse on the fog! Is there never a wind of all the winds I knew
>   "To clear the smother from off my chest and let me look at the blue?"
>   The good fog heard—like a splitten sail, to left and right she tore,
>   And they saw the sun-dogs in the haze and the seal upon the shore.
>   [...]
>   And the rattle rose in Reuben's throat and he cast his soul with a cry,
>   And "Gone already?" Tom Hall he said. "Then it's time for me to die."

With the help of the configuration chart (235), which has the advantage above other kinds of segmentation of being very precise and very objective,[1] we can have a more detailed look at the structure of the one-act play. The chart reveals that it contains seven configurations, each consisting of a particular character constellation. When the chart is read horizontally, we are informed about who and how many are present in each configuration. When it is read vertically, we are informed about in which configurations each character appears. The more frequently s/he appears, the more important s/he tends to be. We need only to glance at the chart for *Cardiff* to realize that two characters, Yank and Driscoll, receive more attention than any of the others. Even a quick perusal of the text leads to the conclusion that of these two, Yank is the protagonist. It is *his* fate that the text focuses upon. Driscoll, his good friend, functions as a helper in need. The chart also gives information about who meets whom and in which order this happens. We here deal with the basic form, the skeleton, of any drama structure. We may, for example, note that in this play the Captain and the First Mate appear in only one configuration; that they do so in the middle of the play; and that they are never seen together with three of the seamen who at the time are performing their duties outside the visualized space. A meaningful question to be posed would be: Why do they appear in [4] and not earlier or later?

The chart also shows who is speaking and who is silent within each configuration, another important choice a dramatist has to make. What is not shown in the chart is the length of each configuration. This can be indicated either by page/line indications of where a configuration begins and ends or by counting the number of speeches per configuration. In the present play the speeches are distributed as follows over the seven configurations: [1] 53, [2] 5, [3] 15, [4] 22, [5] 47, [6] 2, [7] 1. It will be seen that [1] and [5] are the longest configurations. At the same time [1] has six speaking characters, whereas [5] has only two. A closer look at the length of the speeches reveals that these tend to be longer in [5] than in [1]. It is easy to guess why this is so. In [1] O'Neill is working with a broad canvas. We need to be informed about time, space, prescenic circumstances, the present situation, etc. And some of the themes that are later developed need to be touched upon already at this stage. In this particular play it is also of importance to make it clear from the beginning that we are dealing with a group of people sharing the same life conditions. It helps to make us see Yank as a representative of the group and his dilemma as something that *mutatis mutandis* could apply to them all. In [5]—we are now characteristically close to the end of the play— we are confronted with the central configuration of the play: the dialogue between two close friends, both of them realizing that one of them is dying. Contrasting with the (seemingly) everyday group dialogue in [1], the dialogue here deals with fundamental existential questions. Both configurations could be called nuclear configurations, but this they are for very different reasons. [4], the third in length, confirms what has been indicated already in [2], that Yank is mortally wounded. But more important is perhaps that we are here via an outsider, the Captain, plausibly informed that Driscoll and Yank have been shipmates for quite a long time. This explains why they have an especially close friendship and it prepares for Driscoll's role as consoler in the next configuration.

Exits and entrances are naturally motivated. Two sailors (Olson, Paul), we must assume, have entered the forecastle just before the play opens, relieved of their duties up on board. Two more (Smitty, Ivan) are soon to enter for the same reason. These four are replaced by the three (Cocky, Davis, Scotty) who leave the forecastle at the end of [1]. Driscoll, who is the fourth member of this crew, stays behind to care for Yank. The Captain's appearance is motivated by the need to check Yank's health. He here functions as a substitute doctor.

In addition to the change of character constellation from one configuration to another, there is a significant change *within* the configurations, not clearly indicated in the chart. For while the chart's "o" normally means that a character is merely listening, here it usually means that he is not even aware of what is being said because he is asleep. Thus Paul and Olson fall asleep already in [1], Smitty and Ivan shortly after their entrance in [3]. As we shall see, this secures a development from noise to stillness, from togetherness to loneliness, from life to death.

Another fundamental structural device concerns the relationship between the characters and the recipient. Sometimes the recipient knows less than (some of) the characters. This is normally the situation in the beginning of a play. Here, for example, all the sailors know what has befallen Yank before the recipient does. In such cases we may speak of mystification. At other times the recipient may know more than (some of) the characters. At the end of the play, for example, we know that Yank has died; so do Driscoll and Cocky; but the rest of the characters do not. As recipients we are in collusion with the two who know. A play structure is normally characterized by constant suspense-creating shifts between mystification and collusion. The question of who knows what needs to be frequently posed in any drama.

Especially in the beginning, when seven of the nine sailors are present, we are made aware of the narrowness of the forecastle. Swept in dense tobacco smoke, it visualizes the fog outside, made audible by the intermittent blasts of the steamer's whistle.

The melancholy and desolation suggested by setting and sound are countered by Paul's soft playing of a folk song on his "*accordion*" and by jocular talk between the sailors. The play opens *in medias res*. A "*weazened runt*" of an Englishman called Cocky—the name is indicative!—is boasting about an incident on New Guinea, where he had once knocked a "bloomin' nigger [...] silly" when she tried to seduce him. Cocky's attempt to impress the others fails completely. They turn his story into one in which his toughness plays a less commendable part. In their version he is unappetizing to the cannibal "quane av the naygurs" both as lover and as "Christmas dinner." The note of death has been struck, be it farcically.

The dialogue is suddenly interrupted by a groan from one of the bunks behind the men. Driscoll, a "*brawny Irishman*," "*tiptoes softly to [..] the bunk*" and addresses the American who is lying there. A reference to his breath reveals that Yank is sick, and the fact that "*all are silent, avoiding each other's eyes*" indicates that his condition is serious.

We learn that Yank has fallen into one of the holds and hurt himself "bad inside." The sequence is not only expository but also anticipatory, since three of the men express their concern about Yank's chances to survive, whereas a fourth, Driscoll, takes a more optimistic view. Being outnumbered, Driscoll, we sense, has a special reason for his optimism.

The sequence also informs us about Yank's ability to sustain pain and his habit of swearing.

The talk turns from Yank to the man who is officially responsible for his health: the Captain. The Captain is blamed for his inability to help Yank. His trust in science—thermometer and medicine—is ridiculed by the sailors. Behind the blame one senses a naive belief that being their boss, he should have a power lacking in them. Subconsciously sensing the Captain's impotence, which mirrors their own, Cocky states: "Yank was a good shipmate, pore beggar." With its past tense, Cocky's statement takes the form of a necrologue.

In their displeasure at the food on board the sailors raise their voices until another groan from Yank causes Driscoll, by now recognized as Yank's close friend, to summon silence. Driscoll also tells Paul to stop his "organ" playing: "Is that banshee schreechin' fit music for a sick man?" His choice of words reveals what is on his mind. For organ playing is what we expect at a funeral and a banshee, according to Irish popular belief, is a supernatural being who takes the shape of an old woman foretelling death by mournful singing or wailing. The accordion music stops. but instead, as if to demonstrate Driscoll's vain attempt to fight death, "*the steamer's whistle sounds particularly loud in the silence.*"

Davis, an Englishman, damns the fog and Olson, a Swede, joins the chorus of fog-haters when stating that he "yust can't sleep wheen weestle blow." Yet immediately after he has said this he is "*fast asleep and snoring.*"

Fog means impaired visibility and that can be dangerous at sea. All the sailors know that. Especially alarming under the circumstances is that the fog retards the voyage to Cardiff and will thus be responsible if Yank dies. About seven days they still have to go if the fog does not lift. "Sivin mortal days" did Driscoll and Yank once drift in an open boat after a shipwreck "just such a night as this." The shipwreck happened "just about this toime [...] and we all sittin' round in the fo'c'stle, Yank beside me." At that time Yank saved Driscoll's life, we learn. With this new information we understand even better that Driscoll feels a special obligation to try to save Yank's life.

Yank awakes and from now on he more directly holds the stage. The mates try to cheer him up with hopeful wishes, euphemistically phrased as promises. Their forced optimism glaringly contrasts with their former sad forebodings. Yank is not fooled. But he hesitates to spell out the truth; the word "die" is still taboo to him, like a substitute for "*the word he is about to say*" but fears.

The ship's bell is heard heavily tolling eight times. From the forecastle head above the voice of the lookout rises in a long wail.

Aaall's well. The men look uncertainly at YANK as if undecided
whether to say good-by or not.

On the realistic level the lookout's cry is the signal that one team is to replace
another on deck. But the *"tolling"* and the *"wail,"* both suggesting a funeral,
contradict the lookout's hopeful statement which, in the actual context,
evokes the other half of the proverb: "that ends well." Is Yank going to die or
is he not? The contradiction between the message and the manner in which
it is brought makes us uncertain.

Yank appeals to Driscoll to stay with him, making it clear that he can
die at any moment. Fully aware of Yank's precarious situation, we can now
see some of O'Neill's devices in a new light. First, Yank is placed in the far
end of the forecastle where *"the sides [..] almost meet [..] to form a triangle."*
This is the narrowest spot in the room. Apart from illustrating the anguish
of a dying man, here literally cornered, the narrowness, strongly contrasting
with the wide, open spaces around the ship, represents, along with the fog,
the imprisonment of life. When Yank and Driscoll agree that "it's a hell av a
life, the sea," they are seemingly commenting on the hard life of sailors or,
by extension, of the proletarians in this world. But if we see the sailors on
board the *S.S. Glencairn* as a *pars pro toto* for mankind—they characteristically
represent many different nationalities—and "life on shipboard as the world
in miniature" (Downer 1951, 469), the negative evaluation applies to the life
of everyone, to life itself, and the difference between people becomes one in
degree rather than kind. Seen in this way, the ship moving through the fog
becomes a symbol of man's groping his way through a life whose meaning is
obscure to him.

Second, the noise from the sailors in the opening takes on a cynical
shade when we are aware that one of them is facing death in the same room.
At the end, in contrast, when Yank passes away, everyone except Driscoll,
the faithful friend, is either asleep or away. It underlines Yank's insight that
he must face death alone. Although their falling immediately asleep may be
realistically motivated by their being exhausted after their work up on deck,
it primarily illustrates the shortcomings of every man. Willing but unable to
wake, they are, as we have earlier noted, like the disciples of Christ who could
not refrain from going to sleep, leaving the Son of Man alone in his most
difficult moment.

The entrance of the relieved lookout, the English gentleman Smitty,
and another mate, the Russian Ivan, open [3]. Like Olson earlier, they both
crawl into bed and immediately go to sleep. Their snores, together with the
steamer's whistle, form the ironic lullaby to Yank's lonely fight against the silent
sleep that is in store for him. A spasm of pain suddenly contracts his features,

but when Driscoll offers to fetch the Captain, Yank again begs him to stay. Though uncalled for, the Captain and the Second Mate arrive, apparently worried about Yank's condition. Both temperature and pulse are found to be "way up." When they leave to make room for the crucial dialogue between the two friends in [5], Driscoll's attempts to cheer Yank up sound even more in discord with the facts than before. Yank is now heroically trying to accept his fate, and occasionally the roles of consoler and consoled seem reversed. The flashbacks of Yank's life together with Driscoll which the beginning death struggle sets going[2] have different aspects. They are a commemoration between friends of the good moments they have had together, their goodness consisting mostly in the fact that they have suffered *together*. They are also a juxtaposition of life as it has been (roving life at sea) and as it might have been (settled life in a home), illustrating the wish—pipe dream?—of a dying man to relive his life, provided it be a different kind of life. To intensify the sense of grim irony, O'Neill tickles us with the idea that Yank could have escaped his fate altogether, had either of the men dared to speak to the other about his dream to settle down "'way in the middle of the land where yuh'd never smell the sea or see a ship."

Yank's sudden question "How'd all the fog git in here?" refers to the tobacco smoke filling the room. His mistaking the smoke for the fog, suggesting that he is getting delirious, prepares for the hallucinations to come. The moving pictures of his life flash by with increasing rapidity until they slow down before a traumatic memory, a homicide in self-defense. Worriedly he asks whether God will hold this against him, but when Driscoll answers in the negative he "*seems comforted.*"

Nearing the end of his voyage, where time and eternity meet, Yank "makes his will." Aware that his time is up, he gives his watch to Driscoll. His description of this sole property of his, contrasting with the Captain's *golden watch*," is a plain summing-up of his life: "It ain't worth much, but it's all I've got." He then asks Driscoll to buy a box of candy for Fanny, "the barmaid at the Red Stork in Cardiff," and, as if the name of the port he shall not reach proves too much for him, he breaks down and says "in *a choking voice*": "It's hard to ship on this voyage I'm going on—alone."

In this connection the play title alluding to the slang expression "go west," meaning "to die," is a case in point. As Winther (1934, 57) remarks: "His ship was bound east, but he was 'going west', and he knew it." Winther's conclusion is only partially true. For if Yank is undoubtedly "going west," he is at the same time "bound east"—for sunrise, release, and, perhaps, resurrection (Skinner 42). Cocky's announcement, in the final configuration, that "the fog's lifted" shortly after Yank has faced death—in the figure of "a pretty lady dressed in black"—and given up his ghost, verifies that his death coincides with the dissolving of the fog.[3] Yank's last words imply the same, for with the fog gone the starlit night has become visible, "pretty" and "black" like his visionary lady. This means a fulfillment of Yank's wish that the stars and moon were out "to make it easier to go," and an answer to Driscoll's "*half-remembered prayer*" for the soul of the man who once saved his life.

More trivially, "the pretty lady dressed in black" recalls Fanny, "the barmaid at the Red Stork" (Broun 130)—the reference to the beginning of life seems indicated in the name of the pub—for just before Yank has his hallucination, he gulps at the dipper and gasps: "I wish this was a pint of beer." This seems to be his laconic way of saying: "I wish I were at the Red Stork, for then I would stay alive." The black woman figure also recalls the initial "quane av the naygurs" who turns out to be a cannibal. In retrospect we understand that this is an adequate description of Yank's experience of approaching death as at once attractive and repulsive. What constitutes his death struggle is an intensification of what has always been with him, an ambiguous fear of and longing for death. Like his namesake in *The Hairy Ape*, he is virtually—but in another sense—between heaven and earth, not knowing whether he wants to go forward or turn back. When he realizes that he is given no choice, he courageously accepts his fate.

Given the situation in *Bound East for Cardiff*, it is not surprising that there are frequent references to both heaven and hell in the play, where the "Gawd blimey" in Cocky's opening speech is repeated by him in the curtain speech. That we nevertheless experience the same expression quite differently in opening and ending is simply due to the fact that we as recipients have moved from ignorance of Yank's situation to knowledge about it and in the process have become emotionally engaged in it.

The first "Gawd blimey" appears in the middle of the yarn Cocky is telling, and it is surrounded by mockingly good-natured laughter from the sailors sitting around him. At this point we do not realize that next to them there is a dying man. The second "Gawd blimey" follows Cocky's discovery that Yank has died. It is spoken "*in a hushed whisper*" and is accompanied by a gesture of bewilderment, a scratching of the head.

Cocky is apparently irreligious. He mocks Driscoll when he sees him praying. Nevertheless he makes frequent use of God as a testimony to the veracity of what he says, when the mates disbelieve him: "It's Gawd's truth! [...] Gawd blimey, I couldn't stand 'er. [...] Gawd strike me dead if it ain't true, every bleedin' word of it." Why call in as a witness an authority you do not trust? Is Cocky more religious, or at least superstitious, than he himself realizes? Or is he using the name of God to make an impression on those who believe in him?

If the former interpretation seems more meaningful than the latter, it is because it turns Cocky into an interesting counterpart of the protagonist, Yank, who in other respects is his antithesis. "I ain't never had religion," Yank says. But as we have seen, what concerns him in his dying hour is whether or not God will hold him responsible for his murder, whether heaven or hell is in store for him. The very accident that has left him mortally wounded— he misses a ladder and plumps "straight down to the bottom" of one of the dark holds[4]—he experiences as a warning for the *Höllenfahrt* in store for him: "COCKY. [...] Oh, 'ell, 'e says, oh, 'ell—like that, and nothink else." Yank also complains that "it hurts like hell" in his chest and that his throat is "like a furnace." When Cocky calls him "pore devil" and Scotty asserts that "he's verry bod," they refer to Yank's physical ailment: At a deeper level, unrealized by them, the statements refer to his moral condition.

But it is also possible to see the hellish symptoms not as anticipations of what is in store for Yank after death but as disguised references to the pangs of conscience of a dying man, as allusions to his state of mind, or even as references to the misery of life. Driscoll supports this latter view. When he alludes to the devil and to hell, he refers to circumstances in *this* life: the "spindle-shanked" captain, the bosun, life at sea. What is beyond life—the saints, God, heaven—is "love." When Yank talks about death or shows signs of dying, Driscoll invokes the divine love as a counterspell in the form of a compressed prayer or verbalized cross-sign.

The question of what hell stands for mirrors Yank's dilemma. Is he leaving one hell for another, as he himself fears? Or is he leaving it for a better existence, as Driscoll tries to tell him? The answer could not be given unequivocally. But the symbolism of the ending suggests an upward journey for Yank. The fog has lifted. The stars are out. A "pretty lady dressed in black" is waiting for him. This is the resurrection following his initial fall into the dark hold. Reality or pipe dream? Who knows?

The foregoing analysis has emphasized a number of elements in the play which point beyond surface realism: the play title, the narrowness of the forecastle, the fog, the steamer's whistle, the accordion, Yank's watch, the men's sleep, the lookout's cry, the "pretty lady," the references to ultimates. All these elements can be understood on a purely realistic level. Yet by settling for the most worrying universal situation possible—man facing death—and by making all the elements just mentioned implicitly refer to a dying man, O'Neill provides them with an existential and symbolic loading. It is this loading that gives the play its firm texture. Elements which at first sight seem extraneous are gradually or in retrospect found to be exceedingly relevant for the central issue of the play. This goes even for the least interesting fourth configuration. The visit of the Captain and the Second Mate is clearly in the first place included to provide us with factual information about Yank's condition. But aside from this, their mere arrival and their behavior do not justify the sailors' class-determined criticism of them. *They* cannot be blamed for Yank's accident, nor for their helplessness in the situation that has arisen. The antagonist is to be found not on the human but on the metaphysical level.

Notes

1. Cf. for example Condee (13), who applies another kind of segmentation to *Bound East for Cardiff*. Basing it on the concept of suspense, he finds that the play has two major segments." The dividing line occurs, he finds, when the Captain exits. The first segment "establishes the vector," that is, the direction in which the segment is pointing; the second is "virtually a long monologue by Yank." It should be obvious that this segmentation compared to that based on configuration is at once more narrow and more subjective.

2. Macgowan (450) remarks that Yank's "fever of death" is O'Neill's device "of getting out more of man's inner consciousness than a man would ordinarily lay bare to his fellows."

3. The same is true of the death of the child in *Fog*.

4. Skinner (39) sees Yank's fall from the ladder as indicative of his failure to find a "foothold in a life of obscurity."

DORIS ALEXANDER

The Epitaph

Eugene O'Neill's last play arose directly from the two intimate plays about his youth, *The Iceman Cometh* and *Long Day's Journey into Night*. Indeed, he had just finished *Long Day's Journey* when he got his first idea for the new play, and he actually hijacked for it one of the characters from that play—his brother Jamie—and took his story line from the comic story of his father's tenant, called Shaughnessy in his family play. Thus his first note for the new play in his work diary dated October 28, 1941, reads: "S. [Shaughnessy] play idea, based on story told by E. [Edmund] in 1st Act of 'L.D.J.I.N,' except here Jamie principal character & story of play otherwise entirely imaginary, except for J.'s [Jamie's] revelation of self." Immediately O'Neill became convinced, "This can be strange combination comic-tragic—am enthused about it." He got straight to work on it, calling it now for himself "Dolan play," after John Dolan, the actual tenant of James O'Neill who modeled for Shaughnessy, and then, later, changing the name to Hogan as in the published play. He had finished an outline and begun the dialogue on November 10, 1941.

Showing how thoroughly this play was saturated with the themes of ideals and pipe dreams that had nourished the two earlier plays, O'Neill found a title for it expressive of an ideal, calling it first "Moon of the Misbegotten" and then "A Moon for the Misbegotten." The moon is traditionally the image for romantic love, and as first conceived, this play was to concern

From *Eugene O'Neill's Last Plays: Separating Art from Autobiography*, pp. 157–163. © 2005 by the University of Georgia Press.

the romantic ideals of a man and a woman, their divided and contradictory desires of romantic love, and how those contradictory ideals of love made a conventional happy ending between them impossible. (In the final form of the play, this theme remained central.)

By November 26, 1941, when he completed a first draft of his first act, he was writing in his work diary, "getting great satisfaction this play—flows." But his creative push broke with the events of December 7, 1941. He wrote, "WAR! Japs blast Pearl Harbor! (Now the whole world goes into the tunnel!)." He became "glued to the radio" in the next days. Nevertheless he was "determined to finish 1st d. [draft] of this play, war or not." So he labored on, but kept noting, "too much war on mind," or "little done—mind on war." When he finally finished a first draft of *A Moon for the Misbegotten* on January 20, 1942, he wrote, exhausted, "had to drag myself through it since Pearl Harbor and it needs much revision—wanders all over place." Not until a year later, January 3, 1943, did he finally reread it and decide, "want to get this really written—real affection for it—can be fine, unusual play," and set to work, fighting his faltering health all along the way, and arriving at a very different revised draft that did not wander, and which placed a much stronger emphasis on the character of Jamie.

Certainly in many ways the character takes on both traits and story of the Jamie in *Long Day's Journey into Night*. But as history, this play is even less trustworthy than the family one. For instance, *Moon for the Misbegotten* not only mentions Jamie Tyrone's being expelled from university, but also tells of the prank that caused it. The character recalls it in the first act of *Moon for the Misbegotten*, and it fits entirely into the comical, at times almost farcical, tone of that act before the tragic undertones of the drama emerge. According to Jamie, he passed off a prostitute as his sister to the Jesuits, and she let the secret out by concluding her remarks to the priest accompanying them around the campus by saying, "Christ, Father, it's nice and quiet out here away from the damned Sixth Avenue El. I wish to hell I could stay here!" Presumably that put her out, and Jamie with her. As comedy this is funny, and it is plausible, but it cannot be the real story of what happened to Jamie O'Neill at Fordham University. For one thing, with James O'Neill's habit of making friends with the priests teaching his sons, and with his fame and charm, all the Jesuits at Fordham must have known that their brilliant and promising student was the elder of James O'Neill's two sons. James O'Neill Jr. was editor-in-chief of the literary magazine *The Fordham Monthly* as well as winner of almost all prizes for excellence in his studies. He could never have introduced a bogus sister to the faculty, all of whom knew his family well—certainly well enough to know there was no sister. In Jamie Tyrone's retelling of the scene, the prostitute's words don't reveal conclusively that she is a prostitute; she is not misbehaving. And it is unlikely that the student with her would be expelled on the basis of her taking names in vain, particularly if he were a brilliant student at the top of his class. Whatever the actual cause of James O'Neill Jr.'s expulsion, the Jesuits discreetly suppressed all details of Jamie's crime. They even arranged it so he could have transferred the credits of his three successful years at Fordham to another university and taken his degree despite this transgression. Jamie's choice was to end his higher education with his exit from the Jesuits.

In *A Moon for the Misbegotten* Jamie Tyrone has all of Jamie O'Neill's love of poetry and readiness to quote the avant-garde poets of his day, such as Algernon Swinburne and Ernest Dowson. Although Eugene O'Neill speaks of himself in *A Moon for the Misbegotten* only as the distant brother he actually was in the fall of 1923, his own heritage from Jamie in familiarity with the poets of the decadence directed him as he wrote. He had always felt strong identification with his brother in poetry and creativity. Also, he saw his brother, the person who had turned him from his childhood dreams and taught him knowledge of drink and prostitutes, as almost a part of him. Eugene O'Neill certainly was conscious of that feeling when he wrote his first play drenched in the atmosphere of their relationship, *The Great God Brown*, in which one character appropriates the personality of another. Eugene always saw his dissipated self in the admired image of his witty, charming older brother who started him indulging in prostitutes and chorus girls when he was only fifteen years old. In the family play, Jamie calls him his Frankenstein—something he created altogether. In *The Great God Brown* he had seen himself as hiding behind his brother's mask, as if he were secreted within his outer personality.

In *Long Day's Journey into Night* O'Neill had created the strange story told by Jamie of his night at the local brothel. Very delicately he had suggested a resemblance between the pathetic prostitute Fat Violet who has lost her ability to play the piano and his mother with her crippled fingers, so that Jamie's resort to the prostitute serves as an unconscious revenge on the mother under drugs. At this point Eugene O'Neill must have been awakening to the thought that Jamie's wasted life, dissipated among prostitutes and tarts, and his need to have his young brother follow his path, came from an obscure urge to revenge himself on his mother.

In *A Moon for the Misbegotten* Eugene was perfectly clear that Jamie Tyrone's penchant for prostitutes came from an urge to work out his rage and pain, contempt, and pity on a proxy figure. He had Jamie realize consciously what he has been doing. The perception was certainly true for O'Neill, but the story be designed to express it must be largely fictional.

Eugene O'Neill had received a letter from Mrs. Libbie Drummer to Mrs. Phillips, a long-time friend of the O'Neill family, which Mrs. Phillips had then sent on to Eugene. The letter presents Mrs. Drummer's detailed account of the death of Ella in Los Angeles, and Eugene took from it Jamie's agonizing confession to Josie that his dying mother knew he had relapsed into drinking, "saw I was drunk," and was glad to die because of it. Mrs. Drummer had declared that the most pitiful part of Ella's death was that "I think she knew he was drinking before she died and realized everything and was helpless." So this much of Jamie Tyrone's confession is true for Jamie O'Neill. The character's most shocking revelation, however, is that he hired a prostitute for the entire train trip carrying his mother's body back from California to New York. He recalls that this "pig" became for him a proxy for the dead woman: "It was as if I wanted revenge—because I'd been left alone—because I knew I was lost, without any hope left—that all I could do would be drink myself to death." Certainly Eugene O'Neill looked upon his brother's seductions as an unconscious revenge on his mother for her drug addiction and, at the same time, a working out of his pity and love.

But the prostitute story remains in the realm of fiction. According to Ella O'Neill's friend Mrs. Drummer, Jamie O'Neill had been seen off on the train by one of the nurses who had cared for his mother. She reported to Mrs. Drummer afterward that "he had ten bottles of whiskey with him" in his private compartment. Mrs. Drummer commented, "I was so worried. I did not know if Jamie would ever reach New York alive. He was in dreadful condition." Actually, when, the train reached New York, Will Connor and his nephew had to search the entire train at Grand Central Station before they found Jamie finally "in a drunken stupor, with empty bottles all around, beyond knowing them," and unable to do anything but "mumble incoherently." He remained so "broken up" and alcoholic that he could not attend his mother's funeral on March 10, 1922. The story of a blonde pig on the train was surely fictional, but it expressed a profound truth for O'Neill.

Certainly he himself had used prostitutes for revenge during his months of drunken dissipation after being jilted by Beatrice Ashe, and he had put his doing so into his play *Welded* when he had its protagonist, furious at his wife, declare to the prostitute he has picked up; "You have the power—and the right—to murder love! You can satisfy hate!" So although Jamie is the only protagonist of *A Moon for the Misbegotten*, Eugene O'Neill was so powerfully present in him that the play serves even more as his own epitaph than that of his dead brother.

Jamie O'Neill was too cynical to feel Dowson's bitter disillusionment when he woke after a night's dissipation to realize that romantic love was lost in the past and "the dawn was grey." Instead, it was Eugene who was haunted like Dowson by the irrevocable loss of genuine feeling, for it was he who had experienced a shocking destruction of his childhood faith in love and romantic ideals as a young boy. The disillusionment of gray dawns with prostitutes had haunted him all his life thereafter. He had shown his understanding of it in the poem he wrote right after his attempt at suicide, "The Lay of the Singer's Fall." It tells of a poet who became invaded by a devil of doubt who undermined his faith in love and ideals at the moment he learned the meaning of sin, so that he had nothing left to live for. In Eugene O'Neill's world, his brother had played the mocking skeptic, the Mephistopheles, and had given him the knowledge of sin. And it had been in the image of his brother that all his disillusioning dissipations had always been carried out. So although it had indeed been his brother who had set out to drink himself to death after their mother died, Eugene O'Neill was fully with him in his rush to destruction as protagonist of *A Moon for the Misbegotten*.

The play is set in September 1923, when his brother Jamie, like Jamie of the play, had almost succeeded in drinking himself to death, as he had been doing from the day his mother collapsed in California. But Jamie O'Neill had by that time done such destruction to himself with dangerous Prohibition whiskey that he was blind and confined in the Riverlawn Sanitorium at Paterson , New Jersey. Jamie Tyrone was still destroying himself in New London in September, and already dead in his heart if not yet in his life. As such he is one of the two misbegotten of the play, and Eugene O'Neill filled the play character with his own regret for lost innocence and damaged ideals. So all he seeks in his tormented guilt is forgiveness and peace in the innocence of his childhood ideal of love. The other misbegotten of the play, Josie Hogan, the woman born too big and powerful to fit into a male-dominated world, seeks consummation of her humiliating and self-slandered virginity through her genuine love for Jamie. Thus her romantic dream places her at cross-purposes with her beloved, who seeks only release from the self-loathing he has experienced in the gray dawns after nights of dissipation with sluts. As he tells Josie, he shrinks from "the aftermath that poisons you." There have been, he says, "too many nights—and dawns. This must be different." The great scene of *A Moon for the Misbegotten* offers a different night illumined by a genuinely romantic moon that cannot be extinguished into a tawdry gray morning.

Eugene O'Neill found it by his own creation of a resolution of what Jung called the "dual mother image" of mythology and dreams—both an expression of the human unconscious. This Jungian concept had been one of the subthemes meant to recur in O'Neill's planned great cycle of eleven plays. In it the longing to return to the womb in "order to be born again" from a mother symbolic of renewal and life contrasts with the "terrible mother," expressive of the danger of "drowning" in one's "own source," of finding within only death, the peace of nonexistence. Both mother images appear in the surviving draft of More *Stately Mansions* and also in the scenario O'Neill wrote for the play to follow it, "The Calms of Capricorn," which also survived by sheer accident.

In *More Stately Mansions* the dual mother is represented by the womblike Chinese summer house in the garden, which has come to symbolize for Simon his mother's identity. He is both lured by it and terrified of losing himself within. Ultimately, Deborah, his mother, saves him from madness and death by shutting herself up alone in her own depths behind the locked door of the summer house. The dual mother in the scenario for "The Calms of Capricorn" appears in Ethan's ambivalence toward the sea, the mother of life, which he both loves and hates. For him, a victory over the sea by making her carry his clipper ship at record-breaking speed will give him power to possess her and she in return will give him, he says, "freedom and rebirth." But if she turns into a "devil mother" and overcomes his ship with "storms and calms and fogs," he will throw himself to her to swallow and spew "out in death." In the same scenario, O'Neill gave Ethan's mother Sarah a mystical vision of her meaning for her beloved husband Simon, who has just died. She declares that she is overcome with pride because her "heart has borne the man [she loves] into life, and in [her] heart he's become a man" yet "always remained a child, and at the last his death is only a return behind the gates of birth to sleep at peace again forever in the love" of her "heart." It was this mystical perception of the woman as eternal mother bearing her man, by way of her love, into both the gift of life and the endless peace of death that gave O'Neill his idea for the major scene of *A Moon for the Misbegotten* and his own unique unification of the dual mother image into one beneficent source of endless love giving birth to both life and repose.

In the fourth act Josie is able to give a night that, as she says, will end like the promise of God's peace in the sorrow of the soul. She is seen at dawn hugging the deathlike figure of Jamie against her breast, asleep in the love of her heart. So as the great virgin mother of life she has given her child a dawn in which he can awake "at peace with myself," free at last from all the "sick remorse" of his wasted life.

So this last play of all, like the other two set at his rebirth as a playwright, is filled with O'Neill's coming to terms with death. For every minute that he struggled to complete these last three works, he certainly knew he was dying as a creative artist. Looking through his *Work Diary* at any point in those last years, one can see recurring signs of the approaching end. On June 12, 1942, he wrote that he was "at new low." Again and again he noted that he has had "short shift" in his work because he "fades out." Morning after morning he noted, "bad night, prostate pain," and day after day, using the current erroneous diagnosis, he declared "Parkinson's bad." July 28, he confessed, "Tough game—take sedatives and feel a dull dope—don't take, and feel as if maggots were crawling all over inside your skin." August 2, he reported, "in addition to other troubles develop painful hip." August 6, "nothing much done—feel too sick." August 10, "sinking spell—all in," and so on, day after day. Working on his projected play "The Last Conquest" in December, he told himself, "no go—decide will have to quit on this again—or on anything else—one of my old sinking spells is on me—lower than low—mind dead." The next to the last day of December, he admitted, "Parkinson's terrible—got fit in a.m. when I thought I'd hop right out of my skin—just as well I have no will to work because couldn't make it anyway."

Yet only four days after that he resolved to get *A Moon for the Misbegotten*, left in its unsatisfactory first draft, "really written." He certainly was anticipating his own death as a creative artist as he crafted his protagonist's death. On January 31, 1943, when he finished a second draft of *A Moon for the Misbegotten*, he wrote, "What I am up against now—fade out physically each day after 3 hours—page a day because work slowly even when as eager about play as I am about this." With the lack of coordination resulting from his neurological problems, he found it a "constant strain to write." So apparent to him was the approach of the end that he spent part of his time after writing, "destroying old stuff" he had no time to perfect. Thus this last play of all is really an epitaph for both his dead brother and for himself manifestly dying as a creative artist. He as well as his brother—who had actually died on November 8, 1923, not two months after the action of this play—share in Josie's final benediction, "May you have your wish and die in your sleep soon, Jim, darling. May you rest forever in forgiveness and peace." After *A Moon for the Misbegotten* was finished in the spring of 1943, Eugene O'Neill was already dead at heart, even as Jamie in his play. But he had years of cruel affliction to suffer before his last breath on November 27, 1953, granted him the peace and forgiveness and eternal rest he desired.

Chronology

1877   James O'Neill, Sr., marries Ella Quinlan O'Neill. Ella came from an affluent family and was educated by nuns. Biographers note she was not prepared for the life of an itinerant actor. With James O'Neill, she spent time traveling, living in hotels and, in the case of her son Eugene, giving birth in hotels. James O'Neill was one of the most popular actors of the nineteenth century, making his living as the star of a traveling theatrical production of *The Count of Monte Cristo.*

1878   James O'Neill, Jr., Eugene's eldest brother, is born. He would pursue a desultory career as an actor, would be utterly dependent on his mother, and develop alcoholism and eventually die from it.

1883   Edmund O'Neill is born. He dies while still an infant.

1888   Eugene Gladstone O'Neill is born on October 16 in New York City, in a hotel room. Ella had difficulty recovering from the pregnancy, and wound up addicted to morphine, an addiction that plagued her for years.

1895   Eugene starts at Catholic boarding schools, moves around as his parents do. As a teenager, he rarely sees his mother during the school years.

1902   O'Neill learns of his mother's morphine addiction and renounces Catholicism in the same summer. (Some believe the drowning incident referred to in *Long Day's Journey Into Night* to be autobiographical, and the precipitating incident in Eugene learning of his mother's problem.) He persuades his father to let him attend a secular school rather than a Catholic one. Begins learning about drinking, prostitutes, and avant garde writers from older brother Jamie; however, relationship with his brother is mixed.

1906	Starts at Princeton; flunks out within a year.
1909	Elopes and marries Kathleen Jenkins. Father arranges a number of jobs for Eugene, none of which he takes to. But his father pays passage for him on a steamer to Honduras, and Eugene "discovers" the sea.
1910	Son, Eugene Galdstone O'Neill, Jr. is born. O'Neill sails to Buenos Aires, having joined the crew of a steamer. In Bueons Aires, he lives in squalor and drinks heavily.
1911	O'Neill returns to the United States where he lives in a flop house in lower Manhattan. In early 1912, attempts suicide after depressive incident in late 1911.
1912	Divorces Kathleen Jenkins, returns to Monte Cristo Cottage, his parents' home. By the end of the year, O'Neill enters a sanatorium for tuberculosis.
1914	Recovers and decides to change life, to become a playwright. Enrolls at Harvard, takes George Pierce Baker's playwriting class. Publishes *Thirst, and Other One Act Plays*.
1916–1919	Joins theatre company, Provincetown Players, in Provincetown, Massachusetts, and they produce several of his early plays. In 1918, he marries novelist Agnes Boulton, to whom his son, Shane, is born in
1919	Agnes continues her writing career, prompting tension between her and O'Neill. Shane would become estranged from his father, and would die a heroin addict.
1920	*Beyond the Horizon* is produced, wins O'Neill the Pulitzer Prize for Drama. Father, James, sees the play produced, affecting a form of reconciliation with Eugene. He dies shortly thereafter.
1921	*Anna Christie* is produced; wins second Pulitzer Prize. *Gold* and *The Straw* are produced.
1922	Mother, Ella Quinlan O'Neill, dies. *The Hairy Ape* and *The First Man* are produced.

1923	After decades of injury wrought by alcoholism, brother, James O'Neill, Jr., dies.
1924	*All God's Chillun Got Wings, Welded,* and *Desire Under the Elms* are produced.
1925	*The Fountain* is produced.
1926	Daughter, Oona O'Neill is born (she later marries Charlie Chaplin, infuriating her father, who disowns her). *The Great God Brown* is produced. O'Neill begins affair with Carlotta Monterey.
1928	*Lazarus Laughed, Marco Millions,* and *Strange Interlude* are produced. *Strange Interlude* wins O'Neill his third Pulitzer Prize.
1929	*Dynamo* is produced. O'Neill divorces Agnes Boulton and marries Carlotta Monterey.
1931	*Mourning Becomes Electra* is produced.
1933	*Ah, Wilderness!* is produced.
1934	*Days Without End* is produced.
1936	Wins the Nobel Prize for Literature.
1937	Builds "Tao House" in Danville, California, where he writes his last plays. Disillusioned and no longer interested in seeing his plays produced, he essentially leaves the theatre community. The rest of the thirties and early forties are spent writing, particularly his never-finished eleven-play cycle "A Tale of Possessors, Self-Dispossessed."
1939	Writes *The Iceman Cometh*.
1940	Writes *Long Day's Journey Into Night*. O'Neill instructs that the play is not to be produced until decades after his death. Carlotta (Montgomery) O'Neill gives the go-ahead for a production in 1956, three years after O'Neill's death. The play wins O'Neill his fourth Pulitzer Prize, awarded posthumously.
1943	Completes *A Moon for the Misbegotten*. In the mid-forties, he and Carlotta are living in New York, their marriage strained, and his ability to write failing due to health complications related to neurological problems. He helps mount some productions, hires a secretary, but lives in rooms in the Hotel Barclay—feeling camped.
1946	*The Iceman Cometh* is produced.

1947	*A Moon for the Misbegotten* is produced.
1950	Son, Eugene O'Neill, Jr., dies.
1953	Eugene O'Neill dies on November 27, in a hotel in Boston.

Contributors

HAROLD BLOOM is Sterling Professor of the Humanities at Yale University. He is the author of 30 books, including *Shelley's Mythmaking*, *The Visionary Company*, *Blake's Apocalypse*, *Yeats*, *A Map of Misreading*, *Kabbalah and Criticism*, *Agon: Toward a Theory of Revisionism*, *The American Religion*, *The Western Canon*, and *Omens of Millennium: The Gnosis of Angels, Dreams, and Resurrection*. *The Anxiety of Influence* sets forth Professor Bloom's provocative theory of the literary relationships between the great writers and their predecessors. His most recent books include *Shakespeare: The Invention of the Human*, a 1998 National Book Award finalist, *How to Read and Why*, *Genius: A Mosaic of One Hundred Exemplary Creative Minds*, *Hamlet: Poem Unlimited*, *Where Shall Wisdom Be Found?*, and *Jesus and Yahweh: The Names Divine*. In 1999, Professor Bloom received the prestigious American Academy of Arts and Letters Gold Medal for Criticism. He has also received the International Prize of Catalonia, the Alfonso Reyes Prize of Mexico, and the Hans Christian Andersen Bicentennial Prize of Denmark.

LAURIN R. PORTER is Professor of English at the University of Texas, Arlington. Her books include *Orphans' Home: The Voice and Vision of Hortone Foote*, and *The Banished Prince: Time, Memory, and Ritual in the Late Plays of Eugene O'Neill*.

DORIS ALEXANDER is Professor Emerita of English at the City University of New York. She lives in Venice, Italy. Alexander's several books include *The Tempering of Eugene O'Neill* and *Eugene O'Neill's Creative Struggle*.

KURT EISEN is Professor of English and Chair of the Department of English and Communications at Tennessee Technological University. He has written numerous articles on drama and O'Neill, and is the author of *The Inner Strength of Opposites: O'Neill's Novelistic Drama and the Melodramatic Imagination*.

EDWARD L. SHAUGHNESSY taught modern drama and modern Irish literature at Butler University, Indianapolis. He was author of *Eugene O'Neill in Ireland: The Critical Reception* and *Down the Nights and Down the Days: Eugene O'Neill's Catholic Sensibility*, and was a founding member of the Eugene O'Neill Society.

MARGARET LOFTUS RANALD is past president of the Eugene O'Neill Society, Professor Emerita of English at Queens College, and the author of *The Eugene O'Neill Companion* as well as numerous articles on drama.

JAMES A. ROBINSON was Professor of English at the University of Maryland, vice president of the Eugene O'Neill Society, and author of the book *Eugene O'Neill and Oriental Thought*.

BARBARA VOGLINO is a playwright and independent scholar living in Wayne, New Jersey.

ZANDER BRIETZKE is editor of the *Eugene O'Neill Review*. He is an adjunct professor of English at Suffolk University in Boston and is the author of *The Aesthetics of Failure: Dynamic Structure in the Plays of Eugene O'Neill*.

ROMULUS LINNEY has written more than twenty-five plays including *The Sorrows of Frederick, Holy Ghosts, Childe Byron, A Woman Without a Name, Sand Mountain, Three Poets* and *2*. His plays have been produced widely over the past thirty years in theatres across the U.S. and abroad.

ANDREW GRAHAM-YOOLL joined the *Buenos Aires Herald* in 1966 and became editor-in-chief in 1994, after returning to Argentina from a 17-year exile in Britain. Since 1998, he has been the paper's senior editor. His books include the *A State of Fear: Memories of Argentina's Nightmare, The Forgotten Colony. A History of the English-speaking Communities in Argentina*, and *Goodbye Buenos Aires*, among a total of about twenty titles.

PATRICK CHURA is Assistant Professor of English at the University of Akron. He is the author of *Vital Contact: Downclassing Journeys in American*

Literature from Herman Melville to Richard Wright, and has published articles on Eugene O'Neill, Harper Lee, and Shakespeare reception in Eastern Europe.

EGIL TÖRNQVIST is Professor of Scandinavian Studies at the University of Amsterdam in The Netherlands. He has written and edited numerous books and articles on drama, and on O'Neill, Ibsen, and Strindberg in particular.

Bibliography

Ahuja, Chapman. *Tragedy, Modern Temper and O'Neill*, Atlantic Highlands: Humanities Press, 1983.

Alexander, Doris. *Eugene O'Neill's Creative Struggle: The Decisive Decade, 1924-1933*, University Park: Penn State University Press, 1992.

———. *The Tempering of Eugene O'Neill*, new York: Harcourt, 1962.

Atkinson, Jennifer McCabe. *Eugene O'Neill: A Descriptive Bibliography*, Pittsburgh: University of Pittsburgh Press, 1974.

Berlin, Normand. *O'Neill's Shakespeare*, Ann Arbor: University of Michigan Press, 1993.

———. *Eugene O'Neill*, New York: St, Martin's Press, 1988.

Black, Stephen A. *Eugene O'Neill: Beyond Mourning and Tragedy*, New Haven: Yale University Press, 1999.

Bogard, Travis. *Contour in Time: The Plays of Eugene O'Neill*, New York: Oxford University Press, 1988.

Bowen, Crosswell and Shane O'Neill. *The Curse of the Misbegotten: A Tale of the House of O'Neill*, New York: McGraw Hill, 1959.

Cargill, Oscar, N. B. Fagin, and W. J. Fisher, ed. *O'Neill and His Plays: Four Decades of Criticism*, New York: New York University Press, 1961.

Carpenter, Frederic I. *Eugene O'Neill*, New York: Twayne, 1979.

Chabrowe, Leonard. *Ritual and Pathos: The Theatre of Eugene O'Neill*, Lewisburg: Bucknell University Press, 1976.

Clark, Barrett H. *Eugene O'Neill: The Man and His Plays*, New York: Dover, 1947.

Dubost, Thierry. *Struggle, Defeat, or Rebirth: Eugene O'Neill's Vision of Humanity*, Jefferson: McFarland, 1996.

Egan, Leona Rust. *Provincetown As a Stage: Provincetown, the Provincetown Players, and the Discovery of Eugene O'Neill*, Parnassus Imprints, 1994.

Eisen, Kurt, *The Inner Strength of Opposites: O'Neill's Novelistic Drama and the Melodramatic Imagination*, Athens: University of Georgia Press, 1994.

Engel, Edwin A., *The Haunted Heroes of Eugene O'Neill*, Cambridge: Harvard University Press, 1953.

Falk, Doris V. *Eugene O'Neill and the Tragic Tension: An Interpretive Study of the Plays*, Rutgers: Rutgers University Press, 1958.

Fleche, Anne. *Mimetic Disillusion: Eugene O'Neill, Tennessee Williams, and U.S. Dramatic Realism*, Tuscaloosa: University of Alabama Press, 1997.

Floyd, Virginia, ed. *Eugene O'Neill: A World View*, New York: Frederick Ungar, 1979.

Floyd, Virginia. *The Plays of Eugene O'Neill: A New Assessment*, New York: Ungar, 1984.

Frazer, Winifred D. *Love as Death in "The Iceman Cometh": A Modern Treatment of an Ancient Theme*, Gainesville: University of Florida Press, 1967.

Frenz, Horst. *Eugene O'Neill*, New York: Ungar, 1971.

Gallup, Donald Clifford. *Eugene O'Neill and His Eleven-Play Cycle: "A Tale of Possessors Self-Dispossessed,"* New Haven: Yale University Press, 1998.

Gassner, John. *Eugene O'Neill*, Minneapolis: University of Minnesota Press, 1965.

———, ed. *O'Neill: A Collection of Critical Essays*, Englewood Cliffs: Prentice-Hall, 1964.

Gelb, Arthur, and Barbara Gelb. *O'Neill*, New York: Harper, 1962.

Griffin, Ernest G. *Eugene O'Neill: A Collection of Criticism*, New York: McGraw-Hill, 1976.

Hinden, Michael. *"Long Day's Journey Into Night": Native Eloquence*, Boston: G.K. Hall, 1990.

Houchin, John H., ed. *The Critical Response to Eugene O'Neill*, Westport: Greenwood Press, 1993.

Kobernik, Mark. *Semiotics of Drama and the Style of Eugene O'Neill*, Amsterdam: Benjamins, 1989.

Leech, Clifford. *Eugene O'Neill*, New York: Grove, 1963.

Long, Chester, Clayton. *The Role of Nemesis in the Structure of Selected Plays by Eugene O'Neill*, The Hague: Mouton, 1968.

Manheim, Michael. *The Cambridge Companion to Eugene O'Neill*, New York: Cambridge University Press, 1998.

Martine, James J., ed. *Critical Essays on Eugene O'Neill*, Boston: G.K. Hall, 1984.

Maufort, Marc. *Songs of American Experience: The Vision of O'Neill and Melville*, New York: Peter Lang, 1990.

———, ed. *Eugene O'Neill and the Emergence of American Drama*, Atlantic Highlands: Humanities Press, 1989.

Miller, Jordan Y., ed. *Eugene O'Neill and the American Critic: A Summary and Bibliographical Checklist*, Hamden: Archon Books, 1973.

———. *Playwright's Progress: O'Neill and the Critics*, Chicago: Scott Foresman, 1965.

Moorton, Richard F., Jr., ed. *Eugene O'Neill's Century: Centennial Views on America's Foremost Tragic Dramatist*, Westport: Greenwood Press, 1991.

Orlandello, John. *O'Neill on Film*, Rutherford: Fairleigh Dickinson University Press, 1982.

Pfister, Joel. *Staging Depth: Eugene O'Neill and the Politics of Psychological Discourse*, Chapel Hill: University of North Carolina Press, 1995.

Porter, Laurin R. *The Banished Prince: Time, Memory, and Ritual in the late Plays of Eugene O'Neill*, Ann Arbor: UMI Research Press, 1995.

Prasad, Hari M. *The Dramatic Art of Eugene O'Neill*, Carbondale: Southern Illinois University Press, 1965.

Raleigh, John Henry, ed. *The Iceman Cometh: A Collection of Critical Essays*, Englewood Cliffs: Prentice Hall, 1968.

———. *The Plays of Eugene O'Neill*, Carbondale: Southern Illinois University Press, 1965.

Ranald, Margaret Loftus. *The Eugene O'Neill Companion*, Westport: Greenwood Press, 1984.

Robinson, James A. *Eugene O'Neill and Oriental Thought: A Divided Vision*, Carbondale: Southern Illinois University Press, 1982.

Reaver, J. Russell. editor, *An O'Neill Concordance*, Detroit: Gale, 1969.

Shaughnessy, Edward L. *Down the Nights and Down the Days: Eugene O'Neill's Catholic Sensibility*, Notre Dame: University of Notre Dame Press, 1996.

———. *Eugene O'Neill in Ireland: The Critical Reception*, New York: Greenwood Press, 1988.

Sheaffer, Louis. *O'Neill: Son and Artist*, Boston: Little, Brown, 1973.

———. *O'Neill: Son and Playwright*, Boston: Little, Brown, 1968.

Siebold, Thomas. *Readings on Eugene O'Neill*, San Diego: Greenhaven Press, 1998.

Sinha, C. P. *Eugene O'Neill's Tragic Vision*, Atlantic Highlands: Humanities Press, 1981.

Skinner, Richard Dana. *Eugene O'Neill: A Poet's Quest*, New York: Russell and Russell, 1964.

Tiusanen, Timo. *O'Neill's Scenic Images*, Princeton: Princeton University Press, 1968.

Törnqvist, Egil. *A Drama of Souls: Studies in O'Neill's Supernaturalistic Technique*, New Haven: Yale University Press, 1969.

Wainscott, Ronald. *Staging O'Neill: The Experimental Years, 1920-1934*, New Haven: Yale University Press, 1988.

Acknowledgments

"*The Iceman Cometh* and *Hughie*: Tomorrow is Yesterday" by Laurin Porter. From *The Banished Prince: Time, Memory, and Ritual in the Late Plays of Eugene O'Neill*, pp. 63–77. © 1988 by Laurin R. Porter. Reprinted by permission.

"*Mourning Becomes Electra*" by Doris Alexander. From *Eugene O'Neill's Creative Struggle: The Decisive Decade, 1924–1933*, pp. 149–169. © 1992 by Doris Alexander. Published by The Pennsylvania State University Press. Reproduced by permission of the publisher.

"Melodrama, Novelization, and the Modern Stage" by Kurt Eisen. From *The Inner Strength of Opposites: O'Neill's Novelistic Drama and the Melodramatic Imagination*, pp. 38–47. © 1994 by the University of Georgia Press. Reprinted by permission of the University of Georgia Press.

"*Long Day's Journey into Night*" by Edward L. Shaughnessy. From *Down the Nights and Down the Days: Eugene O'Neill's Catholic Sensibility*, pp. 151–162. © 1996 by University of Notre Dame Press. Reprinted by permission.

"From Trial to Triumph (1913–1924): The Early Plays" by Margaret Loftus Ranald. From *The Cambridge Companion to Eugene O'Neill*, ed. Michael Manheim, pp. 51–68. © 1998 by Cambridge University Press. Reprinted by permission of Cambridge University Press.

"The Middle Plays" by James A. Robinson. From *The Cambridge Companion to Eugene O'Neill*, ed. Michael Manheim, pp. 69–81. © 1998 by Cambridge University Press. Reprinted by permission of Cambridge University Press.

"Feminism v. Fatalism: Uncertainty as Closure in *Anna Christie*" by Barbara Voglino. From *"Perverse Mind": Eugen O'Neill's Struggle with Closure*, pp. 35–45. © 1999 by Fairleigh Dickinson University Press. Reprinted by permission of the Associated University Presses.

"Masks and Mirrors" by Zander Brietzke. From *The Aesthetics of Failure: Dynamic Structure in the Plays of Eugene O'Neill*, pp. 59–92. © 2001 Zander Brietzke. Reprinted by permission of McFarland & Company, Inc.

"O'Neill" by Romulus Linney. From *The Southern Review* 38, 4 (Autumn 2002), pp. 842–848. © 2002 by Romulus Linney. First published in *The Southern Review*.

"Eugene O'Neill in Buenos Aires" by Andrew Graham-Yooll. From *The Antioch Review* 60, 1 (Winter 2002), pp. 94–99. © 2002 by *The Antioch Review*. Reprinted by permission of the Editors.

"'Vital Contact': Eugene O'Neill and the Working Class" by Patrick J. Chura. From *Twentieth Century Literature* 49, 4 (Winter 2003), pp. 520–546. © 2003 by *Twentieth Century Literature*. Reprinted by permission of *Twentieth Century Literature*.

"Bound East for Cardiff" by Egil Törnqvist. From *Eugene O'Neill: A Playwright's Theatre*, pp. 167–175. © 2004 by Egil Törnqvist. Reprinted by permission of McFarland & Company, Inc.

"The Epitaph" by Doris Alexander. From *Eugene O'Neill's Last Plays: Separating Art from Autobiography*, pp. 157–163. © 2005 by the University of Georgia Press. Reprinted by permission of The University of Georgia Press.

Every effort has been made to contact the owners of copyrighted material and secure copyright permission. Articles appearing in this volume generally appear much as they did in their original publication with few or no editorial changes. In some cases foreign language text has been removed from the original essay. Those interested in locating the original source will find bibliographic information in the bibliography and acknowledgments sections of this volume.

Index